Tarot for Life

Tarot for Life

Reading the Cards for
Everyday Guidance and Growth

Paul Quinn

QUEST
BOOKS

Theosophical Publishing House
Wheaton, Illinois * Chennai, India

Quest Books
Theosophical Publishing House
P.O. Box 270
Wheaton, IL 60187-0270
www.questbooks.net

The author of this book does not dispense medical advice or prescribe the use of any
information as a form of diagnosis or treatment for physical, emotional, or medical
problems without the advice of a physician or therapist, either directly or indirectly. The
intent of the author is only to offer information of a general nature to help you in your
understanding of the Tarot as a tool for your own intuitive exploration. In the event you
use any of the information in this book for yourself, which is your constitutional right,
the author and the publisher assume no responsibility for your actions.

Except where the author's friends are identified, the names of the students and clients featured in the anecdotes throughout this book have been changed to protect their privacy.

Illustrations from the Universal Waite Tarot Deck® reproduced by permission of U.S.
Games Systems, Inc., Stamford, CT 06902 USA. Copyright ©1990 by U.S. Games
Systems, Inc. Further reproduction prohibited. The Universal Waite Tarot Deck® is a
registered trademark of U.S. Games Systems, Inc.

Cover design by Beth Hansen-Winter

Library of Congress Cataloging-in-Publication Data

Quinn, Paul (Paul Reid).
Tarot for life: reading the cards for everyday guidance and growth / Paul Quinn.
    p.   cm.
Includes bibliographical references.
ISBN 978-0-8356-0879-4
1. Tarot. I. Title.
BF1879.T2Q46 2009
133.3'2424—dc22   2008052129

5   4   3   *   12   13   14

Printed in the United States of America

For my Queens of Wands

Jan Harris
Patricia Hock
Rene Sutor

Contents

Foreword   ix

Acknowledgments   xiii

Introduction   1

  Exercise: Find Your Inner Tarot Teacher   4

Part One: Foundation

  • Tarot beyond Fortune-Telling   9

  • The Structure of the Tarot   17

  • How to Use This Book   23

Part Two: The Major Arcana

  • The Fool   33

  • Major Arcana 1–7: The Essentials for the Journey   39

    1. The Magician   40

    2. The High Priestess   45

    3. The Empress   50

    4. The Emperor   55

    5. The Hierophant   60

    6. The Lovers   64

    7. The Chariot   68

  • Major Arcana 8–14: The Inward Path   73

    8. Strength   74

    9. The Hermit   78

    10. Wheel of Fortune   82

    11. Justice   87

    12. The Hanged Man   92

    13. Death   97

    14. Temperance   101

CONTENTS

- Major Arcana 15–21: The Heat Is On   107
  15. The Devil   108
  16. The Tower   113
  17. The Star   118
  18. The Moon   123
  19. The Sun   127
  20. Judgment   132
  21. The World   137

Part Three: The Minor Arcana
- Wands: All Fired Up   145
- Cups: From the Heart   177
- Swords: To the Point   211
- Pentacles: Down to Earth   247

Part Four: Reading the Cards
- Intimate Conversations: Reading for Yourself   287
- Less Is More: Keeping It Simple   297
- Clarity First: Asking the Right Question   313
- Reading for Others   319

Epilogue   331
Appendix A: Major Arcana   333
Appendix B: Number Meanings   337
Appendix C: Astrological and Planetary Correspondences   339
Appendix D: Chakras   341
Bibliography   343
About the Author   344

Foreword

Paul Quinn and I share a birthday—along with a legendary Tarot reader from Melbourne, Australia; a cartoonist and Wonder Woman scholar in San Francisco; and Mae West and Davy Crockett. A varied group, to be sure, but I think there's a common thread here (leaving myself out of this appraisal): a down-to-earth quality, a love of frontiers and new experience, and fresh ways of looking at things. What did Mae West say? "If I have to choose between two evils, I choose the one I haven't tried yet."

Paul's approach to Tarot involves the esoteric and the mystical, along with Jungian psychological theory, but none of these qualities ever shows up just for itself, to impress or to be obscure for its own sake. They always serve those most vital of subjects, who we are and how we cope with our lives.

It's very easy for books on Tarot to get lost in themselves and become so abstruse—so occult, which is to say, hidden—that only a handful of people can understand them. There are good reasons for this, actually. Whatever the Tarot's origins close to six hundred years ago, over the last two hundred and thirty it has become part of a tradition known as Hermeticism—that is, complex and philosophical—that makes dense symbolism a thing of great beauty. However, it's not easy to present such material in a way that ordinary people can follow.

Coming from the other direction, too many Tarot books dumb down the subject, ignoring the deeper levels in favor of formulaic meanings for every card. What's harder, obviously, is to do both, to make the esoteric not only accessible but in service to people who want to understand the cards for that most practical of purposes, readings. The ability to do this is what makes Paul's book satisfying and exciting.

I've said it before and will probably say it again—the world is full of beginner's Tarot books, so why would we need another one? Because this book is useful. It not only explains the cards in very direct ways, it shows the Tarot in action, in people's lives, through examples and the stories Paul tells from his experiences as a reader, as a teacher, and as someone who has used the cards to help guide his own life. This book is not just theory; it comes from someone who knows.

Paul shares his experiences, but he gives us information as well. I have studied and worked with the Rider deck, that great classic bestseller of Tarot, for nearly forty years, yet as I read this book I was delighted to discover details of its symbolism that were either new to me or forgotten. From the very first card description, the Fool, I learned that the circles on his tunic add up to nine, the final single digit, and thus a symbol of completion, and, because they are circles, wholeness. And since part of the joy of symbolism lies in the ability to spark ideas from one person to another, I might add that nine is the number of pregnancy, so that the famously androgynous Fool could be described as giving birth to himself.

Something else I learned concerns the card of the Empress. It's fairly well known that some older decks, inspired by the French Revolution's overthrow of monarchy, changed the card's name to Juno, the Roman goddess who was queen of heaven in the classical world. Thus she changed from a symbol of earthly power—the original Empress and Emperor borrowed imagery from the Hapsburg Empire—to one of spiritual beauty, a quality she's kept ever since in Tarot interpretation. But now Paul reveals to us that another name for Juno, Moneta, gave us that all-important word, *money*. Thus the Empress card becomes a symbol of the financial world and its importance in our lives. The card returns, in a way, to its original meaning—who had more money than the Hapsburgs?—but now with its spiritual truths intact, so that money and power gain a wider context. This is something I've learned about Tarot, the ability to layer symbolism as it passes back and forth from one person to another.

I paid special attention to the Empress description because, at the beginning of the book, Paul suggests we shuffle the Major Arcana and pick a card for what aspect of ourselves this book is "inviting." I got the Empress, and I have been thinking about it for days. With each Major card, Paul gives us a series of questions to ponder. The ones for the Empress go beyond facts and ideas to challenge us to look at the place of kindness and compassion in our lives. And, of course, to look at the role money plays.

If I may disagree with Paul on one matter—or maybe just add another layer—he attributes the Rider deck's great success to its being a cryptogram, which is to say, a perfectly wrought symbolic structure. To me these classic pictures pull us in because of what artists call storytelling. Every picture seems a frozen moment in a myth, or a fairy tale, or simply a family drama. At the same time, what Paul says is absolutely true, for a complex, and above all coherent, structure underlies all these stories, so that we enter into deeper layers even if we do not know we are doing it.

As Paul knows, a Tarot reading really does form a kind of story, a tale of someone's life. It is not just the cards, but the questions we ask that allow the tale to unfold. Paul tells us, in a wonderful phrase, that we must have "the courage of our questions." And even though he gives us, as do most Tarot writers (myself included), spreads with a fixed set of positions, he also shares his experiences of courageous questions for specific people and situations. In one of my favorite stories in the book, he tells how a woman's view of the Hanged

Man—and much more, of herself—changed dramatically when he asked her what it meant to her that a halo of light shines around the Hanged Man's face.

While many people have seen the Hanged Man as being stuck, or blocked, or signifying a painful sacrifice, I have always looked at it as a joyous card, an image of the spiritual values that sustain us even if everyone else sees us as upside down or backward. Paul manages to capture both these views—the block and the sustenance—in the deceptively simple question, "What's been holding you up lately?"

Tarot for Life is a worthy addition to the literature of Tarot—informative, wise, and, above all, useful.

—Rachel Pollack
Rhinebeck, N.Y.
October 2008

Acknowledgments

*M*y gratitude to Sonia Choquette for her spirited support and constant inspiration; and to my Tarot elders past and present whose published works have deepened my understanding of the cards, with particular appreciation to Christine Payne-Towler for sharing with me her historical research on the origins of the Tarot septenary; Rachel Pollack for introducing me to her concepts of the Trump number reductions and the vertical relationships of the septenary; and Mary Greer for permission to include her many collaborative card-reading techniques in this book. Special thanks to Kenneth James of the Soulwork Center for reading the first draft and imparting his insight into the Four of Cups; Bruce Clorfene and Benjamin Dahlbeck for the initial manuscript edits; Judith Stein for the final copyediting; Sharron Dorr and Lynn Mooney for their proofreading prowess; Cliff Questel for the Chakra Spread illustration; and Susan Schulman, my agent, for stoking my faith during the Hanged Man years.

Love to my students and clients for the invaluable gifts of their teaching, and to my parents, Jack and Jackie Denney, for their lifelong example of embracing the progressive, the spiritual, and the wondrous.

Introduction

*L*ife speaks to us at every moment, in languages of every description. Happily, I have found it to be fluent in Tarot, and on at least one occasion conversant in Cricket.

I dreamed a cricket was resting in the middle of my unmade bed. I was gathering up the corners of the fitted sheet, undecided whether to trap the visitor in the folds of the fabric and set it free outdoors or, in one swift motion, to squash it. Before I could decide its fate, I woke up. For a few moments I lay in bed reviewing the still-fresh images, disturbed by the indifference with which I had considered killing the harmless creature. As a practiced dream watcher I knew the stark scenario meant *something*, but I preferred not to look at it too closely, convinced it would only make me feel worse at what was already a low point in my life.

Rubbing the sleep and dream from my eyes, I sank my feet into slippers and shuffled toward the bathroom. I had traveled only a few feet on that cold, dark March morning when my downcast gaze fell upon a dead cricket on the hardwood floor. In eight years none had ever appeared in my fourth-floor apartment, not even in summer when the evenings sing with them.

I knew I had been sent a particularly poignant message, one that needed my attention.

I pulled out my Tarot cards, an anticipatory sadness welling up as I shuffled them. I asked the question as directly as I could: "What part of me does the cricket represent?" I turned over a card.

It was the Fool.

Here was the archetype of the Wanderer, the Beginner, the Child; a figure poised at the edge of the abyss, the follower of instinct, taker of great leaps of faith. My heart beat a little faster as I made the connection: What do the Fool and the cricket have in common, if not their impulses to *leap*?

The Fool, like the dead cricket, told me I was killing my own impulses for change through chronically safe, uninspired choices in my life and work. Although at that moment I had no clear idea how or where to leap, gratitude for the message itself, for its eloquence and healing intent, began to stir up the vitality that Fool and cricket conspired to reawaken in me. I resolved that no cricket would ever again have to sacrifice itself for me to get my Fool energy moving again!

There is a guiding force that seeks to draw us into a deeper conversation with Life, communicating through the symbolic language of dreams, images, and coincidence. Too often this dialogue is drowned out by the monologues looping through our heads and the noise of the technology on which we've made ourselves dependent. Working with the Tarot is an intimate yet powerful way to say to one's inner and outer universe, "I'm listening."

Acting as the voice of our Inner Wisdom, if not also the voice of the Infinite, the cards tell us what we've been too distracted to hear: the costs and benefits of our choices, powers lost or gained, soul gifts flowering or forgotten, paths too long traveled or left unexplored. The Tarot becomes like a friend who knows your heart, the one you trust to tell it like it is without judging, who gives you wise counsel and helps you feel compassion for yourself even when you've failed to take your leaps.

The Tarot is by no means the sole channel for guidance. We can receive inspired messages just as directly through prayer or meditation, in dreams, in a passage from a novel or a walk through a garden. But the Tarot offers us the advantage of an immediate response.

A deck of the cards and a sincere intention for insight are all we need to engage the sacred conversation and, if we choose, to facilitate that conversation for others.

Using the cards for insight, inspiration, and guidance does not require a particular religious belief. It does, however, demand a respect for the symbolic dimension—an appreciation for life's capacity to communicate with us in highly imaginative and unexpected ways. It invites us to deepen our connection to the source of that voice, whether we call it Life, Inner Wisdom, the Universe, God, the Divine, the Higher Self, or intuition. Ultimately, working with the Tarot nurtures the understanding that, like the cards, we are but physical representations of nonphysical essences and energies. In short, we are spirit.

The Tarot can be a dynamic tool for spiritual development, though the cards themselves have no power to transform us. We evolve in proportion to *the courage of our questions and commitment to act* on the information received. Just as potently, we can use the cards to meditate on the opportunities for soul growth resonating in the Tarot archetypes, using them as catalysts for integrating and maturing their higher qualities within ourselves. With or without divination, the Tarot helps us discover who we are and who we may become.

"Know thyself" is not a private indulgence; it is a global imperative. Our world is in need of radical awakening and transformation, a process that accelerates as we look honestly at the beliefs and motives that drive our actions, observe how those actions play out on the personal as well as collective levels, and learn to make more loving choices. Until we recognize our creative purpose and power—with or without the aid of the Tarot—we weaken under the limitations of conditioned responses, the manipulations of an anxiety-driven media, the bullying of dogmas, and the mind-numbing complacency of escapist lifestyles.

As we pay more attention to the voice of intuition, the craziness of mass consciousness ceases to dominate the discussion. The True Self is amplified. We enjoy a more vibrant exchange with the richer life humming within and around us. We open to the spirit of things, the poetry in the prose, the message in the circumstance, the holiness of Fools and crickets.

Exercise: Find Your Inner Tarot Teacher

It is wisdom to know others; it is enlightenment to know one's self.
—Lao Tzu

Before you begin *Tarot for Life*, why not conduct a simple Tarot reading for yourself? The card that turns up will tell you why you were led to pick up this book—whether you're a Tarot novice, a dabbler, or a pro with a neon "Reader-Advisor" sign lighting up your storefront. Here's what you do:

1. Separate the twenty-two cards of the Major Arcana—the Fool (0) through the World (21)—from the rest of the deck. If you're new to the Tarot, be sure you don't mistake a courtly Page, Knight, Queen, or King for the Major Arcana.

2. Shuffle the cards with the images face down (see Shuffling the Cards, page 295). As you shuffle, ask this question silently or aloud: *"What aspect of myself is this book inviting me to discover and/or develop as I work with it?"*

3. Randomly pull one card from the cards you've shuffled. For the sake of simplicity and clarity (particularly at this early stage), set the intention that *only the card's upright position applies to you*, even if it's upside down when you draw it.

At this time, resist the temptation to read the possible meanings of the card you drew. Just sit with it for now. Notice how the image makes you feel and what associations it conjures. If you pulled a card that looks a little harsh or scary, take a breath and trust that its message for you is unquestionably positive and constructive. There is no force outside of you that seeks to shame or punish you. Tarot study is Self study. *Life* study. And there is always more to discover.

Part One

Foundation

Plants bear witness to the reality of roots.
—Maimonides

Tarot beyond Fortune-Telling

Why stay we on the earth unless to grow?
—Robert Browning

If a national poll were conducted about attitudes toward the Tarot, I could predict the outcome. The majority of people would view it as frivolous—an amusing diversion at carnivals and costume parties. Coming at a close second would be those who see it as a scam luring the flaky and gullible. A slightly smaller number would shiver at the mention, having seen the cards demonized in horror movies or heard them denounced from church pulpits. A handful would express admiration for the Tarot as a fortune-telling tool, and at least one smart aleck would quip, "Turow? He's my favorite author!"

But the Tarot that I know—and can't wait to tell you about—is virtually unknown to the public, unknown even to those who have had their "fortunes told." The Tarot I want to share with you is a treasure box, within which you have the pleasure to discover:

9

- a lifelong key to unlock your Inner Wisdom
- a catalyst for your creativity and inspiration
- flashcards for your intuitive development
- a set of visual affirmations
- a meditation focuser
- a decision-making aid
- a dream interpreter
- a perspective enhancer
- an emotional compass
- a metaphysics teacher
- a spiritual advisor
- a tool for self-understanding

Go even deeper into the Tarot and you'll find a philosophy—one founded on ancient-turned-modern ideas of spiritual evolution. For those on a conscious path of self-realization, this is the Tarot that gives rise to a deeper conversation with the voices of Self and Universe, that enhances the potential for psychological as well as cosmic insights, and that offers a timeless template for transformation.

I should mention that not every Tarot deck illustrates this intent, nor tries to. The *Hello Kitty* Tarot, to no one's surprise, is among many novelty decks absent metaphysical heft. And there are many Tarot decks in my own collection that are beautiful to look at yet short on ideas. But as originally published by Rider in Great Britain, the deck featured in this book has remained the best-selling Tarot in the world for good reason: It's a cryptogram. Arthur Edward Waite and artist/coconspirator Pamela Coleman Smith embedded their iteration of the Tarot with symbols designed to draw us out of the drama and into the recognition that we are spiritual players on a worldly stage. Our task is to choose how we will play our parts.

Six Principles Underlying the Tarot

Natural Law includes paradox, which Logical Law cannot.
—Ram Dass

Below, I've outlined six key metaphysical concepts at the heart of the esoteric Tarot. Could you skip this next section and start reading about the cards? Yes, but many of the card descriptions refer back to these core concepts, and you'd feel horribly left out. Could you interpret the cards without understanding their metaphysical dimensions? You could take a shot at it, but your interpretations would only scrape the surface, and you'd bore yourself to death. The Tarot is an intuitive tool with an intellectual foundation. Like the Magician and High Priestess, one complements the other, completing the package.

The first three concepts—As Above, So Below; the Law of Attraction; and Synchronicity—are part of the Law of Correspondence, which holds that all of life is interconnected. The last three tenets—the Self and Individuation, Integration of Opposites, and Masculine and Feminine—relate to the structure of the psyche and to challenges for personal growth. Together, the six principles sum up the transformative ideas at the heart of the Tarot. Throughout the book you'll discover the many subtle and brilliant ways these concepts are encoded in the card images—*and are at work in you*.

1. *As Above, So Below.* The terms *above* and *below* signify metaphysical, not physical, directions. They point to the presence of the Divine (*above*) in each of us (*below*) and to the spirit of the Divine everywhere in matter. This concept is most vividly symbolized in the upward- and downward-pointing hands of the Tarot's Magician. In Western and Eastern mysticism, there is no separation between the Creator and creation; no notion of inherent unworthiness or spiritual limitation.

The divine Intelligence is as much a part of us as we are of it. The call to claim our spiritual wholeness, thus linking above and below, is symbolized in the journey of the Tarot's Major Arcana (cards 0–21). *Above* and *below* also correlate with the relationship between mind and body—namely, the effect our thoughts have on the state of our physical health.

2. *The Law of Attraction.* Also known as *As Within, So Without,* the Law of Attraction says that everything we experience, all our life conditions and experiences, are created by our thoughts and the emotions stirred by them. Like attracts like. Every thought has its own particular vibrational frequency that pulls in people or situations which match that frequency. Unfortunately, most of us are not conscious of the thoughts we're projecting, let alone the power of those thoughts to manifest tangibly in our experience. But the Tarot offers a tool for noticing where we're placing our attention in any area of our lives and therefore what we're pulling toward us. Where attention goes, energy flows.

3. *Synchronicity.* The term was coined by Swiss psychologist Carl Jung, who defined it as the "meaningful coincidences" that so often leave us marveling at life's uncanny timing and choreography. For events to be synchronistic they must be randomly occurring, such as the haphazard "throwing" of Tarot cards that somehow wind up coinciding with the particulars of our question in that moment. Like wondering what ever happened to your third-grade math teacher and then bumping into him moments later at your hotel in Calcutta, synchronicities defy the odds and challenge causal explanations.

4. *The Self and Individuation.* Here are two more concepts Jung introduced. He described the Self as an archetype of one's core essence or wholeness (as opposed to the more ego-led, lower-case self). He called the unending process of getting to this core *individuation.* Only by individuating, Jung believed, do we have a truly honest, authentic relationship with ourselves and, by extension, with the

world. Individuation involves the conscious integration of all strands of the psyche, including unconscious aspects that we have fearfully repressed and those that we have not yet had the pleasure to meet. Becoming the Self is a lifelong process we can never actually complete. Mindful Tarot exploration, however, can help bring more of who we are to the light of our conscious awareness.

5. *Integration of Opposites.* There's a hero and a hellion in each of us, and each has a role in our development. To recognize and integrate these and other contradictory parts of ourselves is the major task of individuation. Left on their own, our inner opposites "stand off" against each other. They create psychic tension that usually ends with one of the aspects vilified or banished to the unconscious, resulting in the creation of what Jung called the *shadow*. But evolving toward the Self involves a synthesis of light and dark, conscious and unconscious, inner and outer. In bringing our dualities together, we in essence resolve them, awakening the greater power and potentialities of the Self. The interplay of the opposites is depicted in every card of the Major Arcana.

6. *Masculine and Feminine.* Although the concepts of masculine and feminine belong to the integration of opposites, they deserve their own delineation. It is tempting to correlate "masculine" and "feminine" to the attributes stereotypically associated with gender—men ruling the outer world of *Doing*, women the passive inner realm of *Being*. But in the mystical and Jungian traditions, gender is not in the genitals. The process of individuation, of becoming fully human, fully ourselves, leads us to integrate these so-called masculine and feminine aspects.

These terms may be limiting at best, misleading at worst, yet they provide a useful way to understand the dynamic polarities of being. In this way the Magician can represent a woman's "masculine" willpower, the High Priestess a man's "feminine" intuition.

In the dimension of spirit, there are no such distinctions. We simply *are*. The purpose of the Tarot path and of individuation is to become like the figure in the World card, the composite of masculine and feminine, fully integrated and empowered, at peace with all pairs of opposites.

Here are just a few examples of the dualities classically associated with the masculine and feminine principles explored in this book:

Masculine	Feminine
Yang	Yin
Sun	Moon
Fire	Water
Air	Earth
Outer	Inner
Conscious	Unconscious
Left brain	Right brain
Right side	Left side
Extravert	Introvert
Knowledge	Wisdom
Intellect	Intuition
Action	Passivity
Reason	Feeling

What Makes the Tarot Work?

May not such events raise the suggestion that they are not undesigned?
—Daniel Webster

The principle most active when you do a Tarot reading is synchronicity. It's a big part of what makes working with the Tarot awe-inspiring and fun. When seemingly disconnected events converge in related ways, we rightly sense the workings of cosmic forces. Synchronicities, in whatever form they appear, have the power

14

to evoke our humor, wonder, and humility, qualities nourishing to the soul.

My friend Pat will never forget a synchronistic moment that occurred shortly after she was diagnosed with breast cancer. "I was at home watching television, " she recalls, "and at one point I just asked the universe, 'Will I be all right?' I really didn't know. I surrendered. And with that, on TV was a doctor telling this woman with breast cancer, 'You have clean margins; none of it went into your lymph nodes. You'll have the radiation, and you'll be fine.'

"I knew I had just gotten my answer," Pat concludes.

A week later, her oncologist gave her a prognosis identical to the one announced by the TV physician. She lives today free of cancer.

"Synchronicity" does not answer the question, "Who or what is determining where the cards fall?" But if we accept that ultimate reality is *as above, so below* and *as within, so without*, then trying to precisely pinpoint the source of the oracle's animating intelligence is as fruitless as the dog chasing its tail. Consciousness is beyond space and time, beyond "you and me." Tapping into the transpersonal dimension through the Tarot teaches us to relax in the absence of hard boundaries. When we set aside the need to control and let the cards fall as they may, we allow divine mystery to come into play, which may become, with attention, a divine message.

The Structure of the Tarot

The Tarot is a deck of seventy-eight cards composed of twenty-two cards known as the Major Arcana and fifty-six called the Minor Arcana. The word *arcana* is derived from the Latin *arcanum*, meaning "secret" or "key". The name was given to the cards by the nineteenth-century occultist Paul Christian, for whom the Tarot represented the keys to the secrets of life.

The Major Arcana: Universal Costume Party

Whenever we recognize ourselves in a myth, it is empowering.
—Jean Shinoda Bolen

The cards of the Major Arcana, also known as Trumps, are numbered 0 through 21 and bear titles such as the Fool, the Wheel of Fortune, and the Sun. The Major Arcana are universal archetypes—the familiar

17

characters and themes of our shared existence that transcend race, culture, gender, and time.

Take the example of the Hermit. This archetype is expressed equally in a man living alone in a Mongolian forest, a scholar sequestered by studies in Milan, and a Manhattan teenager trying to discover herself in the jottings of her journal. Anyone on the planet— now or at any time in history—who has pondered life's meaning or simply *felt alone* has at such moments embodied the Hermit archetype. Each in its own way, the twenty-two archetypes of the Major Arcana call attention to the unifying threads and timeless challenges of our shared experience.

The Trumps depict distinct stages of self-realization, from the innocent adventuring of the Fool to the transcendent completion of the World. One way to visualize this process is by placing the Trumps into three rows of seven cards, called *septenaries* (see chart, Tarot Trumps Septenary, page 19). The Fool, personifying the essential wholeness of which all the other Trumps are but a part, traditionally floats above or throughout the other cards. Laid out this way, each row begins to suggest its own general theme. To these rows/themes I have respectively given the names The Essentials for the Journey, The Inward Path, and The Heat Is On.

Each card in the septenary can also be viewed in its relationship to the cards appearing directly above or below it. Exploring these vertical correspondences can yield further insights into how the Trumps come together as a philosophy. Keep in mind that your life, no matter how "spiritual," will not follow the neatly ordered progression of the Tarot Trumps. Awakening is a dynamic, lifelong process. In one moment you may know the euphoria associated with the World, and in the next find yourself emotionally unhinged in the Moon. You will acquire the archetypal experiences that the Trumps depict in your own way and in your own time.

Tarot Trumps Septenary

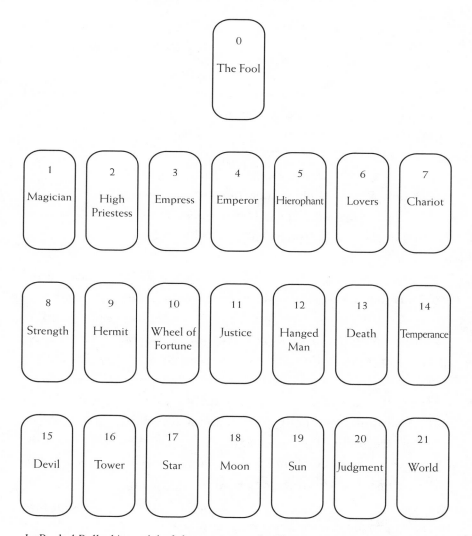

In Rachel Pollack's model of the septenary, the Trumps "story" progresses in the traditional horizontal way as well as in a downwardly vertical fashion.

The Minor Arcana: Life in Snapshots

Life is what we make it, always has been, always will be.
—Grandma Moses

The Minor Arcana are fifty-six cards divided into four suits, each of which represents the characteristic energies of one of the four classical elements—Fire, Water, Air, and Earth.

Wands/Fire—desire, vision, ambition, challenge
Cups/Water—feeling, merging, imagination, depth
Swords/Air—intellect, clarity, conflict, judgment
Pentacles/Earth—physicality, stability, security, money

Each suit is organized from Ace (1) through 10. The Aces are the most abstract cards in the deck, representing the pure elemental energies of their respective suits. Cards 2–10 depict people in various situations and relationships. In contrast with the soul-guidepost role of the Trumps, the Minor Arcana are traditionally viewed as dealing with the "lesser" themes of everyday life. And yet, where else do we find opportunities to grow in spirit if not in the day-to-day challenges and opportunities of family, work, and relationships?

Don't be fooled by the designation *Minor*. As you'll see in the many examples in this book, the Minor Arcana can reveal major insights. Just as a Major Arcana card can have a mundane meaning in a reading, the message of a Minor Arcana card can turn out to be the most provocative, illuminating, and healing.

The Court Cards: Sixteen Types and Temperaments

The Minor Arcana include sixteen Court cards. Although every card in the Tarot is capable of showing us aspects of ourselves, the Court cards articulate specific personality traits. They can depict attitudes expressed in the moment or more permanent ways of responding to life. They can even represent societal roles, from schoolchildren to CEOs. A Court card can represent the *querent* (the person for whom the reading is done), a person involved in the querent's situation, or the general atmosphere of the issue in question.

The **Pages** are the parts of us that, like the Fool, are curious, naive, open to experience, and willing to take risks in the spirit of self-discovery. Depicted as youths in the cards, the Pages can represent children, or the childlike passion for leaping into learning that keeps us young no matter our chronological age.

The Pages are the beginners, the apprentices, the unapologetic amateurs who accept the current limits of their skills and understanding, yet try their hand anyway. Whereas the Aces signal the potentialities of the respective suits, the Pages take the first steps toward activating those potentialities.

As the courtly correspondents of the Chariot, the **Knights** embody the glory-bound warrior archetype. Knightly behavior is intense, given to swearing oaths and throwing down gauntlets. Where there's a cause, there's a Knight riding forth to champion it. Their common mission: to pursue, uphold, and defend the ideals of their suits.

We assume the role of the Knight when energized by tests and challenges, when fueled by opportunities to prove ourselves, and when ennobled by the call to serve, persuade, or rescue others. Whether taking out the trash or taking on the world, an unshakable sense of purpose beats within the brave breast of the Knight.

Unlike the fledgling Pages and questing Knights, the **Queens** are enlivened by a deep reverence for the qualities of their suits, having matured the most creative aspects of those qualities within themselves. They represent the soul of their particular elements, containing, preserving, and cherishing the related essences and gifts. This umbilical connection to essence enables the Queens to recognize the same in others and, like the Empress, nurture it in them.

In readings, the Queens can represent the archetypes of Wife, Mother, Friend, and Confidante. At the most subtle levels, the Queens, like the High Priestess, indicate a private savoring—rather than outward demonstration—of the elemental attributes. Three of the Queens' thrones feature *cherubim*, a word meaning "filled with wisdom."

Whereas the Queens represent the inner soulful connection to their suits (Being), the **Kings** have an external focus (Doing). These monarchs are the models of outer mastery. They play on a larger stage. The elemental passions of the Queens are often the established professions of the Kings. They wear the crown by virtue of their personal accomplishments, professional roles, family leadership, or social status. King-consciousness is the confidence one feels based on proven capabilities. It is the self-trust that comes from operating at one's full powers.

The Kings represent leaders, bosses, fathers, authority figures, and powerful or dominant personalities. In the abstract, the Kings symbolize governments, institutions, and businesses. Their responsibility for the welfare of their subjects connects them most obviously to the Emperor, and in some cases to the moral leadership of the Hierophant.

Despite their royal titles, the Court cards do not depict hierarchical values. A King is not "higher" than a Queen, nor a Queen "better" than a Knight or a Page. In readings, however, the Court cards *can* signify stages of competence. If I had to choose between a Page and a King to remove my gall bladder, I'd hedge my bets on the King. Experience counts!

How to Use This Book

You have to make the leap, and jump on at any point, because
any point is better than not making the leap at all.
— Tom Denney

*I*f you are a beginning reader, you may initially feel book-bound, flipping through this text or others to learn some basics. As with anything, your competence will grow with practice. You'll soon find yourself giving readings comfortably without need of prompts. What's more, your imagination will deepen your connection to the cards. Your musings, fantasies, and intuitions about the images will lead to highly personal and meaningful associations not found in Tarot books. For example, you might decide that the Queen of Pentacles reminds you of your earthy Aunt Molly and get a warm feeling whenever you see the card. You might hear a discordant jazz piano whenever you see the Moon, or remember a perfect retreat in the country at the sight of the Ten of Cups. We come to know these seventy-eight "pictures of the soul" not merely by what we read about them but through the richness of our imagination and experiences.

The private meanings we project onto the images make card reading unavoidably idiosyncratic. Readers base their interpretations on the personal "language" they've developed with the deck. This is why a person who associates the King of Swords with a pompous person, for example, finds that meaning fits most every time. Likewise, the person who attributes intellectual leadership to that card will find it tends to support precisely that in readings. Once you make a strong connection to a symbol, your unconscious will consistently use that symbol as you understand it. Life speaks to us in the language with which we're most familiar.

Yet no matter how distinctive your card-reading system may be, any serious approach must take into account the fact that each card has a range of meanings. For example, the High Priestess could represent neutrality, passivity, secrecy, wisdom, psychic receptivity, apathy, a platonic relationship, or the soul itself, to name just a few possibilities. To determine which meaning of a card is most appropriate, consider the context:

- the person asking the question
- the question asked
- the position in which the card appears in the spread (Recent Influences, Advice, Possible Outcome, etc.)
- whether the card is upright or reversed
- the other cards in the spread
- your gut feelings

In this chapter I outline various factors to consider in your card interpretations—being, doing, reversed cards, shadow aspects, advice, and images with multiple figures. These factors are included at the end of each of the seventy-eight card essays.

Being and Doing

To be is to do.
—Socrates

Each card description is followed by an example of how that card once figured in an actual reading for my clients, my students, or myself. After the card examples, I list a menu of feelings and inner states (Being) and actions (Doing) that could apply in your readings. If what the book says about a given card doesn't fit what you feel, go with what you feel. At the end of each Major Arcana card essay I've included a set of questions for reflection. The questions are designed to help you discover your own "Being and Doing" of the archetypes—how they express themselves in your life. I encourage you to ask yourself these questions as a way to develop a more personal understanding of the cards.

Reversed Cards: A Different Spin

No snowflake ever falls in the wrong place.
—Zen saying

In both small and large spreads, some cards will appear in their upright positions and others upside down (reversed). Reversed cards are not necessarily negative or "bad news." A reversed card may often be interpreted as simply the opposite of the upright meaning. For example, in its upright (or *dignified*) position, the Knight of Wands personifies a fiery, enthusiastic, or impulsive inclination. Reversed, it could symbolize a cautious or cool-headed approach.

Then again, a reversed card may signify a *dilution* or *rejection* of the upright energies. In the case of the Knight of Wands, the card's reversal may not indicate a cautious approach at all, but rather a lack of motivation or flat refusal to engage in the excitement (such as my response to dog-fight invitations). Reversed or upright, every card has several possible meanings. Your intuition and the context of the reading will determine which one resonates as truth.

Don't be afraid of reversed cards. Some cards in their reversed positions have more favorable meanings than in the upright. For example, the reversed Devil usually signifies liberation from an oppressive situation, the reversed Five of Swords an overturning of a "win-lose" way of thinking. However, when the majority of cards in a spread are reversed, it may indicate a substantial degree of blocked movement or suppressed energy. On one occasion, an entire ten-card spread was reversed, which prompted my client jokingly to ask if I had supplied the "reversed deck" by mistake!

Shadow Aspects: The Call to Balance

There is no sun without shadow, and it is essential to know the night.
—Albert Camus

The cards of the Major Arcana depict a perfect balance of the energies symbolized. They show us archetypes—idealized, abstract—not highly advanced human beings. When the High Priestess pops up in a spread to signify your friend Lucille, it doesn't mean Lucille embodies the pristine vibration of that archetype. Rather, it means that your friend is expressing some aspect of the archetype on a very human scale.

Yet, despite the supremely well-behaved impressions given by each Trump (Devil, Tower, and Moon excepted), all archetypes share with us the capacity for light and dark. Expressing the characteristics of any archetype, even the "good" ones, can be taken to extremes, creating imbalances that throw obstacles in the way of our spiritual progress. For example, a person expressing the Empress archetype may be empathetic and solicitous toward others. If taken too far, however, we see a depleted soul groaning, "I give and give and give, and what do I get back—nothing!"

Similarly, too much of the Emperor's order and structure can lead to paralyzing rigidity, if not a compulsion to keep everything in its place. Even a person who strongly identifies with the lovely Temperance card, nobly maintaining the middle ground in every crisis, may be masking a terror of the disapproval he might suffer if he dared to take a stand on the issues.

I use Carl Jung's term *shadow* to describe these excessive or potentially destructive aspects of behavior, aspects of which we are often not aware. (Deficiencies, on the other hand, are shown in reversed cards.) I also identify shadow aspects in the Minor Arcana, although many of those cards already vividly depict excesses as well as deficiencies. In my system, an upright card can signify that the energies are either in balance or are veering toward the excessive (shadow). Your intuition, and the context of the reading, will tell you where the card falls on that continuum.

When Cards Give Advice

Go to your bosom: Knock there, and ask your heart what it doth know.
—William Shakespeare

Many spreads, such as the Celtic Cross (see p. 300), feature a card designated to give advice. Some of the layouts you'll find or design for yourself may involve a question such as, "What action has the most integrity in this situation?" or "What is the energy needed to move forward?" For each card, I've included two interpretive possibilities for how the card might offer advice when drawn in response to a specific request for advice.

Keep in mind that the only cards that advise you in a reading are those which, by virtue of the layout positions, are specifically assigned as advice cards. Be clear about which positions in your spread are designated as advice and which are merely descriptive. This will save you or the person for whom you're reading a great deal of confusion and misdirection. Don't assume a card says you should do anything unless its position in the layout is intended for dispensing advice.

Because the Tarot (i.e., the voice of your Inner Wisdom) only gives advice with positive intentions, it can be baffling when a card you may despise shows up as the sacred advice, or when your marching orders are given by a card you adore—in its reversed position. Could the reversed Sun be encouraging you to feel down about yourself? Is the Five of Cups advising you to curl up in disappointment and regret? Is the crafty Seven of Swords urging you to pocket that packet of pens from the office? Heavens, no! Every card that offers advice has only the highest possible intention for you, and so, it follows, for the greater good of all concerned. Remember too that getting a "no" when you wanted "yes" does not always mean the case is closed. Your Inner Wisdom could simply be cautioning you that the timing isn't right (see A Six of Swords Story, page 224).

In the cases of cards traditionally perceived as "dark," such as the angst-riddled Nine of Swords, I provide examples of how they might serve as advice in their unsettling upright positions—the inferred benefits of their reversed positions being obvious.

Finally, acting upon even the most encouraging advice does not mean we won't encounter challenges or disappointments. No path is free of conflicts. If the unconscious wisdom elicited by the Tarot shows us the best possible advice at the moment, it follows that the accompanying challenges will be tailor-made for our unique spiritual unfolding.

Multiple Figures: Parts of the Whole

All is one.
—Buddha

The majority of cards feature single human figures, though many depict two or three. Some of these cards, such as the Five of Swords and Six of Pentacles, feature people in sharply contrasting attitudes. There are times when you will be satisfied to view all the personalities on a given card, no matter how diverse, as collectively personifying that card's dominant theme. At other times you may feel drawn to one particular figure on a card and feel compelled to explore the possibilities of that singular perspective. I have provided suggestions for what those perspectives might be.

In the Five of Swords, for example, I distinguish the "Being" and "Doing" energies of the Sword holder from those of the people appearing in the background. On one reading you might identify strongly with the man in the green tunic, and at another time find yourself sympathizing with the smaller figures. Yet a reading might also lead you to see in yourself the qualities of the victor as well as the vanquished. After all, we are composites of opposites, capable of expressing multiple and contradictory sides of our natures at any moment.

Part Two

The Major Arcana

All journeys have secret destinations of which the traveler is unaware.
—Martin Buber

The Fool

First you jump off the cliff and you build your wings on the way down.
                                                    —Ray Bradbury

"We are here and it is now," observed H. L. Mencken. "Further than that, all human knowledge is moonshine." Such might be the Fool's toast were he hoisting a glass of the hooch himself. As his name implies, the Fool thumbs his nose at custom, certainty, philosophy, and metaphysical profundities. He would be the first to point out the folly of trying to communicate the unfathomable through a deck of cards, let alone write a book about it! The only thing we can know for sure (and the Fool would agree)

THE FOOL.

is that life is impermanent, unpredictable, and at times absurd. Every time we furrow our brows trying to figure it all out, the Fool is there making faces, for we may as well be trying to smell our own noses.

How then to begin a serious discussion of an archetype that refuses to be taken seriously . . . an archetype so unimpressed with himself that he's numbered zero? "Keep it simple!" answers the Fool.

As a shape, zero is a circle, symbol of the wholeness and totality of the Self. As a number, it's nothingness. From the mystical perspective, being "nothing" is closest to bliss; the ego's not around to pump us up or drag us down. The Fool card shows us the moment before the egoless soul descends into the earth plane and experiences twenty-one states and stages of being known as the Trumps. Surrounding the Fool are mountain peaks, higher places of consciousness that he seeks to attain through this next cycle of incarnation. Two gray peaks below form a gateway to the experiences that await him in the physical world of duality.

The zero is repeated on his tunic nine times, a reference to completion. These circles take the forms of mandalas, emblematic of wholeness and the Self. The wheels intimate as well the cosmic Wheel of Fortune, archetype of death, birth, and rebirth. His boots are as yellow as the light of Divine Intelligence above him, signifying that he walks in accordance with it. Trusting the pure, whole Self that he is, the Fool rolls fluidly along in whatever direction the Universe guides him, for he knows that Self and Universe are one. He knows this in an instinctive way—intellectual constructs being alien and utterly useless to him.

His pole appears to shoot out from the sun's rays, igniting a fiery enthusiasm for the journey ahead. Instinct, symbolized by the dog, will serve as ally and guide. The Fool's satchel, according to one Tarot tradition, carries accumulated experiences from his previous earthly lives that will aid him in the new. Thus provisioned, the Fool, or Self, is ready to leap into the next incarnation of spiritual opportunities.

"Esoteric mumbo jumbo!" chides the Fool. Okay. Let's get back down to earth. . . .

Most of us try to navigate our way through life by collecting information and expert advice. We count on facts and plans to give us a sense of sureness and security. The Fool in us, however, wants only to experience life. It is from our experiences that we gain not just knowledge but wisdom. Jesus tells us, "If anyone among you thinks he is wise in this age, let him become a fool that he may become wise." For our experiences to make us wise, we must enter into them with the openness of a child, "following humbly," as T. H. Huxley urges, "wherever and to whatever abysses Nature leads."

The Fool is the youthful curiosity and daring that enables us to open our arms to the new and unpredictable. It is our willingness to take risks, make dreadful mistakes, and laugh at ourselves. When we can truly accept that we are beginners—unfinished, imperfect— our journey lightens up. We don't have to take life, or ourselves, so seriously.

Whereas the ego has a low tolerance for uncertainty, the Fool romances the unknown and takes great leaps of faith. His tiny satchel demonstrates that he trusts he has everything he'll need for the journey; what he doesn't have will somehow turn up. He leaps without a safety net or a Plan B to fall back on, relying on instinct to point the way. We can almost hear him, like Shakespeare's Romeo, invoking divine guidance: "He that hath the steerage of my course, direct my sail."

Of course, following the Fool is no guarantee that we won't take some bumps. Or fall flat on our faces. But if we're in it for the adventure, we take life as it comes.

The Fool's plucked white rose symbolizes the purity of his childlike spirit. Flower picking requires nothing but a willingness to mosey about with eyes and nose open, wistfully snatching at whatever grabs our fancies. Thus, the Fool is as present in our leisurely meanderings and playful diversions as he is in our courageous leaps into the unknown. Without expecting to, we wander into relationships and job opportunities; while goofing around, we discover solutions to problems our more serious efforts had failed to crack. Success has a way of sneaking in when we stop trying so hard.

A college student was playing with his dog one day when its toy rolled under the young man's secondhand couch. As he reached to retrieve the toy he saw something sparkling next to it—a 1985 Super Bowl diamond-studded ring. Missing for six years, the ring had belonged to the late Chicago Bears legend Walter Payton, who had once left it with the couch's original owner, who then lost it. The student returned the ring to Payton's widow. Like the Fool-inspired Percival of Arthurian tales who innocently stumbled upon the Holy Grail, we often find life's diamonds when not looking for them.

Although the character of Trump 0 is spontaneous and delightfully unselfconscious, there are times when deliberately summoning our inner Fool can pay off. Consciously "playing with" the attitude that life is all too short and way too absurd can make stressful events more manageable. Injecting levity into tense situations lifts and lightens them. Humor, satire, and the ridiculous are classic Fool's tools, following on George Bernard Shaw's advice, "If you want to tell people the truth, you'd better make them laugh." Fools, like Dorothy's dog, Toto, instinctively sniff out pretense, exposing false wizards while coaxing out their humanness.

With his left foot leading left, the direction of the unconscious, the Fool may indeed seem—to the rational mind—to be heading off the deep end. Still, he follows his heart. Stitched almost imperceptibly on his collar is the tetragrammaton, the four Hebrew letters Yod (י), Heh (ה), Vav (ו), Heh (ה). These letters encode the deliberately unpronounceable name of the Almighty as well as the four elements that will become instruments of power for the next archetype, the

Magician. For the Fool, however, the only power that counts is the power of the moment. And this one's about smelling roses.

A Fool Story

The Fool in Samantha's card reading triggered the memory of a dream she'd recently had. In it she was an old beggar whose ragged cloak served as her only means of warmth and shelter. Blind, she traveled through a dense forest with the aid of a dog. A voice within the dream spoke, telling her that if she would pluck out the dog's eyes and put them in her own head, she would see. Horrified, she refused and woke from the dream in tears.

As we discussed the dream I learned that Samantha, like the Fool-beggar in the dream, was now in a wandering place in her life. In her sixties and near retirement, she feared being directionless. "The wandering part makes sense," she said, "but what about the eyes?" I answered that I felt it was her deeper being urging her to enter this next phase of her life with "new eyes," rather than blindly follow the path of old attitudes. The dog's eyes promised faithfulness to the vision she had entered the forest to discover. Were she to let her rational mind alone lead her, she'd never get out of the woods.

Fool Attributes

Key words:	Innocence, Lightness, Trust
Being:	Curious, open, childlike, spontaneous, lighthearted, adventurous, innocent, naive, playful, arbitrary, unencumbered, noncommittal
Doing:	Simplifying, taking a leap of faith, acting on a whim, improvising, traveling, taking life as it comes, enjoying the moment, just passing through, asking "Why not?"

Shadow:	Delayed maturation, irresponsibility, gullibility, absent-mindedness, recklessness, defenselessness, intolerance for detail or complexity
Reversed:	Cautious, risk averse; denying the Inner Child, taking yourself or a situation seriously
	Possible Advice
Reversed:	"Look before you leap, or you may go off the deep end." "Stop wandering. It's time to commit."

Questions for Reflection

What risks have you taken without a safety net?

Where would you leap if you took a leap of faith?

When have others discouraged your Fool qualities?

What would you like to experience for the first time?

When do you express Fool playfulness and spontaneity?

Where in your life could you use some Fool energy?

Major Arcana 1–7:
The Essentials for the Journey

No brims nor borders in myself I see / my essence is capacity.
—Thomas Traherne

In the *Star Wars* series, Luke Skywalker's earliest adventures help him develop the skills, wisdom, and encouragement he will need to master the Force, confront the Dark Side, and meet his destiny. Similarly, Trumps 1–7 represent some of the rudimentary psychic resources required for our own life journey. Where would we be without our basic sense of self the Magician exemplifies, or the moral center represented by the Hierophant? How much would we enjoy life without the appreciation for beauty symbolized by the Empress, or the aptitude for relationship the Lovers embody? Such core capacities fortify us for the soul-seasoning experiences that await us down the road, symbolized in the septenary chart by the second and third rows of Trumps (see page 19).

1. The Magician

As your desire is, so is your will. As your will, so is your deed.
As your deed, so is your destiny.
—Brihadaramyaka Upanishad

At the gateway to the Major Arcana stands the Magician. He is the bright, enduring presence on this journey of awakening that we, by virtue of our birth, have chosen to undertake. The Magician pulls the chain on the cosmic lamp switch, beaming the light of pure awareness onto life. As our guide through the Tarot path, he brings conscious understanding to each of the archetypal encounters that follow.

He is the essence of the conscious mind, the "home office" through which we register every thought and sensation. The Magician represents the ego (Latin for *I*), our basic awareness that we exist, that we have a unique personality that may hate opera or love horse racing. As many occult writers have pointed out, the word *I* and the Roman numeral I are not only identical, they both represent what is primary and singular. In the continuity of life, our *I* is unchanging. We experience everything in relationship to ourselves.

Yet despite the unity implied in the number One, the symbols on the card point to an apparent duality in the Magician, and therefore in us. One hand acknowledges Heaven, the Divine Mind; the other gestures to the physical plane. The Magician is our awareness that, though we are not the Allness of God, that which is God is within us. Trump 1 is our deepest knowing that spiritual power is the only true power, and spiritual reality the ultimate reality. In accepting our responsibility as Magicians, we are called consciously to create the inner conditions that allow divine energies to express through us.

Such an alignment produces extraordinary potential. The Magician's mastery is dramatized by the white rod through which the currents of divine energy are carried earthward. We see the result, the harmony of roses both above and below the Magician. What God desires (*de sire*, "from the Father"), so does the Magician, who acts as agent of divine will. The red roses connote the desire at the root of all creation, here manifested. White lilies symbolize the purity of intention. When our desires are in sync with spirit, we create beauty on earth. The Waite-Smith cards illustrate the timelessness of this truth in the infinity symbol above the Magician.

The Trump's *above-and-below* orientation has another, equally important coordinate. It represents our potential for bringing not only the spiritual and the physical into alignment, but also the conscious and the unconscious, the masculine and the feminine. *The ultimate joining of Trump One and Two, Magician and High Priestess, is the central theme of the Tarot.* These two archetypes, and their capacities for union, are the prototypes for the masculine and the feminine energies depicted in the successive Trumps. In each Trump we see how these forces combine in different ways to offer us new opportunities for growth.

As masculine prototype, the Magician is our basic sense of power—the ability to make things happen. At the most primitive level we experience ourselves as Magicians when, as infants, we first make the connection that our actions have impact: tears bring food and comfort; kicks jingle the chimes above the crib. The degree to which we are able to turn intentions into results determines our overall sense of competence and esteem.

But our true magic is in not merely manipulating the environment to fit our desires; it is in operating from the higher knowledge that as we change our consciousness, we change our reality. Our thoughts, when reinforced with feeling, create our experience. I first learned this key Magician principle by accident. In my midtwenties I cofounded a theater troupe that performed, in local schools, original comedy sketches about self-esteem and personal development. One morning in my hometown of Chicago, I spotted Oprah Winfrey on her morning jog. Having nothing to risk (except possible stalking charges), I trotted alongside her and asked her how my theater troupe might get on her show.

Without breaking her stride she gave me the name of the producer to whom we should send our information. I thanked her and sent a promotional packet that afternoon. From that point on, we began all our school shows with the audaciously bogus announcement, "Watch for us soon on Oprah's show!" We justified the lie because, well, we all knew in our hearts that it *could* and *should* happen some day.

After two years of making the announcement, we got a phone call. A few weeks later, we were performing on a TV special starring Oprah and basketball legend Michael Jordan. The promotional materials—energetically assisted by the power of our intention and the intensity of our desire—had made the dream a reality. "The thing always happens that you really believe in," said Frank Lloyd Wright, "and the belief in a thing makes it happen."

The Magician points up the value of controlling our thoughts, not just so that we may manifest our desires, but so that we may upgrade our consciousness. Unless we are in control of our thoughts, *we're controlled by them.* Without a discerning gatekeeper, the mind will run its programs as randomly as a TV viewer clicking away at the remote control. Inadvertently we give our focus and power to every impulse, obsession, judgment, or diversion that happens to appear. But the Magician points his wand carefully, for he knows that that which plays on his inner screen becomes his outer reality. The Magician challenges us to remain conscious of our thoughts, words, and feelings—in the "magic" of being able to observe ourselves observing. Staying awake to this power is a full-time job; without it, life becomes a crapshoot.

The Magician's table displays the elemental tools with which we create the very substance of our lives. The Wand, instrument of Fire, inflames our passion, drive, and inspiration; the Cup, receptacle of Water, contains our imagination and the deepest pools of psychic and spiritual potential; the Sword, implement of Air, cuts clean through to the truth, sharpens our perceptions, and crystallizes our intentions; the Pentacle, emblem of Earth, grounds us in bodily awareness, physical reality, and taking care of business. With such powers at our disposal, the Magician within each of us asks, "Where will you direct this potential? In whose service? Toward what end?" We are asked to choose wisely, because that upon which we fix our attention determines what grows in our garden—within and without.

A Magician Story

Marta was very close to Don, a man she met at Alcoholics Anonymous. Don credited Marta with helping him stay sober during his rocky recovery. And when he started drinking again, Marta was there for him. Though she tried everything she could to help, he continued to drink. Frustrated and saddened, she began to view Don's decline as her personal failure.

Advice arrived in the form of the Magician, reversed.

"Upright, the Magician has the power to achieve anything," I began, "but the card is reversed here. What is that saying to you?" Marta closed her eyes. "That I don't have the power to work miracles," she said. "I know this, but obviously I need to hear it again." Though she would not cease to offer Don support, his transformation to sobriety would require him to reclaim the Magician within himself.

43

Magician Attributes

Key words:	Vision, Decision, Action
Being:	Confident, focused, inspired, visionary, inventive, quick-minded, clever, resourceful, skillful
Doing:	Pioneering, initiating change, communicating persuasively, demonstrating a mastery of skills or talents, consciously creating your reality, manifesting desires, fixing things, working wonders
Shadow:	Opportunism; overestimating the limits of your power; irresponsible use of knowledge, skill, or willpower
Reversed:	Ineffective communication; hidden motives; nonaction; low self-esteem; inability to manifest desires; randomness; procrastination; lack of ideas, focus, or initiative
	Possible Advice
Reversed:	"Point your wand (attention) in another direction." "Accept the limitations of your power."

Questions for Reflection

What was your greatest inspiration?

What would you like to attract and manifest?

What specific skills or abilities would you like to develop?

When have you deliberately redirected your thoughts
and achieved new results?

In what areas are your powers of focus and concentration strongest?

When have you expressed the shadow aspect of the Magician
and overestimated your ability to control or influence a situation?

2. The High Priestess

There are mysteries within the soul which no hypothesis
can uncover and no guess can reveal.

—Kahlil Gibran

Whereas the Magician personified the thrusting power of intention, words, and action, the High Priestess embodies the receptive power of intuition, silence, and containment. He is the conscious mind, she the unconscious. The Magician perceives through the mind and senses, the High Priestess through an ineffable inner knowing.

Our spiritual progression depends largely on whether we'll accept things at face value or become curious about exploring the reservoir peeking from behind the High Priestess's curtain. The waters she conceals symbolize the unconscious—both the individual and collective unconscious, the full depths and dimensions of which are unknowable. Tarot tradition holds that all water appearing in subsequent cards begins in the pool of the High Priestess. At each step along the path, the High Priestess parts the veil, showing us yet another glimpse of our being.

Like the Magician's oppositely directed hands, the High Priestess's cross is the symbolic intersection of the above and below, the point at which the duality of spirit and matter come together. The black and white pillars amplify the tensions of duality itself—yin and yang, darkness and light, unconscious and conscious, disorder and order. But the Divine is not polarized; it is the ocean into which all contrasts dissolve. (Notice that the archetype's robe flows indiscriminately like water in all directions.)

Despite her symbolic association with the dark pillar of the unconscious, her centering between the pillars reveals her indifference to concepts of opposites. On the psychological level, the archetype is the Zen ideal, the mind that observes all without attachment to labels, opinions, or desires. The High Priestess is holy witness, perceiving the God-force in everything through attentive and loving silence.

The B and J on the pillars flanking her stand for Boaz and Jakin, the names of the pillars of the mystical Temple of Solomon. It was believed that the pillars held within them the secrets of the universe. The Hebrew Scriptures describe the Temple as being garlanded by pomegranates, which Waite has splashed onto the veil. The fruit's profusion of seeds assures that the soul's potential, though hidden from conscious awareness, is fertile. Borrowed from the same biblical passage is the lotus motif at the top of the pillars, symbolizing the flowering of our yet-unseen powers.

The final enigma is the presence of the Jewish Book of Law, the Torah. That the High Priestess partially conceals it in her robe suggests that wisdom cannot merely be handed to us; we must *feel* our way toward it.

The lunar symbols on the High Priestess's crown (that of Hathor, Egyptian Goddess of Life) and at her feet reflect an ancient association with the moon and psychic receptivity. By psychic, I refer not only to abilities such as ESP and clairvoyance. *Psychic* means "of the soul." We access the psychic realm whenever we tap into the interior images and wordless impressions floating just beneath our conscious awareness. By quieting the mind, we more easily lift the veil of the unconscious, revealing more of our depths. We engage the inner life through silence.

Besides enhancing psychic receptivity, silence has another value—it contains that which is best left unspoken. There is wisdom in knowing when to speak and when to say nothing. When Dorothy asks the good witch Glinda why she failed to explain the magic of the ruby slippers *before* the perilous yellow-brick journey, Glinda kindly replies, "You had to learn it for yourself." This is sage advice familiar to anyone who has heeded inner prompts simply to allow others their experiences.

The benefit of containment is also known to artists, who have learned that talking about a work they intend to create dispels the energy required to do it and that explaining a finished work diminishes it. In the same vein, sharing our dreams with the wrong person can open us up to being poisoned by ridicule or jealousy, leading to self-doubt. Like a locked diary, withholding keeps a part of ourselves *for* ourselves and honors the sanctity of the soul.

I unwisely "unlocked my diary" many years ago following an extraordinary experience. While I was listening with closed eyes to a relaxing piece of music, a warm, golden light suddenly filled the entire field of my inner vision. A human hand appeared in the foreground, the fingers outstretched but relaxed. The image was calming, vivid, and intensely present, unlike any mere dream.

When the vision faded, I excitedly told others about it. And yet, in trying to put words to the experience, I began to feel as though I were cheapening it. The blank looks and rolled eyes I got in response only made me regret my disclosure even more. "When you have a gem in your hand," advised Kabir, "you don't go out in the street announcing it." Some gifts are to be savored in private. In our tell-all society, the etymological kinship of the words *sacred* and *secret* is worthy of contemplation.

The High Priestess is the private self and the Self that remains yet hidden. In dropping compelling clues about our deeper identities, the archetype evokes a delight in the nameless and the unknown. "Love the mystery," advised the poet Rilke, for Mystery invites wonder, and wonder, like water to the body, nourishes the soul.

A High Priestess Story

The fickle Wheel of Fortune identified the theme of Amanda's reading—her on-again-off-again relationship with Russ. Though they had once more called it quits, a part of Amanda longed to join him in yet another round. At the start of the reading, she said she hoped the Tarot reading would "decide this once and for all."

In answer to the first question, "What is Amanda getting from the relationship?" the Knight of Wands charged in. Sure enough, Amanda liked the excitement of being with Russ, whose adventurousness led her to experience many new things—recreationally, sexually, creatively—she had never imagined for herself.

"What is Amanda missing from the relationship?" produced the High Priestess. Translation: the relationship lacked depth. Amanda wanted more than a good time. Her frustration about the absence of a more soulful connection had accounted for the repeated breakups. "When I'm with Russ the conversation is always about him," Amanda said. "I've never gotten the feeling he's really interested in who I am." I asked Amanda what she saw in the image of the High Priestess. "She looks lonely," she answered, as if peering into a hand mirror.

High Priestess Attributes

Key words:	Soul, Containment, Wisdom
Being:	Passive, silent, private, detached, aloof, mysterious, neutral, subtle, observant, calm, discreet, intuitive, psychic, soulful
Doing:	Listening within, perceiving essence, recollecting, concealing, observing without judging, honoring the Inner Being, keeping a secret, keeping a relationship platonic
Shadow:	Chronic passivity, fear of exposure; exaggerated purity or delicacy; holding back when engagement is needed
Reversed:	Superficiality, a feeling of soul emptiness; distrusting Inner Wisdom, ignoring hunches, repressing memory, outwardly expressing feelings and sharing observations
	Possible Advice
Reversed:	"Don't hold back. Express yourself. Engage." "Don't expect to find depth and mystery here. Take it at face value."

Questions for Reflection

What mystery intrigues you?

When have you been intuitively directed to say nothing?

Who in your life listens with their whole Being?

What place or experience in your life feels sacred for you?

When have your hunches about a person or situation proved accurate?

Where might it be beneficial to practice emotional detachment?

3. The Empress

Be fruitful and multiply.
—Genesis

Whereas the High Priestess held herself back, the Empress, archetype of Earth, birth, and abundance, simply cannot contain herself. Water rushes into her garden. Towers of cypress flourish in her forest. The sun pours down to prosper the grains from which she will bake her breads. An extravagance of cushions pamper her ("The moment I saw them," she says, "I just had to have them"). There is no want here, no lack; all needs and pleasures are royally indulged. The Empress seduces us, arousing our delight in the sensuousness of physical life. She

waves us nearer with her Earth-orb scepter as if coaxing us to freely "Love! Emote! Savor! Partake!"

The motif on her shield, pillow, and gown is the astrological symbol for Venus, linking her to the planet's namesake, the Roman goddess of love and beauty. On the beauty side, the Empress adores all things pleasing to the eye. She puts a high value on keeping her appearance attractive and her home comfortable and stylish. The loving aspect of the archetype is expressed in acts of generosity, tenderness, and compassion. She is the Universal Mother, patroness of nurturers and caregivers.

Anyone familiar with Dickens's *A Christmas Carol* will recognize the Empress/Universal Mother in the Ghost of Christmas Present. The spirit softens Scrooge's heart to the plight of the destitute and warms the miser's dismal chambers with a breathtaking banquet. In our age, the archetype's compassion has been personified by the likes of Mother Teresa and Princess Diana, and by organizations committed to the guardianship of children, animals, and the environment. Whenever body and Mother Earth are honored as temples of the Divine, the goddess is present.

Nurturer though she is, the Empress deeply enjoys the carnal side of life. Many Tarots depict her sexual passion by showing its outgrowth—a swollen abdomen. Her pregnancy is a reference not only to literal motherhood but to the larger theme of birthing. We become the Empress whenever we deliver something new into the world, be it a child, an ink sketch, or a start-up business. Every birth, at core, is an act of self-expression. As the synthesis of One and Two, Three represents expansion and increase, an out-flow of the creative intent.

The Empress at her most abstract represents Mother Earth, the essential forces of creativity and destruction. With a star for each month at her crown and a field of wheat below, she rules the seasons and the fruits born of them. She is the Mother of Matter (from *mater*, "mother") in all its manifestations. Pomegranates, plump with the promise of fruitfulness, adorn her gown.

The Empress's myriad attributes connect her to a pantheon of love and fertility goddesses, including Juno, mother goddess of Rome. Juno was known also as Moneta, from which the word *money* is derived and in whose temple the first Roman coins were minted. Making money, like making babies, symbolizes generativity and increase, and as such is a vital aspect of the Empress. Yet many spiritually minded people who have no trouble appreciating the presence of God in the physical pleasures of the world tend to draw the line at money. Especially in abundance, it is seen as evil, dirty, a vice of the "filthy rich." But to the Empress, money is just another divine expression, as ripe with creative, nourishing potential as a field of wheat.

The amount of abundance we enjoy in any area of our lives—material, sexual, emotional—is affected significantly by our attitudes toward *receiving*. We don't have what we deserve, the saying goes, we have what we *believe* we deserve. Feelings of unworthiness, consciously held or not, can block the flow of abundance. In such cases, asking and receiving become associated with shame, guilt, or even the fear of punishment. In contrast, the Empress invites us to cultivate a motherly regard for seeing our wants provided. Only when we are rooted in self-love can there bloom a prosperous consciousness free of self-imposed limits on the goodness available to us.

Equally vital to prosperous living is selfless giving. In Thornton Wilder's *The Matchmaker*, the title character says, "Money . . . is like manure. It's not worth a thing unless you spread it around, encouraging young things to grow." Though the quote specifies currency, the principle applies to any resource we may have that, in giving it, benefits others. Whatever the form of our abundance, in sharing it we create new life.

The majestic multiplicity of the Empress was displayed for me one November weekend many years ago. While driving home from college with friends, a sudden blinding snowstorm forced our car off the road. Police eventually escorted us—and more than a hundred other stranded motorists—to a shelter in rural Pontiac, Illinois.

The accommodations were not encouraging. Musty floor mats and fold-up cots promised a skimpy sleep. Most of us went to bed with growling stomachs that night, wondering if the vending machine's snacks would last the length of our confinement. Outside, the snow swirled and deepened, burying the road and all trace of our vehicles.

Early the next morning, a blast of chill wind swept through an open door in the armory. A procession of farmers and locals trudged in, each carrying stacks of foil-covered trays. Our gasps turned to cheers as the smells of hot biscuits, coffee, and farm-fresh eggs and sausages filled the crowded hall. No breakfast ever tasted so good or was more boisterously appreciated. When lunchtime came, another crew blew in with heaps of homemade fried chicken, vats of golden potato salad, and dish after dish of plump fruit pies. This would be topped by an evening feast so resplendent, so finely prepared, that our humble thank-yous as the farmers loaded our plates seemed wholly inadequate. And these people, braving the snow en route from farms and kitchens, fed us in this manner until the roads reopened two days later.

The event moved me with gratitude and awe. In one unforgettable weekend, I had experienced the Empress as Mother Nature in all her fury and as Mother Comforter in all her endless generosity and compassion—one force as magnificent as the other.

An Empress Story

"Last night I asked the cards what would make my headache go away," said Bianca, a Tarot student, "and I got the Empress. What does that mean?" I turned to the class and asked them what the archetype of nurturance might prescribe.

The responses were numerous and creative. "Just relax." "Pamper yourself with a long hot bath." "Ask your husband for a neck rub." "Get fresh air." To our surprise, Bianca blushed at the chorus of suggestions. "But I have kids," she said, as if that automatically canceled all options.

A couple of the mothers swiftly jumped in to challenge her excuse. They told Bianca she was missing an opportunity to model self-care for her children, if not robbing them of the chance to show a little support. Bianca dismissed them all with a skeptical look.

"Do you enjoy backrubs?" I asked her. She nodded. "Good," I said, "For the rest of the weekend I want you to ask your classmates for backrubs. They have a right to say no, but you must ask." Bianca had long ago mastered the giving aspect of the Empress. For one weekend, though, she would have the opportunity to explore the archetype's capacity to receive in full self-worth.

Empress Attributes

Key words:	Sensuality, Compassion, Abundance
Being:	Fertile, creative, compassionate, nurturing, generous, doting, prosperous, lavish, comfortable, healthy, sensual, seductive, emotional
Doing:	Mothering, caretaking, nurturing yourself or others, showing hospitality, freely giving, openly receiving, appreciating or creating beauty, savoring comfort and pleasure, making or spending money, thriving
Shadow:	Taking care of everyone but yourself, being overprotective, overindulging in the sensual or material
Reversed:	Undernourishment, emotional coolness, infertility, denied pleasure, creativity blockage, negative body image, financial lack, frugality, moderation,rejection of mother figure
Reversed:	*Possible Advice* "Let someone else play Mother for awhile." "Don't overdo it (eating, spending, entertaining, etc.)."

Questions for Reflection

How and when do you nurture yourself?

What is the most memorable act of caring ever shown you?

Who could benefit from your compassion, tenderness, or generosity?

What is the most extravagant gift you have ever received or given?

What pleasures do you allow or deny yourself?

What do you find beautiful?

4. The Emperor

Set all things in their own particular place, and know
that order is the greatest grace.

—John Dryden

The Emperor, it must be said, lacks the mystical glamour of the preceding Trumps. In fact, his effect is downright sobering. Many people judge him for looking uptight or intimidating. His power status reminds them of fun-squelching fuddy-duddies or the abuses of the patriarchy. As every archetype has its shadow, these are indeed the Emperor's. But in his purest aspect, he brings order out of chaos, creates safe boundaries, and helps us make useful distinctions in the world.

THE EMPEROR.

The Emperor rules from a solid foundation of logic and reason, symbolized by the sturdy, symmetrical dais and throne. The granite throne ("the seat of reason") demonstrates the Emperor's ability to carve the mountain rock of the Empress/Mother Nature into something useful—a place to sit. The Emperor brings order to what the Empress births. He shapes her unhindered movement into choreography, turns her wild vegetation into cultivated crops, and assigns species to her creatures. With power like that, it's no wonder he holds the *ankh*, the Egyptian symbol of potency.

As Four, the number connoting stability, the Emperor stands for the internal and external structures that give us a sense of solidity and control. The Emperor is the energy that creates and enforces rules and laws, including those that ensure our survival. My friend Kathleen remembers racing through her house and stubbing her toe. "Aww, I know that hurts, doesn't it, honey," her mother cooed, wiping Kathleen's tears. Her father shook his head. "When you run in the house," he lectured, "you're bound to get hurt. Be more careful next time."

The characters in this classic example seem straight out of central casting—the compassionate, nurturing Mother/Empress and the rational, rule-making Father/Emperor. These complementary archetypes show us two different faces of the Divine—God as love and liberality, and God as laws and limits. The Tarot path directs us to integrate the sovereignty of both.

The stream that appears behind the Emperor is a feminine motif that connects him to the feeling, fertile worlds of the High Priestess and Empress. The stream is very narrow, for mature rulership frequently depends upon our ability to minimize watery emotion and imagination and operate on a more rational, objective level. Yet, should the Emperor become too rigid in his thinking or pursue power for its own sake, his royal orb (another feminine symbol) reminds him of his responsibility to the Whole, within and without.

As guardians of the kingdom, our inner Emperors are concerned with enforcing boundaries. This one's armor implies that we may be called upon at times to hold our ground and defend our bodies, territory, ideas, or the people for whom we are responsible—no exceptions. The Emperor is willing to battle for what is rightfully his, and would-be intruders would be wise to consider that the armor he displays is but a glimpse of the full warrior regalia concealed beneath his Mars-red robes. Like the rams adorning the throne, Emperor energy can be headstrong and stubborn, and like the mountains, protective and unyielding.

We manifest the dignity and self-respect of the Emperor whenever we claim our legitimate leadership, authority, rights, or responsibilities.

If we, like the monarch, are coming from a place of inner stability and wisdom, our squaring off against opposition will not be the puffing up of the ego but the genuine expression of our integrity and self-worth.

Most of us, I find, are ambivalent about our power. We're not always sure how to use it appropriately. Our boundaries may be weak around certain people or in certain situations, and we may feel like pushovers or victims. In contrast, a secure and balanced Emperor creates no opportunity for being manipulated, bullied, or taken advantage of and rejects employing such tactics with others. He asks for what he wants without coercion and has no trouble saying "no" when others test his limits.

On the energetic level, the Emperor governs our psychic boundaries. The more finely attuned we become to ourselves, the more easily we are able to distinguish our feelings from those we pick up from others. Then, instead of unconsciously absorbing unwanted energies, the Emperor senses the invasion and rolls up the drawbridge.

One of my students, Mary, told me about a "psychic attack" she'd experienced while visiting her aunt. Within only minutes of her arrival, Mary began to feel strangely wary and agitated. Despite her aunt's gracious smile and harmless small talk, Mary couldn't shake the feeling that the woman was bombarding her with envy and disapproval. In response, she calmly visualized a protective dome of light around herself. Though feeling sufficiently shielded, Mary made an executive decision to leave shortly thereafter, her aunt's polite protests notwithstanding. A brisk walk home served to clear the remaining negative vibrations she'd felt clinging to her, thus restoring her self-sovereignty.

As Emperors we have a sacred duty to manage and protect our inner and outer realms and respect those of others. Yet even here we must exercise the archetype's characteristic caution. Too much order squeezes out spontaneity, sapping the joy from life. Too many reasoned differentiations conceal the truth of the whole. Armoring out of habitual fear only attracts intruders and weakens the spirit. In its most majestic sense, the Trump commands us to act from a place of true authority born of wisdom and self-trust; we hold this space only when our heads rule jointly with our hearts. With scepter and orb held in equal honor, pleasure connects with purpose, compassion joins with reason, peace befalls the kingdom.

An Emperor Story

Alexis wanted to adopt a baby. With a good-paying job and a network of supportive friends and family, she felt ready to make the commitment. We laid out the Celtic Cross Spread. The cards beamed back all her yearning and optimism. "This'll be one loved baby," I thought.

I glanced over to the Possible Outcome position. It showed a major force that would soon play a key role in the adoption process— the Emperor. Here was the archetype of the bureaucratic elements Alexis would confront—the agencies, applications, evaluations, and paperwork. The Emperor would officially decide if her motives, income, and other factors made her a suitable adoptive parent. "I'm basically going to be opening my entire life to inspection," Alexis said. "I have a lot to do to get ready."

Within a year, the Emperor had been appeased. I see Alexis and her daughter often in the neighborhood.

Emperor Attributes

Key words:	Order, Rulership, Stability
Being:	Competent, organized, safe, responsible, firm, rational, specific, decisive, assertive, authoritative, forceful, disciplined, dutiful, self-sufficient, protective, territorial
Doing:	Organizing; prioritizing; creating or defending boundaries; guarding possessions; standing up for yourself; making, enforcing, or honoring rules or laws; exercising authority or leadership; dealing with bureaucracy, fathering
Shadow:	Using authority inappropriately; being bossy, emotionally rigid, overly controlling or overly responsible, rational at the expense of feeling, patronizing, obsessed with security, or tyrannical
Reversed:	Lack of control or structure, inability to say no or draw boundaries, passive-aggressiveness, submission; neglecting responsibilities, feeling inadequate, relaxing defenses, bending the rules, rejecting a father figure
	Possible Advice
Reversed:	"Let go of the need to control." "Loosen up."

Questions for Reflection

What needs to get organized in your life?

When or with whom would it be useful to be more assertive?

When or with whom are you too controlling?

Who in your life most exemplifies Emperor qualities?

How easy is it for you to stand up for yourself?

How easily are you able to act on your decisions without the need for approval?

5. The Hierophant

We are all teachers; the question is not whether we will teach, but what.
—Anonymous

The Chicago newspapers once ran a story about a clerk in a sports-memorabilia shop who, misreading a price tag, sold a $1,200 Nolan Ryan rookie baseball card to a boy for $12. When the store owner discovered the error, he contacted the thirteen-year-old boy, a regular customer and savvy collector, and the boy's father. Reasoning that the boy must have realized the clerk's error, the owner pleaded with them to return the card or pay for it in full. They refused, maintaining that the clerk's ignorance in the transaction was, by law, their gain. For weeks afterward, the local newspapers were choked with letters from readers arguing passionately on both sides of the issue.

In this classic archetypal conflict, we find the Emperor (in its densest sense) defending the letter of the law and the Hierophant arguing that the legality of a situation doesn't make it right. Whereas the Emperor represents earthly authority, laws, and rules, the Hierophant is top dog in matters of ethics. (Put the cards side by side, and you'll notice that the Hierophant's headdress rises just above the crown of his neighbor, indicating the higher matters with which he is concerned.)

Moral development occurs in stages. As preschoolers, we resist the urge to steal so as not to lose parental love and approval. Later, we keep our hands out of Mom's purse to avoid punishment. As we mature, we reject the idea of stealing because it doesn't *feel*

60

right. At this stage, the Hierophant (Greek for "revealer of sacred things") emerges as the internalized voice of conscience, our moral checkpoint. Taking the high road and acting with integrity becomes its own reward—the result of hearing, listening to, and obeying the counsel of our better nature. The theme of listening is accentuated by the Hierophant's attentive acolytes, who represent obedience to principled guidance. The flower motifs on their robes mirror the varieties seen in the Magician's garden, representing here the desire for learning and the surrender to instruction. The Hierophant, too, listens—prominent white earflaps emphasize his mastery in this department. Five's dead-center positioning between One and the final single digit, Nine, make it the archetype for mediation. The Hierophant's ministry positions him as mediator between humankind and the Divine, a facilitator of sacred conversations.

The Hierophant's nearly concealed blue skirt discloses an underlying connection to the sacred vestments of the High Priestess; the red robe and white shirt relate to the active, verbal world of the Magician. The resulting mixture—putting the intangible into words—forms the basis for the Hierophant's deftness with the abstract realms of philosophy, morality, and ethics. The Trump takes hold whenever we consider or give voice to these ideas. The Hierophant's collar is blue, color of the expressive fifth chakra, our communication center; the yokes on the attending acolytes signify their obedience to the higher ideas coming through.

The gray stone fixtures surrounding the Hierophant allude to the pillars of stability provided by well-honed philosophical constructs. As the combination of black and white, gray is the color of balance; as the fusing of light and dark, it is the color of wisdom. At his feet lies a checkerboard pattern, hinting that the pathway to higher awareness must acknowledge this divine interplay of opposites.

Many people flinch at the image of the overtly religious Hierophant. They may look with suspicion on priests, gurus, and any who preach an established doctrine. But a doctrine is merely a set of codified beliefs; to the extent that everybody lives by a belief system, no matter how uniquely one's own, we are all the Hierophant.

Stripped of its religious connotation, the card depicts tribal consciousness—the traditions and expectations of cultures, institutions, families, and peers that profoundly shape us as individuals. Do these influences, like the Hierophant's upraised hand, bless us . . . or do they, like the archetype's shadow, slow our spiritual progress? Using the Hierophant as a tool for self-discovery begins with asking, "What do I believe is good or bad, right or wrong, and how did I acquire these beliefs?" Quite often the answers disclose a startling dissonance: We find we've been carrying around someone else's convictions, living out our lives unaware of just how much the old yoke still binds. For better or worse, our ideas about politics, parenthood, sexuality, religion, money, and relationships are not inspired so much as they are borrowed. Our task is to keep the ones that expand our spirit and retire the rest.

The mystical path leads one beyond concepts, beyond words, to a state of simply feeling the divine presence in each moment. From this topmost perspective, the Hierophant represents not only what one has learned or must learn, but also what one must eventually *unlearn* to nurture the heightened consciousness beckoning in the World card.

A Hierophant Story

When Carleen turned fifty, she decided to break with some long-standing traditions. "Sex wasn't important to my mother," she confided during her reading, "and for years I tried to convince myself it wasn't important to me either. But I want more sex than my husband is willing to give me, and I'm prepared to find it elsewhere if I have to." Considering the Outcome card, the Hierophant, which in its reversed position lay powerless to defend vows or custom, she would likely succeed.

Hierophant Attributes

Key words:	Conscience, Higher Conduct, Doctrine
Being:	Humane, virtuous, philosophical, religious, loyal to a group or to collective beliefs, conventional
Doing:	Focusing on moral or ethical matters, ministering, teaching, learning, receiving counsel, adopting a philosophy or creed, preserving a tradition, following a prescribed path, participating in formalized ritual, making a vow, conferring or receiving a blessing
Shadow:	Unquestioned conformity, dogma, self-righteousness
Reversed:	Acting in ways opposite to your values; breaking a vow; behaving contrary to family, religious, or societal norms; rejecting a prescribed path; stifled speech
	Possible Advice
Reversed:	"Follow your own path despite the pressure to conform." "Listen, don't preach."

Questions for Reflection

What doctrine or philosophy guides your life?

Which of your family or religious traditions do you find most meaningful?

At whose feet would you cherish the opportunity to sit and learn?

What is the best advice you ever gave or received?

What beliefs or ideas would you like to transmit to others?

What long-held beliefs or values no longer serve you?

6. The Lovers

Arms wide, we bend toward each other, and a passing angel pauses
for a moment, standing imponderably on the air, to witness our embrace.
—P. L. Travers

A cartoon by the legendary Charles Addams depicts a stuffy-looking man in his sterile apartment, the door of which is secured by a formidable assortment of deadbolt locks, chain latches, peepholes, and burglar bars. Jaw tight, the man casts a wary glance at the floor where—despite the vault-like entrance—someone has slipped in a valentine card.

The appeal of the image goes beyond the sentimental. It illuminates our fears of connection, intimacy, and the penetration of emotional defenses—the very qualities glorified in the Lovers.

This is not love's first appearance in the Major Arcana. The Empress showed us love through compassion and nurturing, the Emperor through healthy boundaries, the Hierophant through helpful doctrine. But these archetypes reflect love between parent and child and teacher and student, in which there is an inevitable one-up, one-down power imbalance. In the Lovers we see love as *partnership*. The number Six represents cooperation, reciprocity, and the harmony of opposites.

All partnerships, whether between lovers, spouses, friends, or coworkers, offer the potential for personal growth. Through partnership we become less self-absorbed, taking the needs and wants of the other into consideration. Partnerships foster intimacy. They create containers for mutual support and trust. Joining forces creates possibilities not available in solo efforts. Yet even when our partnerships don't meet these ideals, they enable us to discover who we are and who we are not, what nourishes us and what does not—things we could not have learned had we never entered into relationship.

With the Lovers, we are presented with a partnership between the allegorical figures of Adam and Eve. Eve is aligned with the Tree of the Knowledge of Good (truth) and Evil (illusion), representing the receiving of wisdom. Adam is backed by the Tree of Life, afire with potency. Judging by the angel's blessing, it's a match made in heaven. The couple extends their hands to each other, opening in readiness for a union presaged by the intertwining roots of the trees. The angel's robe, resembling a violet rose, symbolizes the higher vibrations blooming in the pairing, the angel's red-hot wings the soaring of their passion.

The Lovers works on two symbolic levels. The first shows an idealized love between two people (of any gender). The second presents a symbol of internal harmony between one's feminine and masculine aspects. Seen through the latter lens, the Trump calls us to integrate the masculine and feminine and thus their corollaries, Magician and High Priestess, head and heart, conscious and unconscious, light and dark.

The halved sun indicates that, at this stage, we may not yet be able to make these inner opposites One. But if we can begin to respect the importance of each, we'll hasten the psychological maturity of individuation—a state foreshadowed by the single mountain rising in the background.

The Lovers is a card of intimacy. Two people have peeled off the protective layers of ego to stand naked before one another. She is the stirring of deep feelings and the surrender to passion no matter how irrational its intensity or direction. He is the *decision* to love, using the mental faculties to make discriminating choices. Their open stances seem to say what all true lovers must: "This is me. I hide nothing from you. I give you my heart."

Sifted down to its essence, the Lovers Trump is not only an exclusive representation of the union of sweethearts and sexual partners (*eros*), it embraces also the deep connections between soul mates and friends (*philia*). And at the other, less personal, end of the spectrum, the Lovers encompasses the unconditional, universal love for all beings (*agape*). The angel hovers to remind us that we are not isolated entities; part of each of us is in all of us. We share connections deeper than our differences, however subtle or tentative the connections may initially appear.

Our common humanity was once the message of a disheveled, ranting Holy Fool who boarded a busy commuter train I was riding. "Ha! You're all pretending you don't see each other," he accurately observed of us.

We stiffened.

"Why doesn't anybody look at each other?" he implored, playfully. "We're all brothers and sisters, right? We're all brothers and sisters!" When the man finally ambled into the next car, the tension broke. People lowered their newspapers and began laughing and talking— out of sheer relief, mostly, but engaged just the same. Our armor hadn't kept out the valentine. As Sufi sage Mahmud Shabistari put it, "There is only One Light, and 'you' and 'me' are holes in the lamp shade." The Lovers prepares us for the ecstatic communion with the divine Beloved, source of love in all its infinite expressions, present and waiting within our hearts.

A Lovers Story

As part of the Tarot presentations I give for organizations, I often fan out the Major Arcana (face down) and invite someone to randomly pick a card. After briefly discussing the card, I'll ask the person to comment on how that archetype may have personal meaning for her. In most cases we discover the card either represents a current theme in her life, or a quality she'd like to develop.

I once used this format at a small church-group presentation. By the end of the evening, only one person, a middle-aged woman, prim and guarded, had not drawn a card. Prodded by the others, she reluctantly took one. When it was shown to be the Lovers, the group members shot each other looks of surprise and embarrassment. I talked briefly about the archetype and then invited the woman to share how it may have spoken to her. She declined to comment.

When the session ended one of the attendees took me aside and said how impressed he was that the Lovers had come to the most emotionally closed-off member of their group. I nodded. The Lovers had called attention to the very sensuality and connection the woman ached for, a prescription direct from her Inner Healer.

Lovers Attributes

Key words:	Attraction, Cooperation, Harmony
Being:	Alluring, emotionally open, trusting, intimate, sexually attracted; a soul mate
Doing:	Finding commonality, making harmonious choices, appreciating differences, creating win-win situations, forging deep connections with others, loving passionately
Shadow:	Possessiveness, overidealization of the relationship, codependency
Reversed:	Separation, fear of intimacy, antagonism between opposites, absence of trust, diluted passion, emotional or sexual rejection
	Possible Advice
Reversed:	"The attraction is misdirected. Make another choice." "Stop looking for the 'perfect' relationship."

Questions for Reflection

How do you express your "masculine" and "feminine" sides?
What relationship brings out the best in you?
When have you been surprised by your attraction to another?
What lessons learned in relationships have served your growth?
Where is cooperation most needed in your life?
When have you expressed the shadow aspect of the Lovers and
   acted possessively?

7. The Chariot

Climb high; climb far. Your goal the sky; your aim the star.
   —Inscription at Williams College

Meet the Graduate. The splendid young man strikes a regal, ready pose, as though pausing for the flashbulbs of admirers. He faces away from the walled confines of the community of his childhood, preparing to venture forth to prove himself to the larger world awaiting him.

In his purest sense a spiritual warrior, the charioteer is primed for the conquest of Self. He must charge courageously, purposefully into the archetypal tests and challenges of the greater adventure. The card's number, Seven, is associated with tests and advancement.

Though he will make his journey alone, he takes with him many parting gifts, which symbolize the qualities he has assimilated from the core family of archetypes in the first line of Trumps. The yellow boots that led the Fool so spontaneously to life's daring edges have been transformed here into more ambitious means of conveyance, the wheels of the Chariot. The Magician's wand ignites the charioteer with vision and the power to manifest it. The High Priestess's crescent moons proffer the guiding presence of Inner Wisdom.

A laurel wreath and star crown, blessings of the Empress, urge compassionate choices. The Emperor's armor serves to shield the young adventurer's still-developing ego from the lances thrown at questing heroes. And from the Hierophant's temple, pillars remind the lad of the values driving his journey.

At the front of the vehicle, resembling a wheel and axle, are the interpenetrating Hindu *lingam* and *yoni*. Emblematic of his quest, they connote the dance of polarities personified in the Lovers (the winged sphere of unity recalls the angel). Empowered by the gifts and blessings of his archetypal allies, the charioteer is ready to roll.

Unlike the Fool's innocent meanderings, the Chariot's movement is fueled by planning and willpower. We become the Chariot when charging toward goals for which we have carefully prepared or when putting muscle behind causes that stir the blood. The driver's lower half looks poured into the foundation of his vehicle, as if to dramatize his fusion with his mission or a need for protection in its pursuit. The expansive presence of the city backing the charioteer inspires us to ensure that the goals we go after are not merely self-serving, but in some way benefit others, if not the world at large. Without genuine ardor behind our ambitions, our victories will be short term and hollow.

Will and action belong collectively to the masculine archetypes. A balanced ego enables the Magician to initiate meaningful change, the Emperor to rule comfortably in his authority, and the driver of the Chariot to declare himself worthy of his cause. Yet unless the ego is kept in check, we become vulnerable to shadow forms of our power, such as pursuing a goal so zealously that people stepping into our Chariot path get flattened.

Although the charioteer is in possession of his power and emboldened with purpose, he is not completely alone at the helm. The invisible reins are controlled by a higher Intelligence. The charioteer's apparent ease with the reins' invisibility indicates that he has moved beyond the ego-driven belief that he is solely in charge. He understands that his success, inner and outer, ultimately requires copiloting with unseen guidance. This awareness will keep him from succumbing to hubris and grandiosity or delusions of invincibility —attitudes that the Tower archetype would eventually call to his attention in its earthy and humiliating ways.

His quest is not free of pain. Like the masks of comedy and tragedy, two faces affixed to his crescent shoulder plates serve to remind him that, in the words of William Blake, "Joy and woe are woven fine / a clothing for the soul divine." Seeing adversity as useful a teacher as success will keep him from falling off the wagon in despair or cynicism and getting left in the dust. Traditionally, the faces are said to denote the Urim and Thummim, two oracular stones worn on the shoulders or breastplate of priests in ancient Israel. The stones became luminous in response to the priest's questions and directed him according to divine will.

For all his preparation and readiness, the charioteer's team of sphinx chargers appear to be conflicted. Both creatures face slightly different ways, which suggests the possibility that they might pull their driver in opposing directions and throw him off track. What could be more daunting? "I long to pursue a life of public service, but I'm such a private person." "I long to go after what I want in life, but I question my own abilities." "My humility says 'Stay,' my curiosity says 'Go.'" Without a warrior's self-trust and determination, such tensions can undermine our missions and keep us paralyzed in indecision. Rather than waiting for conditions—inner or outer—to be perfect (when are they ever?), the charioteer cries, "Damn the contradictions, full speed ahead!" Eventually he will reconcile these opposing forces.

The water behind the Emperor is narrow to allow for more stable, rational influences. The river behind the Chariot compels us to move, to ride in the direction of our emerging Selves with spirit and purpose. That impulse will lead us to a road filled with new tests and opportunities in the second line of the Major Arcana.

A Chariot Story

I received the following e-mail from Elizabeth, a Tarot student: "I did a reading about whether my sweet little nineteen-year-old cat, Emily, was ready to transition from this life. The card was the Chariot. My sister and I took her to the vet the next morning. She was beginning to fail very quickly, and we did not want her to suffer. It was one of the hardest mornings of my life. She and I were so very close, but that card gave me such comfort that she was ready to move forward."

Human or animal, the Chariot signifies the energy of commencement, carrying us onward to the next levels of the journey.

Chariot Attributes

Key words:	Commencement, Challenge, Victory
Being:	Purposeful, brave, driven, disciplined, ambitious, idealistic, victorious, heroic
Doing:	Pursuing or completing a goal, overcoming obstacles, proving yourself, moving forward, accelerating efforts, staying on track, overriding your doubts

Shadow:	Bravado, workaholism; feeling compulsively driven, feeling worthy and loved only through achievements
Reversed:	Purposelessness, doubt about direction, inability to harness energy for moving forward, stalled by a lack of support, low drive, "falling off the wagon"
	Possible Advice
Reversed:	"Hold your horses—now is not the time to move forward." "Change direction."

Questions for Reflection

What mission have you completed, or are committed to completing?

When have you boldly moved forward despite doubts or criticism?

How easily are you able to ask for support in the pursuit of your goals?

Over what "insurmountable" obstacles have you triumphed?

In what area do you feel compelled to make your mark on the world?

What do you feel is your life purpose?

Major Arcana 8–14:
The Inward Path

Vision is the art of seeing things invisible.
—Jonathan Swift

Trumps 1–7 gave us the relative familiarity of self, parents, church, love, and achievement. In Trumps 8–14, we encounter cosmic forces that call us to probe more deeply for answers or meaning. Life will ask us to be strong and to examine the consequences of our choices. We will wrestle with the workings of justice and divine order. We will confront our limitations and our mortality. And at the end of this Trump line, we'll find ways to make peace with our conflicts and contradictions, distilling wisdom from the whole unlikely mix.

8. Strength

He who reigns within himself and rules his passions,
desires, and fears is more than a king.
—John Milton

In Strength's lion, we see a symbol of that which pants beneath our pressed suits and modest blouses. Here is our physical and emotional power at its most raw: the baring of teeth, the licking of chops, the raising of hindquarters. The golden beast is the instinct for survival, sex, gratification, and the freedom of spontaneously expressing these impulses. It is our basic vitality—sinewy, earthy, primal.

Accepting one's animal nature can be difficult when the ego worships rationality and keeping things cool. Many people reject all but the intellectual view of themselves. Others may suspect a shaggier counterpart lurking within, yet lock it away, terrified of the consequences of raw, unmuzzled feelings and instincts. But if we habitually beat back these impulses—in effect, demonizing them—they will stalk us unmercifully in the archetype of the Devil.

If the lion represents such a vital source of energy, why does the woman seem to be closing its mouth? Certainly not to punish the animal or protect herself from it, as the calmness of her expression makes clear. Rather, she tames it. Although our lion qualities make us feel truly alive, without the control of a higher intelligence (the woman) they weaken us. The woman in Trump 8 maintains the ascendancy, thus keeping the passions from running amok.

The role of Strength's lion keeper is similar to that of people who have wolves and wolf hybrids as pets. While they may respect the animals and enjoy their exciting companionship, the owners are aware of the need continuously to assert top-dog status. Failure to do so can bring trouble. I once read about a man who was forced to crawl as a result of a sudden painful back injury. When his two-year-old wolf-dog noticed him in the lowered, vulnerable position, it saw its chance for dominance and pinned him, snarling, its teeth exposed just above the man's neck. He escaped unharmed when family members distracted the animal with their shouts.

In contrast to the placid woman on the card, keeping our lower natures in line can be a challenge. The call of the cheesecake may drown out our dieting affirmations; the smirking face of our belittling boss may tempt us to throw our coffee at him. Though it seems paradoxical, one method of self-control is negotiation. By seeing the lady's gesture as stroking, not closing, the lion's mouth, and the lion licking her hand, we have a symbol of respectful *partnership*. From partnership, negotiation—not mere taming—becomes possible.

The lady honors the biological and emotional needs of her beast; she works with it toward a satisfying coexistence. If we choose the low-cal fruit tart over the cheesecake, we pacify our raging sweet tooth and keep our diet promise. If we wait to roar *after* leaving the boss's office, we discharge the rage and stay employed. Strength promotes a win-win dynamic—feed the lion (in right proportion), and it won't eat you in the form of ulcers. A fed lion won't rattle your cage with a menagerie of troubling symptoms in an effort to reconnect you with your basic needs and feelings.

Trump 8 shows a balanced interchange between upper and lower energies. "Too much of the animal," said Jung, "disfigures the civilized human being; too much culture makes for a sick animal." Just as the number 8 signifies ebb and flow, the infinity symbol hovering above the figures suggests that what is occurring is a symbiotic relationship between raw power and the consciousness that uses it wisely. The woman aligns with the lion's power yet maintains creative control, channeling it into the service of a higher expression. When balanced in this way, we are able to live and love with passion and courage, becoming a positive force within and without.

In the most obvious sense, Trump 8 is about being strong. This is not the same as fearlessness, for even lions tremble. Nor should it be confused with the kind of sheer determination seen in the Chariot. Rather, Strength is that power we call upon to help us remain resilient in fear's midst. Though our initial animal impulse may be to attack or run away, when the archetype is activated we intuitively recognize the need to refine those urges and find more steady ways of responding. While soothing the beast, we channel its fiery force into the fiery conviction that we will survive no matter what.

I recently read about Irena Sendler, a Polish Catholic social worker credited for saving 2,500 Jewish children from extermination during the German occupation of Poland. In 1942 she joined Zegota, a Polish underground organization that secretly moved children from the Jewish ghetto into orphanages, convents, and homes. Irena Sendler was captured by the Nazis in 1943. Her captors tortured her, yet she refused to identify her coconspirators. They broke her feet and legs. Still she gave no names. Though severely crippled, Irena Sendler escaped and immediately resumed her rescue efforts. In 2005 she told a British newspaper, "I was taught that if you see a person drowning, you must jump into the water to save them, whether you can swim or not" (*Chicago Tribune*, May 13, 2008).

When others tell us of having survived momentous trials—physically, emotionally, or spiritually—we may find ourselves saying, "I don't know how you did it. I don't know what I'd do if I had to go through what you went through." The fact is, we *don't* know how we would manage. All we can do is trust that we too would find the lionlike strength within to meet it with courage. Strength of that magnitude can only be found, not willed, which gives Trump 8 its quality of grace.

A Strength Story

Roger was preparing to leave for his company's annual winter retreat. Despite his descriptions of a snowy paradise and luxury resort, his manner seemed tense and evasive. At his request we did a two-card spread: the energy that would support his greatest good on the trip (Strength) and the energy he should leave behind (Two of Cups). Roger sighed, though I couldn't tell if it was in relief or disappointment.

Shifting in the chair, he explained that a coworker with whom he shared a mutual attraction was going to be at the retreat. He was excited by the likelihood of a sexual encounter but was fearful of the complications such an action could impose on his fifteen-year marriage. Recognizing the cards' petition for faithfulness, the visibly chagrined Roger had been put on alert to keep his animal impulses in check—and his tail between his legs.

Strength Attributes

Key words:	Courage, Constancy, Self-Control
Being:	Strong in spirit, buoyant, self-disciplined; a survivor
Doing:	Showing grace under pressure, holding steady despite challenges, controlling fear, loving with boundaries intact, "taming" baser instincts and desires, forgiving
Shadow:	Excessive self-denial; stifling vital emotions, needs, or desires
Reversed:	Poor impulse control, timidity, weakness of spirit, depression; yielding to temptation
	Possible Advice
Reversed:	"Let go of your idea of what it means to be strong." "Let the lion roar."

Questions for Reflection

What makes you feel most vital and alive?
When have you been surprised by your own strength and courage?
Which of your drives or impulses do you routinely try to subdue?
What fears have you minimized or tamed?
Whose strength inspires you?
Where in your life do you most need strength?

9. The Hermit

Be ye lamps unto yourselves.
—Buddha

THE HERMIT.

A glance around the average home reveals an almost endless supply of things designed to keep us entertained, informed, productive, and busy for busy-ness's sake—round the clock, if we choose. We wire ourselves with gadgets to keep the conversations going, the music pounding, and the schedules crammed. The relentless overstimulation of modern life, and the superficial priorities it promotes, are endemic to the pervasive feelings of emptiness that plague our population. When that psychic hole becomes too great, we try to fill it with yet more stuff—food, stimulants, time fillers, trivia. Still we are unhappy. Why? In philosopher Blaise Pascal's diagnosis, "All men's miseries derive from not being able to sit quietly in a room alone."

High above the masses stands the solitary figure of the Hermit. In the tradition of holy men, he has ascended the mountaintop to come closer to the wisdom of his Highest Self. The stark peaks offer no distractions from his inner quest. Even the season supports his aims. It is winter, a time for retreating to interior places.

The Hermit's white beard places him in the winter of his years. As the last single digit, 9 is the archetype for completion and the ends of cycles. The Hermit has integrated the lessons of Trumps 0 through 7 and now calls upon Trump 8 for the Strength to withdraw, wander, and wonder at the Big Questions: *Who am I? Why am I here? Where have I been? Where am I going? What does it all mean?*

Whether terrified of not finding the answers—or not liking the ones we get—many of us exert great effort to avoid these questions altogether. And society is more than willing to assist in that deterrence. Answering the Big Questions takes reflective solitude, which many look upon as selfish, antisocial, cause for concern, or just plain odd. With such a stigma, why would anyone choose to leave the warmth of the community campsite for the cold, dark unknown of the woods? For most people, it takes a crisis.

Jung decreed that the search for the Self is the central mission for the second half of life. Awareness of mortality turns attention inward. Priorities shift. Long-held external values become the source of disillusionment. We react against a lifetime of approval seeking, selling out, playing the game. With growing intensity, we hope that life holds something richer and truer, yet sense that the key to this possibility can only be found within. When the inner-directed call comes to discover more lasting truths, we instinctively pull away—psychologically, physically, or both—from the clamor of outer forms.

The quest for truth through self-examination is in no way limited to the classic midlife crisis. The need for time alone is a hallmark of adolescence, as is the knack for penetrating (if gloomy) self-scrutiny. Like the Hermit's cloak, the "Keep Out" sign on the teenager's door enables her safely to disappear for a while. Removed from the attention and expectations of family, friends, and society, she is free to figure out who she is—outer influences no longer competing to define her.

Many tribal rites of passage sanction the temporary isolation of the young. Girls are confined to special chambers for menses. Boys are left in remote locations from which they must, with the help of animal or ancestral guides, find their way back home. In many cultures, the ability to function alone effectively signifies emotional maturity. Of course, simply being alone does not lead to the nourishing introspection symbolized by the Hermit. The archetype's way of aloneness is organized around self-discovery, self-improvement, or unlocking the mysteries of life.

No peephole-peering recluse, the Hermit's "time out" is only temporary. The insights he acquires on this retreat will restore and refine the sense of meaning in his life. Others will benefit, too. We simultaneously become the Hermit and awaken the archetype in others when we use the light of our wisdom to guide them to a deeper understanding of who they are—not through preaching, but by example, or in the posing of questions leading to their own self-discovery. The way-shower energy of the Hermit can also take the form of counselors, therapists, mentors, vision quests, and self-development books and workshops—"lanterns" leading us back to ourselves in intimate ways. The Hermit's glimmering lantern symbolizes the kindled self-knowledge illuminating his path. The radiant flame is the six-pointed Seal of Solomon—two intersecting triangles representing the union of yin and yang.

In contrast to the High Priestess's nonverbal, felt ways of knowing, as the Hermit we plumb our depths through conscious evaluation and analyses. And whereas the Hierophant offered a useful set of guidelines for the path, the Hermit teaches us to follow an internal compass so that we may follow paths of our own making, discovering truths more profoundly personal. With patience, we may eventually perceive the map of the road we've been traveling—its windings and bridges, ditches and dead ends—as revealed in the Wheel of Fortune.

A Hermit Story

Norma-Jo's dedication to her art demanded extended periods of solitary work in her studio, a forest cabin alongside the Willamette River in Oregon. But the solitude that produced soulful and extraordinary works of art also strained her marriage. It surprised neither of us to see the Hermit in her reading.

"My husband knows how important my work is to me, " she said, "and he's very supportive. But he'd like for me to be more available to him, so . . . " Her words trailed off, merging into the silence of the woods.

The Hermit may teach the value of aloneness, but it falls to us to negotiate the costs.

Hermit Attributes

Key words:	Solitude, Study, Self-Examination
Being:	Alone, private, serious, studious, unhurried, shy, introspective, contemplative, austere, discriminating; an outsider
Doing:	Slowing down, distancing yourself from others physically or psychologically, mentoring or guiding others, researching, investigating, seeking answers, soul searching, renouncing all but the essentials
Shadow:	Feeling isolated, being a shut-in, hiding from others, overthinking; perfectionism, extreme self-absorption or self-denial
Reversed:	Fear of aloneness or self-examination, poor concentration; coming out of your shell, being less serious or studious
	Possible Advice
Reversed:	"Get out of yourself." "Don't overanalyze this."

Questions for Reflection

To what questions are you looking for answers?

For whom are you a mentor or guide?

From whom do you seek sage advice?

How comfortable are you in undistracted solitude?

When do you feel the need to retreat into yourself?

What activities do you most enjoy alone?

What area of study completely absorbs you?

10. Wheel of Fortune

Everything goes, everything returns; eternally rolls the wheel of being.

—Nietzsche

In the Chariot, the wheels turned per the driver's intended direction. In Trump 10, we encounter a single, mystical wheel powered by the Great Mystery. One of the most complex Tarot archetypes, the Wheel of Fortune represents the cosmic Wheel of Life, destiny, karma, laws of cause and effect, and the apparently random ups and downs that compose our life experiences.

The Wheel of Fortune was an image familiar to people of the late Middle Ages and early Renaissance. A king was typically shown at the bottom of the Wheel, while a pauper or vagabond ascended to the top, underscoring the fickle, indiscriminate turns of fate. When the goddess Fortuna

82

cranked the Wheel, it was without any apparent consideration of one's deeds or status. All were subject to radical and unforeseen shifts.

In the eighteenth century, the card was reimagined by French occultists who attributed Egyptian origins to the Tarot, an influence reflected in Waite's design. Typhon the snake and jackal-headed Anubis together symbolize life, death, and rebirth—the Universe coming full circle. The occultists further encrypted the card with anagrams, Hebrew letters, alchemical glyphs, and astrological and Christian symbols (icons of the four apostles grace the corners of the card). The meaning of these symbols can be summed up quite simply: no matter which way the Wheel turns, no matter our circumstances, it's all an opportunity to evolve on our soul path, to expand in awareness of our spiritual opportunity. God is everywhere and in everything. In many religions, the circle is the symbol of the sacred.

Like the human figures shown riding the Wheel of Fortune in earlier decks, we cannot escape the ebbs and flows of earthbound existence. We are inextricably part of the Wheel of Life. At times the Wheel's fluctuations are the result of our efforts: a project we'd begun is completed; an invitation sent is received; the Wheel turns as expected. Less predictably, change blows in and takes our breath away: a lost love reappears; a stalled career takes off; a fortune vanishes. Some may dismiss such events as random, but every turn of the Wheel fulfills an appointment on the cosmic calendar—a schedule created without our conscious participation.

In concert with the Magician, the Wheel of Fortune invites us to notice how what we're spinning out gets spun back to us (in one form or another). The more awareness we bring to this dynamic, the less bewildering is the synchronization of events. The card's value, 10, symbolizes fulfillment. The joining of the Magician (1) and the Fool

(0) suggests the moment at which the apparent, free-wheeling nature of circumstances comes to consciousness. We discover the degree to which our own hands turn the Wheel and humble ourselves to the greater workings of hands unseen.

Contemplating the Wheel of Fortune helps call attention to the patterns in our lives that appear like clockwork. I once found myself driving behind a motorist who, as each red light turned green, would linger distractedly for a few moments. With each of his delayed starts I became newly annoyed, only to become immersed in other thoughts moments later—and this cycle continued for several blocks. It wasn't until the fourth repetition on that road that it finally dawned on me: I was stuck in a pattern; the pattern felt uncomfortable; I had created it myself; and, simply by changing lanes, I could alter it. The least-mysterious teaching of the Wheel of Fortune is also the most practical: Be mindful of what shows up in your life; notice what works and keep doing it; and, for what doesn't work, change course.

Naturally, some causes are beyond our ability to perceive, and some effects beyond our ability to alter. We are not always capable of comprehending the Wheel's arc. We may find ourselves asking, along with author Gregg Levoy, "How might this be a plot twist that I won't understand for another two hundred pages?" When the catalyst or meaning of events eludes us, we may be inclined to regard it as fate.

The question of whether certain features of our lives—or every moment of them—are predetermined is central to the development of a personal philosophy. When the wind blows your "sailboat of life" on an unexpected course, do you take it as a sign that that's where God wants you to go, regardless of the conditions of the ride? Or do you see the wind shift as a God-given opportunity to overcome obstacles and muscle your way back toward the direction you had intended? While there are no right or wrong answers to this question, the wisest response may be, "It depends." Ultimately, the decisions we make are not as important as the motivation behind them and the feeling with which we carry them out.

Atop the Wheel of Fortune sits a Sphinx—the totality of the human and animal figures on the card. Just as the Hermit's mountaintop perch gave him the distance necessary to see his life more objectively, the Sphinx's heightened elevation enables it calmly to survey the turnings of the Wheel below. This cool blue character may know the blueprint of our soul paths and the outcome of every action, but unless we're game for riddles, it isn't about to give up its secrets. For now, we might consider borrowing the Sphinx's sword to detach psychologically from the need to figure it all out or find someone to blame. Taking our cue from the zero in Trump 10, when we can't comprehend the ways of the Wheel, we might as well play the Fool and roll with it.

A Wheel of Fortune Story

"What life-changing event happened for you recently?" I asked Scott, prompted by the Wheel of Fortune in his layout. The forty-four-year-old tradesman, his voice halting, talked of his son's recent suicide attempt. The teenage boy had overdosed on the drugs to which he had secretly become addicted and was now slowly making strides in rehab. The reverberations of the event shook everyone within the family sphere. "It was very troubling to me as a dad that I didn't see it coming," said Scott. "We had had a good day together. He seemed to be in a good place. And that night he tried it."

In the most basic sense, "Fortune smiled" on Scott and his son—the suicide was prevented; the boy survived; his life was now turned in a more positive direction. As the archetype of cycles and patterns, the Wheel symbolized Scott's new understanding of the phases of addiction and recovery, which would alert him to any warning signs in the future. And the spiritual meaning? Scott got that, too. "There's a higher power," he said flatly, "and a reason these things happen. I'm just glad it turned out the way it did."

Wheel of Fortune Attributes

Key words:	Cycles, Cause and Effect, Karma
Being:	"On a roll," lucky, fickle, fatalistic, aware of cycles or patterns
Doing:	Recognizing the effect of past lives on the present, experiencing a change in circumstances (usually positive), accepting the course of events, taking advantage of good timing, putting plans into motion, getting results, gambling
Shadow:	Joyless repetition, resigning yourself to fate or destiny to avoid making empowering choices, wishful thinking
Reversed:	Absence of motion or fruition, interruption of a cycle, breaking a pattern (or failing to see that one exists), a false start, counterproductive behavior
	Possible Advice
Reversed:	"Break this cycle." "Put on the brakes—this is not the right time to plan and do."

Questions for Reflection

How are your actions (or nonactions) today sowing the seeds of your future?

What patterns or cycles tend to repeat in your life?

What seems to be the "blueprint" of your life up to this point?

When has timing made all the difference in an outcome?

What big change would you like to see happen?

To what recent change are you still trying to adapt?

11. Justice

To be perfectly just is an attribute of the divine nature; to be so to
the utmost of our abilities is the glory of man.

—Joseph Addison

Trump 11 sits at the very center of the Major Arcana and governs the balancing of the opposites seesawing in every Trump. The archetype is the force that keeps the Lovers attracted, the Chariot on track, the lion and lady in rapport, and so on throughout the Major Arcana. Justice's unerring balancing function is an allegory of the Divine overseeing the equilibrium through all of creation. Everything, Justice assures us, is in divine order.

In concert with the precept *As above, so below*, the same intelligence that weighs and balances the doings of the cosmos has its counterpart within each of us, known as the Higher Self, Expanded Being, or the soul. The Universe and Higher Self work as an indistinguishable unity; together they calibrate our psychic balance. We partner with the Justice archetype whenever we pause for a self-check: "What do I need to do to right myself and be kinder to my body?" "Is my behavior in harmony with the loving capacities of my Highest Self?" "How am I 'off kilter' right now, and what will bring me into alignment?" Like sensitive aircraft instrumentation, our Justice mechanism detects when we're wobbling off-center.

When we neglect to notice that we're acting in ways that throw us off balance, and fail to take responsibility to correct them, unconscious forces move to restore equilibrium. As a result, we experience conditions *customized* by the Higher Self/Universe to adjust the imbalance, though we may be ignorant of their true corrective purpose. These soul interventions do not always match our personal or collective ideas of balance. In fact, we may point to our circumstances as proof of the fallacy of divine Justice—a universe out of whack—so terrible are our feelings of being forsaken. At such times Justice's chief tenet, that everything happens in balance with the greatest good, can seem a callous platitude. It is only through initiation into and contemplation of the deeper mysteries that we come to know Justice as unfailing, paradoxical, supreme.

Compensation is the chief operating principle in Trump 11. And the archetype is highly inventive here. For example, despite an over-achiever's griping about his punishing workload, the scales might be balanced by the sympathy and admiration he craves from others. Lying beneath an unhappy couple's constant squabbles could be the mutual conviction that they deserve each other. On a more redemptive note, many people who have suffered wrongdoing have found a life-altering sense of purpose by creating reforms that spare others the same pain. "For everything you have missed," wrote Emerson, "you have gained something else; and for everything you gain, you lose something else."

Justice presents one of the most challenging tests of the Trumps: to accept complete and total responsibility for our lives; and to view all our experiences as steps necessary to advance us along our unique, soul-chosen path of development. As we grow in that acceptance, our capacity to handle truths both personal and cosmic expands. Whereas Justice's scales symbolize equilibrium, the upraised sword signifies the shining, transformative power of truth.

Truth—avoiding it or being shielded from it, searching for it or having it thrust upon us, being liberated or ruined by it—is the story at the center of the human drama. How will Oedipus handle the news about Mother, or Hamlet the scoop from Dad? What will Harry Potter do when he discovers he is not a typical English lad? The prospect of facing *what is* fascinates and frightens us because we instinctively recognize the seismic power of truth to shift our platelets. We nod sagely at maxims about the truth setting us free, yet tremble at the costs those freedoms may incur.

For this reason we may well prefer that truth come in trickles. It is surely for the ego's protection that the searing light of divine Intelligence is partially concealed behind Justice's veil. The whole concentrated, awesome, timeless truth of our Being, were we exposed to it all at once, could zap us like a lightning bolt; without adequate preparation, the flash could fry our circuits. Such instantaneous illuminations (though of lesser magnitude) are typically the job of the Tower. Justice, impersonal enforcer of divine order, arranges our Tower events when only an emergency jolt of reality will restore balance.

The Trump's numerical value, 11, suggests the Magician (1) recognizing in his mirror image the one who tilts the scales. Eleven reduces to 2, the High Priestess, the neutrality underlying the Law of Compensation. Notice too the calm expression of Lady Justice. Her handling of the sword bears no trace of condemnation or vengeance. The jewel on her crown intersects with the sixth chakra or "third eye," symbol of clear seeing. She instructs us to look honestly at ourselves and to strive for discernment in the choices we make.

In its purest archetypal majesty, Justice is silent on worldly matters of right and wrong, fairness and unfairness. In readings, however, the card can indeed address these issues. Yet even in the most mundane Tarot spreads, Justice's unflinching gaze might compel us to perceive our situations, even seemingly inequitable ones, as karmic justice. Unrelated to ideas of punishment or repayment, karmic justice is the precept that every "good" and "bad" experience is a result of the consciousness that created it, whether moments or lifetimes ago; we are the architects of our circumstances.

Unfortunately, this concept of responsibility is often distorted to justify guilt and shame: "I must've been a rotten person in a past life to deserve the life I'm living now." "If only I were more spiritually conscious, I could've prevented myself from getting ill." But Lady Justice offers some reassurance here: The only proper response to our circumstances is love. Clasped at her heart center is a symbol of the perfection of the spiritual within the physical. At her breast hangs a cape of green, the color associated with Venus, goddess of compassion. Accepting our self-responsibility will knock us off center unless we take equal responsibility to love ourselves unconditionally.

A Justice Story

Brendan, a forty-year-old Tarot student, was uneasy about a rare visit he planned with his older brother, Chuck, in Albuquerque. "I've always found his lifestyle completely depressing," said Brendan, who described decades-old clutter and decrepit furniture in his sibling's oppressively dark apartment. "As if that's not bad enough," he said, "my brother surrounds himself with losers. A two-day visit is all I could stand."

We asked, "What energy will help Brendan during his stay with Chuck?"

I told Brendan the card, Justice, was his cue to try to stay balanced in the chaos of Chuck's life. I asked Brendan also to consider that Justice was a reminder that, troubled as Chuck's life seemed to be, his brother was living it on his own terms, including the "losers" he welcomed. The spiritual challenge for Brendan would not only be to find the inner balance to cope during the visit, but to trust that the scales of Justice were balanced for his brother.

Justice Attributes

Key words:	Equilibrium, Integrity, Self-Correction
Being:	Discerning, reasonable, fair, honest, scrupulous, precise
Doing:	Acting with integrity, accepting responsibility for your choices, striving for balance, rectifying a situation, keeping promises, telling the truth, trusting divine order, dealing with legal issues
Shadow:	Telling the truth with hurtful intent, judging harshly
Reversed:	Disequilibrium, psychic or physical imbalance, unjust decisions, bias, unfairness, integrity lapse, inequality, self-deception; cheating, denying responsibility
Reversed:	*Possible Advice* "Don't play Judge." "Embrace the chaos."

Questions for Reflection

What was the most difficult truth you've ever spoken or were told?

What decisions are you currently weighing?

Where does your life feel unbalanced, and what would balance it?

What once seemed unfair or unjust but seems wise in retrospect?

What have you accepted responsibility for that you used to blame on others?

Where do you most passionately feel the need for justice?

12. The Hanged Man

Humility that low sweet root, from which all heavenly virtues shoot.
—Sir Thomas Moore

There are times when life seems to slow to a standstill. Yesterday's momentum becomes a memory. Dreams get put on hold. The Chariot spins its wheels. The clarity that sharpened us in Justice dims, and we find ourselves strung up by feelings of uncertainty and powerlessness. Even the will of the Magician is unable to help us get things moving again. We look to Strength, hoping it will supply us with the endurance needed to simply wait things out. Welcome to the Hanged Man.

In our society, the criteria for tolerable waiting times gets shorter by the second. Delays trigger outrage. We take our slowdowns and setbacks personally. Feeling stuck or helpless becomes proof of our vulnerability, and we fight desperately to maintain a leg up on life. Likewise, the figure in Trump 12 has entirely lost his foothold on the world. The legs that ground him to his business-as-usual activities are upended, tethered, leaving him immobile and defenseless. His bound hands prevent him from extricating himself from this extreme predicament.

Curiously, the Hanged Man does not appear to struggle or shout for help. He maintains a peaceful expression. And despite the fact that he might easily have lost consciousness in this position, he remains awake.

The secret of the Hanged Man's composure lies in his nonresistance. He has surrendered to his limbo state. Though he knows not when or how, he trusts he'll be on his feet again. The wait may be long, but also ripe for spiritual awakening in spite of the holdup.

Shooting up through the center of the picture is Waite's symbol of the World Tree, representing the sacred source of life. In surrendering, the Hanged Man has aligned himself to the wisdom of the mystical tree. Its roots deep and eternal, the tree gives him stability during his enforced timeout. That the stripped-down "tree" in Waite's design more closely resembles a hitching post offers an additional analogy: the hero is compelled to "hold his horses" until the time is right to ride again.

Significantly, it is his right leg that has been fastened to the rope— his conscious world of action put on hold. But his unhitched left leg moves freely; when life spins out of our control, heeding the inner call to surrender to *what is* can provide flexibility and adaptability in even the most challenging times. As many Tarot observers have pointed out, the Hanged Man's lower half resembles the dancing legs of the figure on the World card, implying that even in our ordeals the potential for liberation is alive and kicking. However, it is not a literal unsnagging that frees the Hanged Man, but a spiritual one. The glowing sphere around his head shows that it is an illumined perspective, rather than a changed situation, that brings him peace.

The key to the Hanged Man's illumination is his inverted position. In his downswing he has no choice but to view things from a different angle—a perspective he would not likely have discovered were it not for being in this fix. This aspect of the Hanged Man archetype is familiar to many parents, who learn that loving a child sometimes requires doing virtual headstands in order to see things from the child's vantage point. With parental logic and expectations temporarily suspended, new levels of empathy and understanding may emerge.

The nourishing qualities of a reversed outlook are further suggested in the archetype's blue tunic. The fabric cascades like a waterfall into the area of the heart chakra. In surrendering to the wisdom of the unconscious, The Hanged Man allows the integrating power of the Self to swing him, pendulum-like, into alignment. His number, 12, brings together the will of the Magician (1) and the soul receptivity of the High Priestess (2). The sum of their union is the Empress (3), who reminds the Hanged Man that his suspension, like her pregnancy, is but a precursor to a new awareness.

The Hanged Man dangling from the mighty tree shows us the heady ego lowered, come humbly down to earth. The archetype thus has an anchoring effect. In our trials we come to feel the full, inescapable weight of our humanness, stripped now of all notions of being in control or of being somehow greater or more special than others. Concerns about status and propriety gradually lose substance.

Anyone who has ever spent time in a hospital bed, for example, knows that having one's body routinely exposed and bodily functions asked about makes dignity (in its fussiest sense) impossible and pointless; healing is the sole priority. The Hanged Man reacquaints us with the wholeness of our simpler, scaled-down Selves. He permits us to admit our fragility—moreover, to embrace it—and thereby learn to love the parts of which we might have been ashamed.

Whether he has consciously chosen to surrender or has been made to do so, there is an element of sacrifice in the Hanged Man's impossible situation. The Latin root of *sacrifice* means "to make sacred," which provides another clue to the figure's shining aura. The Hanged Man perceives divine purpose in his suffering and consecrates it as a spiritual test—atonement, purification, initiation, creative incubation, or preparation for greater things to come. As Nietzsche concluded, "Who has a why to live can bear most any how." When we are able to see meaning in our suffering—or choose to assign it meaning—we transmute it into spiritual power.

Seen another way, the glow radiating at the Hanged Man's head just may be the light at the end of the tunnel. But with the peace born of trusting the partnering intent of the unconscious, there is light no matter where we happen to be in the tunnel. As the Hanged Man himself might say, it all depends on how you look at it.

A Hanged Man Story

"What's been holding you up lately?" I asked Chelsea, a fifty-five-year-old social worker, as I turned over the Hanged Man. I learned that she had been fired soon after reporting corruption within the government agency in which she worked. The damning reasons given for her termination were false but stained her record nonetheless. Two years later, she had not found another job.

She was touched that the card seemed so sympathetic to her "sacrificial lamb" ordeal. But I wanted her to see more than just the victim aspect of the archetype.

"Make up a reason for the Hanged Man's halo," I said. Chelsea cocked her head. "His integrity," she said. "He did the right thing." I turned the Hanged Man onto his toes. "How does he look to you now?"

"Strong. Focused." she answered.

"Yes, but he's hung up!" I said. "How does he survive this adversity?"

"Oh, you'd be surprised," she said, a trace of defiance in her eyes.

Hanged Man Attributes

Key words:	Suspension, Sacrifice, Reversal
Being:	Humble, self-sacrificing, frustrated, lost, "in limbo," powerless to effect change
Doing:	Surrendering, coping, suffering, waiting, experiencing delay, sustaining short-term deprivation for long-term gain, losing position or ground, seeing from a different perspective
Shadow:	A persecution complex, martyrdom, unremitting suffering, resentful submission, a pariah, a victim
Reversed:	An end to a trying time; getting back on your feet, fighting a delay, refusing to surrender, avoiding suffering or grieving, refusing to see things differently
	Possible Advice
Reversed:	"The waiting is over. It's time to act." "Take back your power."

Questions for Reflection

What is the greatest sacrifice you were forced to make or chose to make?

What, if anything, are you waiting for? What is "on hold"?

Where in your life could you benefit from surrendering control?

What limitation that you initially struggled against have you come to accept?

When has being "out of your element" given you a new perspective?

When have you felt ridiculed or ostracized for being true to yourself?

13. Death

There is no death! What seems so is a transition.
—Henry Wadsworth Longfellow

My friend Sandra came home one eve-ning to find her apartment ransacked. But to her relief (and the astonishment of the police) none of her possessions was missing. Even her jewelry was untouched, though the drawer she kept it in had been yanked open, its glitter-ing contents nakedly exposed. As the police examined the intended loot—so mysteriously intact—one of the officers pointed quizzically at Sandra's Tarot deck nestled amid the rings and brace-lets. At the top of it, face up, was the Death card. Their official conclusion: the intruders had been spooked!

Fear of what is loosely called the *occult* (meaning "hidden") and fear of death are closely linked. The ego fears the unseen, as it fears what will remain of the personality upon the final passing on. Fortunately for Sandra, the superstitious would-be burglars didn't know that the Death card symbolizes not physical death but endings of all kinds and the new energy that emerges from them.

Life is an inevitable cycle of beginnings and endings. The end of one thing is the beginning of another. Consider the sun shown in the Death card. Its position makes it unclear whether it is showing the end of day or the end of night. Either way, a new orb will come forth to cast its beams upon the earth—a continuous celestial passing of the baton. The whole of existence thrives on cycles of creation and destruction; cells continuously die as new cells are born; forests burn to yield new growth; salmon perish to ensure the survival of hatchlings.

Womb to tomb, the only constant is change. Old forms die, things fall away, people leave, and in their wake, new choices must be made, fresh possibilities explored. Every ending thus has the power to transform by propelling us to new opportunities to live from the psychic bare bones of our Inner Being. This alone remains permanent in the midst of change and loss.

Enter the skeletal Knight. He is armored in black, the color of the void, mystery, and mourning—aspects threatening to the ego desperate for certainty and gain. Like all knights he is on a mission, carrying out higher orders. Riding up from the unconscious, he has one goal: to clear away old energy to make room for new. The white rose on his banner heralds his pure intention. Its five petals promise the flowering of the Self when the soil of old forms is broken through.

The Black Knight straddles a magnificent white charger. Skulls and crossbones dot the animal's head strap—nature harnessed inevitably to the cycles of life and death. The horse represents the power of instinct, a sense of knowing in a basic way when it's time to let go, move on. The ship in the background, inspired by the Egyptian ferries to the land of the dead, carries away the old way of being.

Even though physical death is not the true meaning of the card, the ego's fears of losing control are as intense as its terrors of a literal demise. At the top of their hierarchy, few kings abdicate when their leadership becomes outworn; most must die or be overthrown for new leadership to emerge. In the card's toppled king we see the permanent destruction of the old self, the outmoded attitudes and agendas. The presence of the priest recalls the Hierophant, who shows up here to honor ritually the transformative opportunities presented by Death so that we may find ways to let go peacefully.

Forgiveness, too, is a kind of death. To "bury the hatchet" is to let go of our anger and resentment, an act as freeing to the forgiver as it is to the forgiven. It is interesting to note the Bible teaching to forgive seventy times seven times. The sum of that equation is 490, which adds up to 13, Death.

Trump 13 unites the Magician (1) with the Empress (3)—a conscious recognition of Mother Nature's continuous interweaving of life and death. Thirteen reduces to 4, the Emperor, underscoring Death's "take no prisoners" approach to reorganizing the psyche. Devastating though it may be, Death's handiwork will be regenerative, birthing a whole new order of awareness and growth.

Unlike the Death card's kneeling maiden, few of us submit easily to change. Deep down we may know it is time, yet the prospect of a painful transition inspires an inventive barrage of excuses for staying put. Comedian Woody Allen summed up this attitude in his famous quip, "I'm not afraid to die, I just don't want to be there when it happens."

Like Susan's thwarted burglars, the ego-mind is paralyzed by terror of the unknown, even when the reward outweighs the risk. We all feel the fear of letting go. We clutch for dear life onto old habits that no longer serve us (and may even kill us) but provide a security blanket. The relationship may be toxic, the job a dead end, the thinking rotted and reeking, yet we cling to the familiar for fear of what lies beyond.

Look again at the card. In the thick of all the destruction and denial is the trusting child, who openly welcomes Death with a bouquet of flowering acceptance. When we let our resistance to change die, we are born to a more authentic life. Made lighter in our shedding, we move more swiftly through the journey, drawn forward by the sun shining through the card's portals of spiritual evolution.

A Death Story

I once saw a theater production so inspiring, I sent the company a $500 check in an effort to match the richness of the experience they'd given me. All that week I smiled as I pictured the fledgling troupe's surprise and joy in receiving my gift. Strangely, a month went by with no thank-you note. Then two months. Not a peep. The check had cleared, so what was the problem? My good will gradually gave way to righteous anger.

One afternoon I composed a searing letter about the company's ingratitude when, almost as an afterthought, I decided to pull a Tarot card about the situation. "What is the appropriate response to this?" I asked, fighting the temptation to add the word *outrage!*

The Death card suddenly made the answer painfully obvious.

"Let it go."

Weeks of harrumphing ended with those three little words. I sat there until I could feel the original joy of sending the gift and accept that that was enough.

Death Attributes

Key words:	Dissolution, Transition, Letting Go
Being:	In psychological or spiritual transition, unattached to outcomes
Doing:	Letting go of someone or something, experiencing loss and endings, accepting impermanence, giving up old habits, creating closure, divesting, ending financial or emotional debts, forgiving, reaching a point of no return
Shadow:	Prematurely ending relationships or projects, affecting an attitude of nonattachment as a defense against the fear of loss

> Reversed: A partial death in which some things are held onto, inability to let go or move on; denying the reality of loss, keeping a good thing going
>
> *Possible Advice*
> Reversed: "Stay with it. There is yet more to learn."
> "Don't throw the baby out with the bathwater."

Questions for Reflection

Who do you need to forgive?
What do you no longer need but are afraid to let go?
What relationship needs to pass quietly away?
What loss do you still find difficult to accept?
What is absolutely certain and permanent in your life?
When has the loss of something created space for transformation and growth?

14. Temperance

You carry all the ingredients to turn your existence into joy.
Mix them, mix them!

—Hafiz

Two irises rise up near the feet of an angel—Waite's modest allusion to the myth of Iris, a winged messenger of the gods. To create an access point between Earth and Olympus, Zeus brought forth the rainbow, down which Iris descended to convey divine missives to mortals. Iris thus became known as the goddess of the rainbow, representing in classical times a bridge between Heaven and Earth.

Heaven and Earth are synonymous with the spiritual and the physical, the above and below. Trump 14 oversees the process by which these and all opposites begin to morph together. Tarot's Temperance (from *temper*, to mix or modify) traditionally signifies alchemy, a metaphor for the process by which the raw materials of the psyche are combined, tested, and refined in preparation for more harmonious stages of consciousness.

As angelic emissary and alchemist, Temperance works patiently in each individual's psychic laboratory to vaporize the denser contents, dilute deep inner discord, meld warring opposites into more compatible concoctions. In doing so, she creates the right inner conditions for us to continue on the pathway to the gold within. On the card, a road stretches toward a shining crown of self-mastery, a state further indicated by the alchemical symbol for gold at the angel's forehead.

Temperance's continuous tinkering is usually so subtle and gradual that we are rarely aware we are part of an alchemical process. But the evidence is there. Most of us can look back at times when our personalities had rougher edges, but few of us can account for how those edges managed to smooth out. Or we may have a vague sense that we are *being prepared* for something, yet have no idea what we're being prepared *for*, or *what* is preparing us. Temperance reminds us that we are works in progress.

Temperance glorifies paradox, the essence of universal truth. Paradox defies simplistic "either-or" thinking. It challenges the narrowness of our tidy self-definitions by showing us to be a vast amalgam of opposites—selfish and generous, deliberate and spontaneous, forceful and gentle, caring and cruel. Until we come to accept these contradictions, we cannot embrace the full paradox of life—that to be human is to contain opposites. The angel throws it *all* in the soup, thus seasoning the soul.

Temperance (14) mixes the resourcefulness of the Magician (1) with the orderliness of the Emperor (4) to work constructively with the energies freed up by Death. The combination (5) gives us the Hierophant, who has in common with Temperance a mediator function, though the angel represents a more direct line to the Divine. As they did on the Fool, the four Hebrew letters at her collar spell the name of the Almighty.

Temperance is the peacekeeper. Whenever we strive to bring together clashing forces—inner or outer—we are, in effect, "working on our wings." There is the story of a woman who moved to a small town. While she was shopping at her local florist the owner made a catty remark, and the two exchanged a few curt words. The woman later complained about him to her neighbor, who listened patiently but encouraged her to give the fellow another try. When the woman reluctantly returned to the florist a few weeks later, he greeted her warmly and proceeded to give her exceptionally gracious service. Within moments the pleasantries had become mutual, and the woman left with a smile.

"I don't get it," the woman later told her neighbor, "Two weeks ago he acted like a jerk. What on earth could've happened?" The neighbor flashed a sly grin. "I was in his shop the day after your run-in with him," she replied. "I told him that you told me that you loved his shop and that he was a wonderful florist!"

Whether we view the intercessor in the story as inspired or meddlesome, there is no arguing her role as angel Temperance, successfully blending oil and water to create harmony for two opposites, who were unaware of the alchemical magic going on behind the scenes!

Every Major Arcana card depicts a balance of the energies symbolized. However, the most literal images of balance are the measurement instruments of Justice and Temperance. Yet the two have different functions. On one level, Justice's scales compel us to weigh options and choose between this or that. In contrast, Temperance's chalices inspire us to blend this *and* that. Our winged alchemist pours together yin and yang, softening their starkness, and reworks them into new, creative solutions fluidly, artfully, on our behalf.

Though a largely mysterious process, Temperance has aspects we can consciously employ, such as moderation and synthesis. Moderation is simply the doing of things in right measure. Synthesis is the creative combining of familiar things in unfamiliar ways. The results of synthesis may be genius. For example, the unlikely fusion of Shakespeare's star-crossed lovers, mid-twentieth-century gang warfare, and musical theater gave us Broadway's classic *West Side Story*.

Inner assets, too, may be consciously blended, like an artist dabbling at his palette. Take a teacher who blends the anything-is-possible spirit of the Magician, the spontaneity of the Fool, and the Hermit's talent for inspiring investigation, and you're looking at someone with the power to transform an ordinary classroom into a place of breathless discovery. Creative synthesis draws from a variety of resources, both inner and outer, and combines them into something fresh and new. When we embrace the energy of Temperance, we stay creative, flowing, and elastic in proportion to the work before us.

Like all archetypes, the angel represents an ideal. Though we cannot achieve its perfection, Temperance reminds us that we are already "enough" as well as works in progress—a message as contradictory as the opposites the archetype seeks to intermingle. If we accept our own paradoxical nature, we will not lose sight of our light when forced to confront our darkness. In this way, Temperance becomes an essential guide on the bridge across the next stages of consciousness, of which the Devil is the gatekeeper.

A Temperance Story

Lance's conflicts with his wife, Makeda, were always short lived. A professional psychologist, he prided himself on his ability to stay temperate in almost any argument. His pattern was to "allow space" for his wife to fully vent while he went into professional mediator mode—rationally sorting out her feelings, then his, until the issue was resolved to mutual satisfaction. He acknowledged that his clinical approach "sometimes drives Makeda crazy."

Lance shared this background with me before telling me about a Tarot reading he'd recently given himself. There had been a sizeable issue brewing between him and Makeda. As always, his impulse was to go into neutral and "process it" with her. But the more he anticipated playing the controlled peacemaker, the angrier he became. He asked the card what energy to bring to the situation. It was Temperance, reversed.

"I didn't hold back my emotions from Makeda," Lance says. "We really went at it. I think it cleared the air faster than if I'd played psychologist!"

Temperance Attributes

Key words:	Synthesis, Creativity, Harmony
Being:	Accommodating, patient, conciliatory, tolerant, adaptable, moderate, modest, healthy, resourceful
Doing:	Integrating opposites, consolidating, combining things creatively, working toward win-win solutions, keeping the peace, behaving temperately
Shadow:	Intolerance of extremes, fear of conflict

Reversed:	Excesses or deficits; wastefulness; disharmony; improper combinations; extreme attitudes or behaviors; refusal to mediate, placate, or come to agreement
	Possible Advice
Reversed:	"Don't play the peacemaker. Let the opposites clash." "Moderation does not suit the situation. Make a bold choice."

Questions for Reflection

What conflicts are you working to bring to harmonious resolution?

What in your life could be improved by adding new energies or resources?

What opposite energies are you learning to combine and integrate?

When have you played the role of mediator or peacemaker?

Where is moderation most needed in your life?

Who, given your differences, is your most unlikely friend?

Major Arcana 15–21:
The Heat Is On

One does not become enlightened by imagining figures of light,
but by making the darkness conscious.

—Carl Jung

In the final line of Trumps, intense concentrations of light—fire, electrical, stellar, lunar, solar—illuminate the journey toward the Self. The Devil's torch may burn us, but it can also expose that which has been hiding in the dark and tripping us up. The lightning strike on the Tower is but a momentary flash, but that may be all it takes to shock us out of complacency. In the wavering light of the Moon, the seen world becomes less substantial, acclimating us to the spiritual and the formless. And the end result of this convergence of lights? Dancing, of course!

15. The Devil

If thou hast not seen the devil, look at thine own self.
—Rumi

As far back as the Stone Age, a horned, cloven-hoofed deity was worshipped in Europe as the god of the hunt, animal fertility, and winter. Its *pagan* (Latin for "country dwellers") worshippers invoked and celebrated the god's blessings through food offerings, ecstatic sexual rites, and animal sacrifice—practices that, in later millennia, jangled the nerves of the Christian Church. Church strategists effectively demonized the horned god and transformed it into an icon for the Satan of the Christian Scriptures, an image that has lasted to this day. The

newly conceived Devil provided an effective justification for wiping out paganism (and lots of pagans) and served as a scapegoat for all beliefs and activities that did not conform to Church doctrine.

On the psychological level, we are both the power-seeking Church and the Devil. Posing in its pulpit, the righteous, fragile ego is quick to repress or deny any thoughts or feelings that threaten to make it look less than ideal. Rather than claim ownership of our darker predilections, we unconsciously project the rejected contents of our psyches onto external figures—namely, other people.

The dynamic is played out in the perpetual pleaser who cannot abide phonies, in the scolding prude who dreams of orgies, and in every conceivable example of pots calling kettles black. In friendly card games I often found myself silently and harshly judging players who displayed too much competitive zeal, and I have only recently discovered that beneath my "Let's play nice" façade has lived a cut-throat dying to take all without apology!

The self-protective propensity for assigning flaws to others is amply evident on the world stage. Just one such illustration can be found in the American reactions to the domestic dominance of Japanese auto sales in the early 1980s. Though the public conceded the inferiority of U.S. auto manufacturing, some Americans blamed the Japanese for the industry's mass layoffs of employees. The situation took on tragic proportions when two Detroit autoworkers fatally bludgeoned an American man of Asian descent. At the root of our small-scale finger-pointing and full-scale wars lies a terror of self-examination—and the accountability that goes with it.

Carl Jung said, "The shadow personifies everything that the subject refuses to acknowledge about himself." Failing to recognize our blind spots is to be, like the people in the Devil card, chained in ignorance. My friend Gail had an old pal who came to the dawning realization at age thirty-five that he was not, as it turned out, hetero-sexual. She and other longtime friends of the man expressed great relief at his admission, assuring him they had always assumed he was gay and had never judged him for it. As if informed he'd spent the day with a piece of spinach in his teeth, he moaned, "Well, why didn't anybody *tell me* I was gay?" The Devil of Tarot is not the bibli-cal Lord of Darkness, but the composite of those parts of ourselves we have denied and displaced, albeit unconsciously.

Our shadows form in childhood when we begin to lock away those behaviors devalued or shamed by our tribe. To be sure, socialization has its useful purposes; a child unable to control hostility or aggression is a danger to himself and others. It is through the maturing influence of Strength that he learns to manage these impulses and keep them in check. But when our impulses are shamed consistently and unconditionally, they get banished, forced into the background and the underground, which leaves us with a sense of badness at our core.

The categories of shadow shame are in no way limited to the usual suspects of vice, sexual taboos, and selfish motives. Exuberance, tenderness, and hope may also be sealed within the unconscious vaults of those who, to find acceptance or safety, learned to disown these qualities. For some, the mere fact of having human needs is a shadow matter of extravagant dimension. What is life-giving to one person may to another have horns and a tail attached.

Trump 15 shows a corruption of both the creative power of the Magician (1) and the conscience of the Hierophant (5). Fifteen reduces to 6, the Lovers, in whose shadow we find the possessiveness that can occur only in the absence of love. Traditionally, the tails of the humans are seen as representing sensual attachments and animal desires to the exclusion of spirit. In place of the infinity symbols that hover above the figures in the Magician and Strength, the Devil sports a five-pointed star turned upside down. This reversal symbolizes twisted priorities—anything and everything that we make more important than self-empowerment. The flimsy foundation on which he is perched speaks for itself.

The demon looms behind the couple unacknowledged, giving it power to control them in ways of which they are unaware. Our unseen shadow aspects and unexamined motives make us vulnerable to an A-list of deviltry—self-defeating behavior, fears, delusions, psychosomatic illnesses, obsessions, compulsions, addictions, and oppression by (and of) others. The Devil is the archetype of enslavement to forces inside and out that limit our awareness and chain us to suffering and illusion.

Yet the Devil, like the Hierophant, raises his hand in a kind of benediction. Tattooed on his palm is the astrological glyph for Saturn, which alludes to the planet's astrological association with redemptive restriction. In its transformative aspect the Devil functions as Lucifer (Latin, "light bearer"), shining awareness on the diabolic (Latin, "thrown apart") regions of our psyche. Like a flashlight beamed into the psychic basement, the Devil offers us the gift of his torch so that we may see in the shadows the games we've been playing to hide our pain and fear. If we resist the urge to turn away, we will see the self-condemned, rejected parts of ourselves. Deny these parts, and we remain chained to them. Judge them, and we compound shame. Suppress them, and the trap is set for a first-class self-sabotage.

We may be surprised, then, to discover that our darkest parts are not asking us to act them out, but simply to recognize them as ours, boils and all. The Devil represents an inescapable route on the path to wholeness. The archetype invites us to humanize, not demonize, our shadows, to give them our compassionate understanding. We may just find, as the poet Rainer Maria Rilke proposed, that "everything terrible is in its deepest being something that needs our love." Paradoxically, in loving our shadows and forgiving these imperfections, we loosen the chains that bind them to us. Inner peace becomes a very real possibility.

A Devil Story

Marcus, a participant in one of my presentations, shared that he once received a brochure for a five-day personal growth workshop led by a spiritual teacher he admired. The dates coincided with his vacation time, but he had tentative plans to spend that week snorkeling in the Bahamas. His friends called him crazy when he told them he was genuinely torn between a week of sparkling water and sunshine or a windowless seminar room at an airport hotel.

He told our group that he had asked his spirit guides, "What do I stand to gain from these two options?" and pulled a card for each.

The Nine of Cups promised pleasure and relaxation for the Bahamas trip; the Horned One endorsed the workshop!

Devil be damned, Marcus chose the workshop. "Intuitively, I didn't feel like the card was warning me away from danger," Marcus explained, "but that it was challenging me to deal with some parts of myself I'd been avoiding, which terrified me at the time. It was a powerful workshop, and I grew a lot in that week. In many ways it was the best thing I've ever done for myself."

Devil Attributes

Key words:	Restriction, Fear, Shadow
Being:	Ashamed, jealous, codependent, deceitful, ill-intended, self-destructive, shackled by ignorance, chained to the need for approval
Doing:	Experiencing restriction, acting in ways that impede your growth, struggling with (or denying) addiction or depression, projecting your faults onto others, abusing others or being abused
Shadow:	(The Devil *is* the shadow.)
Reversed:	Throwing off restrictions; liberation from internalized or externalized oppression
	Possible Advice
Upright:	"Accept the restrictions of the current situation." "Face your demons."

Questions for Reflection

To what do you feel bound or enslaved, and what will free you?

What negative trait that you possess has only recently come to your awareness?

What fears get in the way of living your life, and how can you move through them?

Who or what brings out the worst in you, and how do you allow it?

In what ways do you sabotage your own well-being and success?

What personal "demons" have you reconciled or conquered?

16. The Tower

We turn to God for help when our foundations are shaking,
only to learn it is God who is shaking them.
—Charles C. West

You are looking at the only card in the Major Arcana that depicts a moment of actual *drama*, and a harrowing one at that. The image looks to have been torn from the pages of a fairy tale. Here, a man and woman live in a tower of stone hewn from a spiny crag. They have put themselves so high that all they see are cloudy, distorted thought forms through which their reality is filtered.

In their confining little world, the woman has crowned herself queen. Her cohort imagines himself a superman, complete with red cape of invincibility.

Convinced of the supremacy of their high-and-mighty status, they have capped off their tower with a crown of exaggerated scale (the bloated Emperor!). But their conceit will be their downfall. On this night a bolt of lightening zaps the tower. In a flash, the woman discovers the uselessness of her crown, while her companion learns the limits of his flying abilities. Their nosedive forces them into a more down-to-earth perspective.

Pride and arrogance may be the obvious "sins" flushed out by the lightening bolt in Trump 16, but the archetype has a more inclusive hit list. All corners of the false self—every pretense, disguise, and empty ideal, every foundation built on illusion—must be incinerated, brought to rubble, before spiritual renovation can begin. The Tower's great distance from the ground and its conspicuous lack of a door isolate the inhabitants from life and keep them, as towers do, in a defensive position. The ego is blockaded within the mortar of fear or ignorance, so that a tension is created between it and the true Self. When the pressure is on from within to move out, something's got to give.

The Tower card depicts the lightning-flash moment when the roof blows off of our illusions and lets the light in. Jung identifies the catalyst for such explosive change as "an archetype that has been at work for a long time in the unconscious, skillfully arranging circumstances that will lead to the crisis."

The Tower escapade concludes the vertical line, as if the Universe arranged a crash course for the ego on the wisdom it missed in the High Priestess and Hermit. Trump 16 combines the perceptive force of the Magician (1) with the unshielded nakedness of the Lovers. As the sum of 1 and 6, the Chariot (7) assists in driving out the false self and putting us back on track for the opportunities for liberation that lie ahead.

A humorous twist on an old maxim has it, "The truth shall set ye free . . . but first it shall make ye miserable." The expressions of the card's characters tell us that sudden revelation can come as a rude awakening.

I once permitted a friend who was staying at my home to have her new friend, Dana, move in with us for a month. When I met Dana the following day, my inner voice literally shouted, "She's bad news!" But my need to be accommodating was stronger, and I managed to convince myself that if my friend could trust Dana, so could I.

Several weeks later, I was sitting in the kitchen when the coffee pot lid violently and inexplicably blew off, splattering angry constellations of hot grounds onto the walls and ceiling. As I cleaned up the mess there came a bigger explosion—a phone call from the bank. The account representative asked if I had authorized several unusually expensive transactions on my credit card in the last few days, including some hefty airfare.

It turned out I had been far more accommodating to Dana than I'd intended. I unknowingly picked up the tab for her getaway (literally) to Los Angeles, among other things. A subsequent police investigation turned up outstanding warrants for Dana's arrests for theft, battery, forgery, and mail fraud. Within the span of a few moments, the Universe had blown the lid off my coffee pot, Dana's cover, and the suspicions I had suppressed. I deluded myself into seeing my trust of Dana as the Fool's leap of faith, but had set myself up for a dizzying spill from the Tower.

Even so, Tower experiences are not always calamitous, not always betrayals. The fire bolt can bring the sudden "Aha!" of a painless awakening—a breakthrough in the science lab or the realization that we've been singing the wrong song lyrics all these years. But in most readings, the card signifies the avalanches and earthquakes that rock our private and collective worlds.

The Tower is one of the few completely unambiguous images in the Tarot. Our primal fear of falling and its associations with failure are vividly expressed in our language. Reputations "take a dive," stocks "plummet," conflicts lead to "fallouts," relationships "crash and burn." For some, descent is seen as punishment from an angry

God. But the deeper meaning of the Tower is not falling, failure, or divine retribution, but illumination—accomplished here by the immediate disintegration of the obstacles to higher consciousness. Our apocalypse (from the Greek *apocalypsis*, to unveil) will free us to rebuild a more lasting foundation, one grounded in an indestructible connection to that which is deepest and eternal.

Golden *yods* (a Kabbalistic analog for "hands") float upon the Tower's violent nightscape. Their number represents the combined mystical power of the twelve signs of the zodiac and the ten points of the Kabbalistic Tree of Life, totaling twenty-two, the number of Major Arcana. Their presence promises that even in our upheavals, the hands of the Infinite are at work.

Stricken towers are not automatic tickets to illumination, however spectacular the wreckage. If we fail to see our delusions in the ruins, we may become even more determined to rebuild them—lying to cover lies, reviving false dreams. A friend once described her own Tower denials as "constantly running into the same wall at ninety miles an hour." The Tower challenges us to learn from the strike of the lightning and find its luminous intent. Until we do, we are destined to sift through the cinders again and again in the vain hope of salvaging our personal and collective illusions.

A Tower Story

On the first day of Tarot class, Sally expressed concern that the Tower appeared in response to her question, "What does the Tarot have to teach me?" I offered several possibilities: major shifts in her understanding might occur suddenly and be met with her own resistance; she could find the "old baggage" of her beliefs tossed without her ego's permission; or the level of sharing in class could weaken old defenses. "How does that sit with you, Sally?" I asked. "It scares me!" she blurted, laughing nervously.

True enough, as the weeks advanced Sally was jolted by some of the basic metaphysical concepts of the course. Her questions revealed her struggles to accept that the "negative" cards in her readings had instructive, not punitive, intent, and that the key to happiness lay within, not outside her. Most disruptively, I believe, the Tarot shook her Tower with its implications that she had bricked herself into thought forms that reinforced a basic distrust of herself and life. Despite the rocky road, Sally stuck through the course, offering few clues as to how deeply her learning had penetrated. "I really thought it would be fun to learn about the cards," she said on the final day of class. "But I had no idea what I was getting into!"

Tower Attributes

Key words:	Upheaval, Rupture, Release
Being:	Emotionally shaken, physically stricken, shocked out of complacency, stripped of defenses, suddenly exposed or enlightened
Doing:	Falling, failing, losing a secure position, experiencing an injury or betrayal, detoxifying, driving out obstacles to greater awareness, shaking up the status quo, angrily confronting, learning the hard way, evacuating
Shadow:	Defeatism; destroying someone's dreams
Reversed:	Imprisonment; trying to keep the lid on an explosive situation, denying the inevitability of collapse, trying to preserve a façade, avoiding a calamity or meltdown
	Possible Advice
Upright:	"Shake things up." "Let it crumble, and let the light in."

Questions for Reflection

What cherished foundations crumbled yet liberated you?
What "rude awakenings" accelerated your growth?
What "towers" keep you isolated from the world?
When have you sensed a pending Tower-like collapse and taken
    steps to change or avoid it?
What upheavals do you no longer experience?
Who seems ready to fall from their Tower?

17. The Star

It is the nature of goodness to pour itself out.
—St. Thomas Aquinas

We faced our darkness in the Devil and
survived the transformative turmoil of
the Tower. It's time for a little peace. We
long for tranquility and consolation, for
assurance that all has not been illusion,
for confirmation that we are whole in
spite of feelings of self-doubt and loss.
In the Star we find an oasis.

THE STAR.

The drama of shadows and shake-ups
is gone for now. Here we discover ourselves naked in the midst of water, sky,
stars, a bird in a tree. The image sighs,
soothes. Even the dreamlike strangeness
of the immense stellar display doesn't
disturb, for whether the stars are intruding on daylight or banishing
the darkness, we sense that all is well.

118

Stars inspire a conviction of the presence of the Infinite. Beholding the vastness of a star-swept sky lets awe and wonder fill us full. We sense something of our own boundlessness. Even in their great distance, an intimacy prevails, as though we are in the company of guides as wise as they are old, who gaze back at us with interest, blinking calmly in the quiet of the night.

The guiding lights on Trump 17 lead us to sacred waters in which we may heal (from *haelen*, Old English for to "make whole") from the lightning strikes of the Tower. Whatever the magnitude of that destruction, the wellspring of wisdom reflects what remains untouched—our naked, divine essence. We see our original faces; the soul is adored. Peace washes over us, and we are refreshed. Strength (sum of 1 and 7) has seen us through the dark night. The energy released in the Tower has made us wiser, and we commence—like the Chariot (7)—toward a new cycle of growth.

The woman uses the red jug in her right (conscious) hand passionately to pour out her gratitude into the spiritual spring that sustains her. The jug in her left (unconscious) hand spills the curative waters onto the outer world of daily life, creating a revitalizing flow between the mundane and the sacred. Five rivulets drench the earth—the sensual outer life nourished by the inner Source. Symbiotically, five ripples stir the pond, for the act of becoming more conscious, of bringing our true nature to expression, is a gift we give back to the Divine.

The marvel of the woman's floating foot suggests a spiritual grounding from the holy spring. The central star in the picture represents a vision of what we are becoming—the soul in all its radiance. It is encircled by seven smaller stars, which form a container for the core Being.

As a symbol of inflow and receptivity, the woman's body forms the base of a chalice—an implement of holy rites—and the clustered, cup-shaped stars depict the receiving vessel. The contours of the pond resemble a cauldron, a fitting receptacle for the cosmic pool from which she draws her wisdom. Even the outstretched limbs of the tree appear to be cupped in eager receipt of the Ibis, the bird favored by Hermes, messenger of the gods.

In the classical world, *augury*—the oracular interpretation of the flight and songs of birds—was considered to be mostly *favorable* or *auspicious* (both words from Latin, *avi*, meaning "bird"). An equally accepted form of divination was the ritual pouring of libations from sacred vessels onto fires, basins, earth, or statues of the gods. Even today, astrology shows which "stars" are aligned in one's favor. In Trump 17, bird, vessels, and stars draw together to dispense a unified message of hope.

Both the Hierophant and the Star depict sacred rituals, one through the veneration of ageless wisdom, the other through a loving outpouring of praise, gratitude, and service. Like the stars themselves, the expressions of devotion that may rise up from within are limitless. Standing at the ocean has moved my friend Louise to sing spontaneously in tribute to the foaming waves. Between two fallen trees in the forest near my father's home, he once left two of his watercolor paintings—symbolically giving back something of beauty to the nature spirits that inspired his art. At the conclusion of anatomy classes in many medical schools, students perform ceremonies of appreciation for the cadavers they studied, including writing poems and songs and placing flowers in bowls when the donors' names are finally revealed. The Star shows us the concurrent offering and receiving, the replenishing inflow and outflow, that comes with tending the sacred.

The Star shines whenever we pour out our devotion and get back as much, if not more, than we have given. The archetype thus combines the Empress's generosity with the natural give and take of the Wheel of Fortune (the vertical line) and feeds our faith in the inexhaustible gifts of the spirit.

Though the vessels of Trump 17 never empty, ours do. We all experience times of depletion, whether triggered by staggering Tower traumas or low-grade malaise. Some experience it as writer's/ artist's block, where the creative imagination dries up. Yet, there are ways to coax back the flow of fullness. Mark Twain advised, "When the tank runs dry you've only to leave it alone and it will fill up again in time." Meditation, too, replenishes. Sitting in stillness empties the mind of rattling doubts and clears space for the ripples of pure Being. As we raise our vibration through meditation, prayer, or acts of devotion, our Star reappears, the waters collect, and our brimming nourishes the world. The Star ascends to renew our confidence in the existence of inner reserves and the conviction that our true nature is, like the cosmos, timeless, shimmering with creative possibilities.

A Star Story

After months of searching, twenty-one-year-old Carrie located the mysterious man she'd never met—her father. "It was so weird," said Carrie of her phone conversation with him just days before. "We were both pretty nervous." She learned that he had never married and had no other children. She asked to meet him for lunch the next week, and he agreed. Carrie wanted advice on how to prepare emotionally for the momentous visit.

I turned up three cards. The Star was there, reversed. "Carrie, what result do you want from this meeting?"

Her answer sounded like a question. "Well, I guess it would be nice if he became a part of my life?"

I proceeded delicately. "It's good to go in open to that possibility, Carrie, but the reversed Star is telling you to keep your expectations in check. It may turn out that your father doesn't have a lot to offer the relationship. He may not have your relational skills."

The reversed Knight of Cups warned against idealizing the relationship. The third card was the Queen of Wands, who wanted nothing more than for Carrie to appreciate her courage in taking the emotional risk.

Star Attributes

Key words:	Replenishment, Well-being, Devotion
Being:	Hopeful, peaceful, cooperative, charitable, devoted, self-accepting, nurturing, appreciative, spiritually replenished
Doing:	Aspiring to an ideal, giving from a sense of infinite supply, reviving the spirit, forgiving, consoling, pouring out gratitude, nurturing a dream, trusting life, offering hope
Shadow:	Intolerance for anything but the ideal
Reversed:	Dimmed hopes; putting a dream on hold; losing sight of ideals; lack of inspiration, reciprocity, or sustainability; energy deficit; withholding emotional energies; artist's block
	Possible Advice
Reversed:	"Be less starry-eyed and more realistic about your expectations." "Conserve your energies, or pour them elsewhere."

Questions for Reflection

What replenishes you?

What brings you hope?

How are you helping make the world a better place?

What are you in the process of healing?

In what activity do you receive back as much, if not more, than what you give?

When have you experienced a cleansing and renewal?

18. The Moon

Behold, this dreamer cometh.
—Genesis

Look closely at the face on Trump 18. Perhaps it's my Moon-induced imagination, but the outline of an embryo appears to conform to the profile. I like to think that Waite is providing a subliminal link here between the Moon and our primitive, watery origins. There is a moment in that liquid, membranous state when we are alike in appearance to nonhuman prenatal life forms. Never are we as close to such a purely wild condition or as close to the world of pure spirit.

The howling canines remind us of the ancient linkage between wildness and the moon. So too does the water, over which the moon holds dominion as agitator of the tides. Both wildness and water symbolize the unruly depths of the unconscious, of which the Moon is an archetype.

Our rational minds would rather we ignore the strangeness of our lunar dimensions, but the Moon represents an inevitable passage in soul development. When we explore our moonscapes with full consciousness (the Magician, 1) and courage (Strength, 8), the water and wildness work to take us to yet higher planes of awareness. At the very least, the Moon will prove that there is far more to us than meets the eye. The Moon abandons the Emperor's order and all semblance of Justice's balance so that we may explore our uneven, uncharted psychic territory; the sum of 1 and 8 is 9, the Hermit, a reminder that at this phase of the journey we're on our own.

You'll recall that lunar imagery appeared in an earlier card, the High Priestess. In that scene a quarter moon lay elegantly at her feet quietly to induce intuition, memory, and wisdom. In Trump 18 the moon has assumed its celestial proportion and sternly eclipsed the sun—an aggressive intrusion of lunar changeability onto solar stability. The placid waters of the High Priestess won't still us now. The Moon is in command, and the seas are at its mercy.

When the spell of the moon pulls back the tides, things that had been submerged become exposed. The Moon rules whenever the stuff of the unconscious has its way with us—dreams, sudden mood shifts, psychic revelations—with no guarantees that we'll make sense of them. On the morning that I began this essay, a client, George, told me about his own Moony experience. A dream he recently had—but only sketchily remembered—had left him with a vague feeling of apprehension. The next morning, still troubled over the dream fragments, he drove out to visit his mother. From the instant he arrived, both of their moods seemed "off." Every word between them was tinged with agitation. Resentments between them began roiling to the surface, and within minutes he left, shocked by the intensity of his anger. Driving back home, he was shaky at the wheel, envisioning gory accidents at every intersection.

At the end of this most upsetting day, George was struck by the confluence of the unsettling dream, the dread during the drive, the rough upsurge of emotions, and the presence that night of a full moon—the sphere linked astrologically with Cancer, ruler of maternal energy! When the Moon brings things to the surface, good luck trying to resist. You might as well throw back your head and howl.

Still, there is meaning in the madness. The Moon's intent isn't just to mess with our heads, but to get us to see better in the dark.

For example, instead of trying to shake off a bad dream, Moon wisdom directs us to *work* with it—write it down, talk about it, turn it into a poem, dance it. In doing so, we dilute its terrors, open a dialogue with the unconscious, and take steps toward better understanding ourselves. The Moon functions to release our psychic and creative energy and to introduce us to deeper mysteries of Self and Universe.

The Moon is also known to cast its beams in more sensational ways. Apparitions, premonitions, visions, déjà vu, and other non-ordinary experiences blur the lines between the real and the imaginary, the five senses and the sixth, the seen and unseen. While such phenomena may be jarring for the uninitiated, they serve, at the most basic level, to remind the ego that the material plane is not the only reality. There is a lot going on behind the scenes. The Moon is a tour bus through the multidimensional, and its destinations are often a surprise.

The surreal image of Trump 18 evokes the dream world. Just as each character and object in a dream represents aspects of the dreamer, so do the animals on Trump 18. We are the crawfish moving fluidly between the solid (conscious) world and the aquatic (unconscious) realm. We are the wolf and its domesticated cousin, who each respond instinctively to the raw emotions evoked by the moon.

The French idiom *entre chien et loup* (literal translation: "between dog and wolf") describes the time just before nightfall when the light makes these two animals indistinguishable. And there's a point to that confusion: The Moon asks us to put no greater value on the friendly and familiar parts of our psychic makeup (the dog) than the parts unknown-and-seemingly-dangerous (the wolf). The emotional changeability of the latter doesn't make us crazy, only human, and has the potential to unleash our wildest creativity.

Beneath our Moon instabilities lie spiritual opportunities. The archetype broadens the feeling of psychic boundlessness we sensed in the Star and prepares us for the extraordinary consciousness of the World. Meanwhile, the falling golden petals of the Divine bless our progress.

A Moon Story

Years ago, one of my clients paid me to do a phone reading for her nineteen-year-old niece, Lauren. I agreed, but felt uncomfortable about it. Shortly before the appointment I asked myself, "What's going on with Lauren?" and pulled the Moon, reversed.

At her session Lauren asked for a general reading, so I laid out the Celtic Cross. The Moon again appeared reversed, along with the Devil and a few other heavy hitters. The dominant theme of emotional restriction was unmistakable. But as I shared my impressions, Lauren, in a flat, faraway voice, claimed she was unable to see how any of it applied to her. And I knew she was being honest. Her emotions, like the Moon, were alien territory to her; the reading would not penetrate. I suggested we shift the focus to another topic, and she quickly agreed.

Moon Attributes

Key words:	Imagination, Dreams, Changeability
Being:	Creative, imaginative, empathetic, emotional, artistic, psychically adventurous, easily influenced, moody
Doing:	Experiencing fluctuation, delving into emotions, sensing or exploring other dimensions, dreaming, fantasizing, facing emotional tests, behaving erratically, discovering that not everything is as it seems

Shadow:	Living in a fantasy world; deception, moodiness, emotional instability, psychosis
Reversed:	Suppressing or denying psychic or unconscious material, ignoring instincts, avoiding the inner or outer unknown, behaving as if everything is okay, taking a more rational approach

Possible Advice

Reversed:	"Don't let your emotions or imagination get the better of you." "Go in a more solid and steady direction."

Questions for Reflection

What glimpses have you had of other dimensions or realities?
How much time do you spend in daydreams and fantasy?
What are your reccurring dreams, and what is their message?
When have your own strong emotions taken you by surprise?
Where are the emotionally charged atmospheres in your life?
What things have not turned out to be as they appeared?

19. The Sun

Life is a pure flame and we are lit by an invisible sun within us.
—Sir Thomas Browne

In the Moon we found ourselves swimming in images and emotions that at first seemed too alien, too wild, to have been part of us. However disturbing, we sensed that there was something initiatory about the plunge, a kind of baptism into yet another stage of self-knowledge.

Now, as the Moon gives way to the Sun, our instinctive lunar nature carries us into the bright light of day. We feel lighter, emboldened, no longer a stranger to our depths. Light floods into us and from us. With blazing clarity, we see there is nothing that can hold us back but ourselves.

A red flag unfurls in triumph over inner discord. Wavy and straight currents, representing feminine and masculine, inner and outer, shoot out from the Sun. Each current numbers 11 (Justice), which signifies a balance of these energies. The balance is reflected in both the androgyny of the child and in his/her perfect equilibrium atop the horse. Saddle, bridle, and reins are absent— mere baggage when higher and lower forces are in such harmony.

Four sunflowers bob approvingly toward the child, their number representing order and stability. The Sun is felt as the happy awareness that the parts once at war are becoming congruent, moving in a mutually declared direction. What we think, say, and do reflects our implicit self-worth and positive perspective. There are no cross-purposes at work, no competing agendas. All systems are go.

The light of the Sun filters our perception to reveal the brilliance in things. "Light is above us, and color around us," observed Goethe, "but if we have not light and color in our eyes, we shall not perceive them outside us." The brighter our inner Sun, the more apt we are to see the Sun in the world (*as within, so without*). This principle accounts for the common experience of everyone and everything seeming beautiful after we've received good news or been smitten by love. When the heart is opened, one's universe lightens up, priming the pump for joy. We become more expansive in energy and outlook, fed by an unstoppable faith that life is a gift, and resolve to live it fully.

The Sun figure's arms reach out to embrace existence. Here we witness the coming out of the Inner Child. To this part of us, the world is a wide-open space bursting with opportunities for spirited self-expression. Flagstaff in hand, the Sun child stakes claim to joy. Not merely the transitory joy that comes in response to fortunate events, but a hard-wired joy—our divinely intended basic operating system.

Living in joy is not an unattainable archetypal ideal, nor is it an escape from or denial of life's pain and bitterness. Being joy based is a core resilience that enables us to claim life as good—if not glorious—even as we sing our sorrow and dance our anguish. It is the sense that something within shines brighter, bigger, and longer than the aches and obstacles. The Sun commands us to break through the clouds of doubt and despair and to step confidently into our own light and feel the radiant presence of divine energy.

Once alive to this inner light, we can never again completely buy into the illusion that we are separate from spirit. Any lingering attitudes of unworthiness will be unable to withstand the solar intensity of Sun consciousness and will be burnt to a sizzle—not by a Tower-like intervention of the unconscious, but by an intelligent decision to love ourselves more. At long last, we're comfortable being who we are, able to accept our basic nature, free of the self-punishments once meted out by unrecognized shadow shame.

Ironically, the greatest obstacle to shining so brightly is that we'll call attention to ourselves. The ego warns us away from making joy and faith conspicuous by filling us with fears that we'll arouse envy, tempt cruel Fate, or endure mocking from our cooler, more cynical friends. If that's not enough to douse the flame, we might question our right to be happy when there's misery in the world. Or make it our personal duty to suffer along with everyone else, forgetting that the healing of the world requires the very light we're attempting to hide or deny.

But once the Sun is activated, it knows no restraints. We are warmed by the rays of self-acceptance. We celebrate our unique gifts and allow them to flower. Like the Fool's feather waving in the Sun child's cap, there is a flamboyance about expressing oneself so authentically and openly, a pleasure in being and in being seen for who one truly is. In contrast to "how special I am," Sun consciousness exudes "how *much* I am, and how much I have to contribute"—the largeness of the spirit uncensored.

In the septenary (page 19), the Sun lines up vertically below the Hierophant and the Hanged Man. The Hierophant's traditional belief system got turned on its head in the Hanged Man so that a deeper sense of spiritual alignment could emerge. The Hanged Man's sunlike halo, which signified his dawning understanding, has exploded into the full solar brilliance of Trump 19. For the first time since Trump 0, life is fun!

From the looks of things, the journey could quite satisfactorily end here. But two Trumps remain: 19 reduces to 10, the Wheel of Fortune, promising further evolution. The child, though joyful, is a child nonetheless, not at full maturity. And the wall behind the figures suggests that there may be something too exclusive, too isolating, about the feeling enjoyed here; the blossoming must be shared with a larger audience.

Arms outstretched, feather and flag aloft, the Sun child will carry the adventure to even greater levels when it hears the call of the Judgment Trump.

A Sun Story

My life partner, Rich, was ambivalent about making the five-and-a-half-hour drive to his parents' home in southern Ohio. Aside from the gas costs required for the three-hundred-mile excursion, the trip would take him away from the novel he'd been working on and thwart his desire for a productive weekend at home. He decided to get input from the Tarot and asked, "What is the greatest good of going to Ohio?"

The Sun card arose, providing the encouragement he needed to make the trip. Rich said that when he walked in the door of his parents' house, his three-year-old nephew, Matthew, ran up to him with open arms. "I immediately thought of the child on the Sun card," Rich said, "and I was so glad I came." What might have been another mentally immersive weekend of writing at home had turned into a restorative weekend of laughter and play with his nephew and nieces.

Sun Attributes

Key words:	Radiance, Optimism, Clarity
Being:	Warm, optimistic, joyful, fortunate, charismatic, magnanimous, healthy, outgoing, playful, successful, confident; a leader
Doing:	Seeing the good in others, letting your light shine, looking on the bright side, expressing your Inner Child, empowering others, seeing things clearly, achieving goals, cheerfully defying obstacles
Shadow:	Compulsory cheerfulness, denial of the shadow; expecting everything to revolve around you
Reversed:	Hiding your light; low self-esteem, failure to see the good, doubt, burnout; a killjoy
	Possible Advice
Reversed:	"Turn down the wattage—consider a more subtle approach." "Notice if you're being too self-centered."

Questions for Reflection

What is your most powerful form of self-expression? (Where do you shine?)

What doubts or insecurities have you overcome?

Who championed you and helped you appreciate or develop your gifts and talents?

Where in life are you a leader, and how do you help others thrive under your leadership?

What could you do to bring more joy into your life?

What are you most optimistic about?

20. Judgment

God had sounded through them as though through trumpets.
—Marsilio Ficino

The Sun brought us to the peak of self-acceptance and the fullness of personal expression. The opposing strands of the psyche came together. In Judgment, the coming together continues—this time, in community. In the state of consciousness symbolized here, we are less preoccupied with what makes us different from everybody else. We begin to sense our place within the human family and embrace a feeling of unity.

A majestic angel, its hair aflame with spiritual fire, sounds a golden trumpet. The blast has literally awakened the dead, who rise from their coffins and welcome the vision of unified consciousness soaring above. The angel calls them to leave behind the past, let go delusions of separateness, and merge with the cosmic All. Their nakedness intimates their spiritual readiness; they have stripped away all worldly resistance to the divine summons to blend and ascend.

The figures are connected and fortified by the river of Life at the center of the scene as they prepare for the Great Melding. The Trump unites the fluidity of the High Priestess (2) with the ego-unencumbered wholeness of the Fool (0). The combination initiates the process that will lead to the spiritual homecoming symbolized in the World.

In the Septenary, Judgment falls below the Lovers and Death. In that vertical triad, the exclusive relationship honored in the Lovers was relieved of its possessiveness in Death. In Judgment we see the Lovers reborn and the creative possibilities (their progeny) that emerge upon the death of the old self. As the individuals behold the angel of the realized Self, they take in the presence of other awakening beings with whom they are spiritually identical. Their sense of a cosmic community will grow, extending beyond their shores until it encompasses the whole Earth.

Judgment's angel breaks through the density of mass consciousness with the revelation that we are all one in spirit. Every so often a catalyst arrives on the world stage to assume the angelic role and hasten that message. The archetype has appeared in the all-are-one teachings of ascended masters such as Jesus and Buddha, in Martin Luther King, Jr., calling the nation to honor its pledge of equality for all, and in every heaven-on-earth effort to wake global consciousness to the fact of our interconnectedness.

Therefore, the Angel of Judgment does not seek to judge us (as the name of the card might imply) but *to lift us out* of our judgmental consciousness. Like the waves of sound shown issuing from the angel's trumpet, Judgment pitches our vibration at a higher frequency and remakes us as instruments of the Divine.

Thus far we've focused mostly on Judgment's collective emphasis. But the card speaks equally to the individual (which inevitably affects the collective). Judgment is the archetype of callings, the summons to a new life. We receive our angelic visits in the guise of break- throughs, whether in the form of a newly discovered path, a healed relationship, a forgiving of self, or the finding of a more authentic way of being. The messenger might come through a passage in a book that lifts us to the next level of growth or a conversation with a friend that transforms our perceptions.

Many elements of the Waite image are consistent with those of the earliest Judgment cards. Features of this particular design may be seen in paintings such as Piero della Francesca's mid-fifteenth-century masterpiece *Resurrection of Christ*. In that work Jesus, swathed in a robe as pink as the wings of Waite's angel, heralds his arrival with a banner of the four-armed Greek cross, a symbol employed by Constantine, the first Christian emperor. Both the title of the painting and the period of its creation, the Renaissance, mean "rebirth"—the essence of Judgment. The people on the card, long dead to their true spiritual identities, revivify in the trill of the angel's trumpet. The purity of its tones calls them into awareness of their closeness to the Source and to the inevitability of being transformed by it.

When we hear the call to leave behind the confining percep- tions of the past and act upon a new, progressed vision of the Self, we may be skeptical. Or, like the fellow on the left side of the Judgment card, we may be interested, yet hesitant. The higher we perceive our calling to be, the more undeserving we may feel, perhaps because it rings of divine selection: "Who am I to do, or be, this thing?" It's enough to make us burrow deeper in our boxes, where the cold, dark corners confirm the illusion of isolation and limitation.

Being singled out was inconceivable for Mary when told by archangel Gabriel she would bear the Messiah. Muhammad protested fiercely when that same angel appointed him Prophet of Islam and channel of the Koran. Yet each of us is equal in potential for light bringing. What inner stirrings have we kept sealed for having thought ourselves too lowly or too flawed to give them wings?

Despite the operatic overtones of Trump 20, our marching orders are more likely to be whispered, not trumpeted and incremental, not instantaneous. Ultimately, our highest calling may simply be the decision to be happy; to let love, not fear and judgment, lead our lives. And our happiness is no small matter. Consciousness is contagious. As more of us awaken to our joy, to our cosmic kinship, and to the power of these perspectives to heal the world, we rattle the tombs of those still asleep.

A Judgment Story

Doug received a phone call from his high-school friend, Michael, with whom he'd had no contact for twenty-five years. "We just fell out of touch," Doug says, "but within the first two minutes, it was like we'd never missed a day."

Toward the end of their conversation, Michael invited Doug to stay with him in California for a few days. Doug said he'd consider it. Later that day he did a reading.

"What's the greatest good of visiting Michael?" Doug asked. He drew the Sun, which seemed encouraging. But the answer to his second question, "What energy shall I bring on the trip?" was Judgment, reversed. "Isn't that a contradiction?" he asked during Tarot class.

I replied with a question. "How might you be tempted to play the role of Judgment's Awakening Angel, and how might that get in the way of an otherwise pleasant visit with your friend?" Doug pondered this a moment. "I get it!" he said, snapping his fingers. "Michael made a few right-wing statements on the phone that really bugged me. I feel it's my duty to bring him into the twenty-first century."

The choice was up to Doug, but as his Inner Wisdom made clear, trying to enlighten Michael would spoil the sunshine in an otherwise friendly reunion.

Judgment Attributes

Key words:	Calling, Awakening, Rebirth
Being:	Deeply inspired, uplifted, awakened, reborn, summoned to a higher awareness, redeemed, on the same "wavelength" with others; motivator
Doing:	Awakening to your purpose, experiencing a breakthrough, getting a second lease on life, leaving the past behind, thinking "out of the box," uniting in the common good, rallying others
Shadow:	Waiting to be rescued, inappropriately assuming the role of awakener/savior
Reversed:	Complacency, entombment in old habits, the road not taken; doubting or denying a call; refraining from trying to convert, rescue, or "save" others
	Possible Advice
Reversed:	"This call is not yours to answer. Or, perhaps, not yet." "Don't try to change others."

Questions for Reflection

What moment marked the beginning of a whole new life for you?
What "calling" have you answered or ignored?
What makes you feel spiritually uplifted?
What "angels" have awakened you to greater possibilities?
What breakthrough would recharge your life?
In what group or community do you experience a shared feeling of
  interconnection or inspiration?

21. The World

*Give me beauty in the inward soul; may the outward and
the inward be as one.*

—Socrates

In the Sun we saw the opposites fuse in what appeared to be the perfect finale— the androgynous being astride a powerful white horse. Yet the Sun child's ride had barely begun when Judgment's angel flew in and stacked more rungs up the evolutionary ladder. The Sun's "integrated-but-separate-me" was now asked to become the "interconnected-and-interdependent-we." A tall order, but once attained, surely the summit of spiritual progression. Or so it seemed.

In spite of Judgment's all-is-one elevation, yet higher altitudes await. The World points the way to the Ultimate. The Unbounded. The Inmost.

States indescribable even to Zen mystic Alan Watts, who concluded, "No one's mouth is big enough to utter the whole thing."

Where the Chariot forged ahead despite the tension of opposites, and Temperance worked to integrate the opposites, the World transcends them. A naked figure dances, encircled by a triumphal wreath. According to Tarot tradition, she is a hermaphrodite. Trump 21 joins the prototypical masculine and feminine archetypes of Magician (1) and High Priestess (2), thereby fulfilling the marriage of opposites at the heart of the esoteric Tarot. Their union adds up to 3, the spiritual fruition of the Empress.

Red ribbons form infinity symbols to signify the potentialities birthed at this highest sphere of consciousness. The dancer has reached the spiritual perfection that mystics call Self-Realization, *sahaja*, nirvana, enlightenment, the awakened Buddha nature, living in the Tao, and Christ-consciousness. Such a state is so advanced that people who've reached it are said to have no other karma to work through. They've framed their certificates of completion and hang around to serve as models for the rest of us.

At these egoless levels, there are no distinctions between above and below, within and without. Awareness enters the timeless; love is unconditional. There is no judgment of self or others. The mind is focused only on the One, the Most High, having no desires except a longing for that which is God.

We do not need to be ascended masters to experience Trump 21's bliss, freedom from inner strife, and abiding love. But for most of us, such states are fleeting. A spontaneous spasm of universal oneness while atop a mountain may be transcendent in that instant, but by the descent it has become an anecdote. Nevertheless, each whiff and glimpse of liberation hollows out the ego a little bit more, creating deeper receptivity to spirit. The dancer's pair of wands suggest the number 11 (Justice), an indication that World consciousness finds both balance and joy in the certainty of divine order.

Like the twenty archetypes preceding it, the World in readings also relates to more commonplace experiences. In many cases, it speaks to the happy completion of tangible, earthbound goals. As the archetype of completion, the World is resolution after struggle—the inner and outer worlds are working beautifully together, tying up the loose ends (for now, anyway). We are in a state of flow, graceful as the purple sash floating about the dancer. Time and space expand amid feelings of lightness and liberation.

From her sky-riding perspective, the dancer sees life globally. In this spirit the archetype asks us to see ourselves as world citizens; to claim and celebrate our connection to people beyond our neighborhoods and nations, beyond borders of race, country, culture, and religion; to see that we are more alike than not while marveling at our inexhaustible diversity.

World consciousness expresses a deep respect for the value of the individual as well as the collective. We begin to take a holistic view of the planet and its inhabitants as integrated, mutually dependent. From there it is a relatively small jump to consider that everything is linked by a greater universal energy—a divine spark—even if that understanding is at first intellectual. Through meditation and contemplation, we take the idea more deeply into the heart, moving us closer to a permanent *knowing*, not a mere believing, that the Divine is in all and is all.

The inclusiveness of World consciousness naturally extends to those outside the human family. The spirituality of Native Americans is rooted in a profound connectedness to animals, plants, and the earth itself. This "sacred hoop" holism is mirrored in many of their languages, in which the articles *a*, *an*, and *the* do not exist. People of these tribes would refer not to *a* mountain or *the* mountain, but simply "mountain," as in "we went to Mountain, followed Sun, saw Fox and Bear." (Doesn't that sound a lot friendlier?) Directly addressing the object—"Hello, snowfall"—further enhances the sense of connection and engenders almost instant feelings of intimacy. We start to see the soul of the thing. "The eye that sees a 'thou' is not the same eye that sees an 'it,'" said Joseph Campbell. "Your whole psychology changes when you address things as an 'it.'"

Animal and human faces surround the World wreath, a reappearance of the Elemental Beings/Four Apostles of the Wheel of Fortune. Here, wreath replaces wheel as the androgyne moves at the hub in a dance of joyous detachment from past and future, us and them, win and lose.

Centered in the expanse of World awareness, we too rise above the dramas of life. Though not transcending the chaos, perhaps, we find more creative ways of perceiving order in it and moving through it more fluidly. Anxious "Ohmygod!" reflexes give way to "Hmm, what have we here?" mindfulness. Appearances become less real and far less important than the essences underlying them.

Fittingly, the wreath's oval mirrors the Zero of the Fool. View life with a little distance, and the humor is impossible to ignore. Bemusement mingles with pain, like estranged family members patching things up at a deathbed, weeping and laughing over past animosities and marveling together at the absurdity of having taken everything so seriously.

Suddenly we love it all, the whole shebang. From the vast inner sky the world is clear. Ordered. Perfect. Divine.

A World Story

It took four years for this book to find its publisher. As each year came and went without a contract, I felt increasingly like the whiny, shadow side of the Hanged Man—"When is it my turn?" In that time I never once asked the cards to show me *if* the book would be published, because I knew anything but a promising response could wreak havoc with the positive expectations I worked hard to maintain.

During the second year of the wait, I decided to ask the Tarot if there was anything I could do to help the book along. "What energy should I bring to the publishing of my book?" I was surprised to see the archetype of completion—the World—reversed, which seemed to say I had more work to do on it.

I soon got the inspiration to follow each of the seventy-eight card descriptions with an anecdote, such as this one. Two years later, the book got the green light from Quest Books. My World card had finally righted itself!

World Attributes

Key words:	Universality, Wholeness, Completion
Being:	Victorious, fulfilled, euphoric, on top of the world, at home within yourself and in the world
Doing:	Seeing the Divine in everything, thinking holistically, taking a global perspective, completing something, reaping rewards, celebrating, dancing, engaging in life fully without despairing in its dramas
Shadow:	Trying to transcend earthly limitations rather than work spiritedly within them, being unable to make useful distinctions or focus on details
Reversed:	Incompletion, alienation, the world turned upside down; focusing on the parts rather than the whole
	Possible Advice
Reversed:	"Completion is premature. Give it time."
	"Attend to the details. Get specific."

Questions for Reflection

In what area of your life do you seek completion?

How safe and "at home" do you feel in the world?

What triggers your deep sense of connection to the planet and the living beings upon it?

When have you felt "on top of the world"?

What boundaries are you dissolving?

When has a larger perspective made your problems smaller?

See appendix A, page 333, for a chart summarizing the Major Arcana.

Part Three

The Minor Arcana

Our highest business is our daily life.
—John Cage

Wands: All Fired Up

Fierce fire reveals true gold.
—Chinese proverb

Element: Fire
Astrological signs: Aries, Leo, Sagittarius

The skyward thrust of Fire fulfills the human desire to rise rapidly, gloriously above earthly limitations—the old self crumbling in ash, the new ascending in greater intensities of light. Fire is the life force; vitality, the divine spark. Fire's inspirations come to us in flashes, generating insight and genius. Fire leaps and dances, igniting creativity, drive, ambition. It sizzles as desire and roars into passion. The heart rate accelerates. We burn with vision, and confidence climbs. Contained within the hearth, cheerful Fire comforts, lights, and warms.

Except perhaps for its flammability, a stick of wood may seem an unlikely symbol for so electrifying an element. Waite called the suit *Wands* (known as *batons* or *staves* in the earliest Tarot decks) to give it a more magical connotation. His addition of the budding leaves is a biblical reference to Aaron's miraculous blooming staff, believed to have earned a place in the Ark of the Covenant. Since the ancient Mystery cults, rods have served as magical implements and masculine power symbols, conduits of spiritual fire.

Ace of Wands

Man is so made that when anything fires his soul,
impossibilities vanish.
—Jean de la Fontaine

The Ace of Wands represents the highest potentials, opportunities, and gifts offered by the elemental energy of Fire. Here, the hand of pure spirit forces our attention on all that ignites, rises, blazes, and consumes. The eight falling leaves refer to the 8 in the Major Arcana, Strength, emblematic of the life force. Sexuality, the very essence of that force, is graphically portrayed in Waite's phallic rendering of the Wand.

Like the passing of a cosmic Olympic torch, the Ace of Wands is the glowing rush of desire to create, expand, push past restrictions, and win, whether the aim is for gold medals or the gold of spiritual perfection. The Ace gives us an enthusiastic thumbs up to go after whatever has us fired up.

An Ace of Wands Story

If there were ever a "Mr. Wands" contest, my friend Brian would take the title unopposed. Possessed of an entrepreneurial spirit, an appetite for risk, and boundless creativity, Brian had never held a job other than the businesses he created for himself. If one venture failed (a rare thing), he had half a dozen others to jump on.

Like many driven type-A personalities, Brian's response to personal problems was to throw himself even harder into his work. But now in the middle of a wrenching divorce, years of neglected emotions ripped fresh wounds. He increased his psychotherapy appointments to twice a week, and he asked me for a reading.

"I have some opportunities to take my business into a couple of new areas," said a visibly sleep-deprived Brian. "Should I pursue them?"

Brian's Higher Self answered with a thudding thumbs-down from the reversed Ace of Wands. "This is a not a time for creating more work for yourself," I said. "Right now you have no energy to throw into your business. Your inner work needs priority."

Brian gave me the look of a prisoner who had just been pulled off a forced march.

Ace of Wands Attributes

Key word:	Ignition
Being:	Inspired, encouraged, empowered, excited, sexually potent
Doing:	Planting the seeds for growth, initiating creative endeavors, pursuing sexual opportunity
Shadow:	Overdevelopment of, overreliance on, or exaggerated importance given to the qualities of the suit

Reversed: Lack of faith, potential, or opportunity; a premature start;
             cooled passions

Possible Advice
Reversed: "Thumbs down. Move on. No sparks here."
             "Wait. Now is not the time to fire things up."

Two of Wands

Faith dares the soul to go farther than it can see.
—William Clarke

Two Wands frame a wealthy lord. Though the lands he owns stretch to the distant mountains, he is not content. His towering success, so ambitiously forged, now seems to him too confining. One of the Wands is clamped to the foundation; this creates a problem, for Fire does not like to be tied down, especially when the first winds of opportunity begin to fan its flames.

He grasps the untethered wand. Its height suggests the priority of new inspirations. He looks with yearning to the water, across which lie unknown worlds of experience. But adventures must wait. For now he turns a small globe, just toying with possibilities for expanding the reaches of his considerable powers.

The Two of Wands illustrates the tension between stability and mobility—the gulf between where one is now and where one longs to be. Though we may feel secure in our present situation, there is restlessness for change, a hankering to find what the world may hold for us beyond the familiar edges of our experience. Like the sea-gazing figure in the card, we are eager to get our feet wet, even if the destinations luring us flicker only faintly on the horizon.

A Two of Wands Story

My forty-something client Anika described herself as "a brilliant interior designer pretending to be a paralegal." Although there were many cards in her spread, she was fascinated by my read on the Two of Wands. "I *am* this card," she said. "As much as I'd love to leave my law job and go out and start a design business, I'm afraid of the drop in income. It's a constant conflict for me."

While discussing the card with her, I referenced a story by the Irish novelist Frank O'Connor, in which a boy tosses his cap over walls he's afraid to climb. To get his cap back, he has no choice but to climb the wall. He commits to following the goal before knowing how to get there.

Anika laughed. "Then I guess I want a guarantee that I can climb the wall before I throw my hat over it!"

"In that case," I replied, "the only guarantee is that the world will be denied one brilliant interior designer!"

Two of Wands Attributes

Key word:	Aspiration
Being:	Restless, eager for change and expansion, torn between security and risk; a visionary
Doing:	Contemplating a move, longing to explore, dreaming of bigger and better things
Shadow:	Never acting on the desire for change

Reversed:	Making your move or, conversely, being complacent
	Possible Advice
Upright:	"Decide where you want to go." "Pursue your desire."

Three of Wands

Good fortune is what happens when opportunity meets with planning.
—Thomas Alva Edison

The creative tension and longing in the Two has shifted to a more tangible formation of potential. What was once a dream has become decision and follow-through. The figure's powerful crimson cloak suggests great initiative; he is the impetus behind the movement of the three ships, the commander mobilizing his forces. In him we see the likes of Joshua, who led the Israelites from Mount Nebo on a three-day journey into their spiritual homeland. On a less epic scale, the Three of Wands is the corporation attracting investors and the

student taking on more challenging courses. Outside of a specific context, the card represents the lifelong process of managing the commerce of ideas and opportunities that expand one's ability to know, be, and do.

Except for a few minor costume details, the figure appears to be the Magician. The headband calls attention to the sixth chakra's visionary function, by which we apply the natural magic of picturing

150

the outcomes we desire and so draw them to us. Such intense concentration requires the kind of panoramic view shown on the card, with no obstructions to our inner sight. When we direct time and energy into our dreams, we get them moving, like the wind that powers the ships' sails. The Three of Wands shows us that commitment.

A Three of Wands Story

On my last day as a student in my first Tarot class, I drew one card to show how the week's insights and discoveries might serve me back home. I got the Three of Wands and groaned. The Tarot books described a golden waterway, but I saw a man looking sadly at three beached ships on a desert. After my euphoric week of inspiration and spirited community, the card seemed to show me the dearth of both awaiting me back in Chicago. I suddenly felt very alone and grieved the return to business as usual.

Though my response to the card was personally meaningful, it proved to be only a projection of my fears. Within days, the sand turned to water and the ships began moving. I was devouring every book I could find on the Tarot, doing readings for friends and myself, and supplementing my studies with metaphysical texts. I met some- one with whom I could "talk Tarot," collected some wonderful decks, and developed a Tarot journal to assimilate my learning. Everything I drew to me influenced not only my understanding of the Tarot, but the way I looked at life. Like the image on the card, my "ships" were sailing, and the view was terrific.

Three of Wands Attributes

Key word: Assimilation

Being: Self-directed, entrepreneurial, enterprising, forward thinking, resourceful, capable

Doing: Strategizing, planning, acting on intentions, exercising creative powers, broadening horizons, building an enterprise, managing operations, appropriating resources, gathering input, delegating

Shadow: Overreaching

Reversed: Doubt, inability to put energy into planning; lacking direction, keeping ambitions in check

Possible Advice

Reversed: "Refocus your goals, or scale them back."
"Stay flexible with your plans."

Four of Wands

And young and old come forth to play / On a sunshine holiday.
—John Milton

Of all the Wands pictured in the Rider-Waite deck, these four Wands are clearly self-standing. That which was intuited in the Two of the suit and planned for in the Three has come to an initial phase of fruition in the Four. The energy has been expended in the support of something wonderful; a bountiful garland bends like a smile over the celebrants below.

The castle from which the figures emerge may provide them with a sense of protection or a reminder of their prosperity, but it is dwarfed by the Wands, symbol of the enduring spirit they have gathered to glorify. The Wands are decorated like maypoles, ancient centerpieces for public jubilation, particularly fertility celebrations. There is ripeness here. The card heralds arrival, rejoicing, and commencement. Life pats us on the back and exclaims, "Well done!" The bough's red ribbons signify that the loose ends of an endeavor have been tied up and brought to temporary completion. It's time for a party, which the outgoing nature of Wands never fails to appreci-

ate. Once the excitement settles and the last guest has gone, the Wands' continuous drive toward growth will spark the next flurry of creative activity.

A Four of Wands Story

Unless there's such a thing as having *too good* a party, or an ill-intended celebration, the Four of Wands is a card for which I've never found a shadow aspect. At an elegant fundraising event, the card sat whistling in the Present position for a young male guest. Glowering from the Past was the Devil. In the Future the Page of Cups raised a glass to continued progress. I felt like breaking out the champagne!

"Congratulations on overcoming whatever 'demons' you've been wrestling with," I said. After his eyes returned to normal size, the man looked around to make sure our conversation was private. In a lowered voice he told me he had recently sworn off visiting Internet sex sites, to which he had been addicted for several years. He added that he never expected to tell anyone about it, let alone a Tarot reader, least of all at a ritzy black-tie gala. The Four of Wands stood as a spiritual validation of his very private victory.

Four of Wands Attributes

Key word:	Celebration
Being:	Happy, triumphant, liberated, sociable
Doing:	Reaching a milestone, celebrating, graduating, marrying, enjoying festivities, reaping rewards
Reversed:	Incompletion, delayed reward, muted celebration, insecurity; feeling unworthy of the party
	Possible Advice
Reversed:	"Don't hire the caterers just yet." "Sit this one out."

Five of Wands

One must have chaos in him to give birth to a dancing star.
—Jean-Jacques Rousseau

In the volatile world of Wands, nothing remains stagnant for long. After the achievements of the Four, the Five of Wands rumbles in to shake things up. Old forms are challenged, lose their hold, and break apart in the rush of new energy.

A restructuring is inevitable, but now there is only agitation and struggle. Five young men clash in confrontation. Each of them attempts to advance an aggressively singular vision. There is no cohesion, consensus, or unifying force.

However, the men's youthful faces appear nonthreatening, and their bright garments are disarmingly cheerful; perhaps such

disharmony is not a failure of cooperation, but merely the cost of entering
the fray. Like sibling rivalry or the routine
jostling and shouting on the floor of the
stock exchange, the hostilities hinted at
in the Five of Wands may be impersonal,
burning out as quickly as they arise.

Change draws us into conflict, scram-
bles the rules, and heightens the very
friction necessary for finding inspired
solutions. As abrasive as the rubbing of
sticks may be, with the right conditions
light may come of it.

A Five of Wands Story

Erin came to see me a few weeks after being fired from her job as the
manager of a real estate office. She saw her dismissal as an opportunity to do something more fulfilling with her life, but she couldn't
decide whether to start her own marketing consulting business, go
into business with a friend, sell her own brand of homemade toffee,
or apply for school loans for an advanced degree. The Five of Wands
in the layout perfectly summed up Erin's feeling of being pulled in
all directions. The only thing she knew for sure was that her next
employment situation had to match or exceed her previous income
and put her in a leadership role. We set the intention that the cards
would show us each option's potential for meeting her criteria (see
Exploring Options, page 308).

Two of the cards/options invited further consideration, one
was so-so, the other a recipe for financial disaster. "That makes
this easier," said Erin, placing the two encouraging cards together.
"These happen to be the directions I was leaning toward." With

fewer options noisily competing for her attention, she was free to move forward in a more focused way.

Five of Wands Attributes

Key word:	Unrest
Being:	Agitated, competitive, contentious, combative, confused
Doing:	Struggling to unify inner or outer disparities, inciting rebellion, quarreling, jockeying for position, restructuring, brainstorming, working at cross-purposes, enjoying rivalries, playing devil's advocate
Shadow:	Being a brawler, crazy making
Reversed:	Cooperation, resolution; establishing priorities, refusing to play the game, stifling a conflict
Upright:	*Possible Advice* "Shake things up and see what new creative energies come of it." "Jump in! The process may be messy, but worth it."

Six of Wands

Skill and confidence are an unconquered army.
—George Herbert

The rider in the Six of Wands wears no armor, weapon, or insignia. He enjoys a purely ceremonial procession, the strife of the Five of Wands now behind him. The two sets of rods that flank him recall the gateway of the Four of Wands, while an intersecting center Wand creates a *V* for the victory that has prompted his hailing. The haloing swirl of laurel branches is matched in the lanced triumphal wreath, proof that acting with courage has paid off.

Just as Prometheus brought human-kind the gift of fire, our greatest individual achievements serve to light fires under others and incite them to act on their dreams. The rider displays the crownlike wreath for the people, as if to say, "This one's for all of us—if I can do it, you can too." He turns his face to acknowledge those who supported him, for he knows that no one succeeds alone.

Artist Pamela Coleman Smith has layered the otherwise straightforward image with a little mystery. Why the contentious expressions of the background figures? Does the horsecloth hide something? What is the intention in the steed's backward glance? (My pick: "Hey, boss, don't let this go to your head.") Although these contrary elements may invite us to contemplate the potential *costs* of success, they don't detract from the card's central message of optimism, victory, and reward.

A Six of Wands Story

Matt, an energetic man of twenty-six, had completed six weeks in a substance abuse program. I read for him just a few days before he was to return home. The Eight of Pentacles in his Present position confirmed the disciplined progress he'd been making in recovery. A confirmation of a different sort lay in his Future position, and I didn't like what I saw.

The Six of Wands, reversed, gave me the feeling that Matt's sobriety would find no support from his friends back home. Even more troubling, I felt he might soon fall off his triumphant white horse and return to his addiction. "The Future shown here is not inevitable," I began, "but stay in close touch with your sponsor. This card is your Higher Self's way of putting you on alert to stay on course." He signified his understanding with a single gruff nod, and I silently sent him prayers.

Six of Wands Attributes

Key word:	Triumph
Being:	Confident, proud, optimistic, heroic
Doing:	Receiving a welcome, accolades, or rewards; basking in glory; carrying the day; leading others
Shadow:	Grandiosity, the overachiever
Reversed:	Self-doubt, unsuccessful ventures, fear of falling short of expectations
	Possible Advice
Reversed:	"Point your horse in another direction." "Assume a lower profile. Be more humble."

Seven of Wands

The best lightning rod for your protection is your own spine.
—Ralph Waldo Emerson

"Back off!" bellows the man in the Seven of Wands. Six opposing Wands loom menacingly. Judging from the direction of his gaze, more challengers may be fast approaching. Though he is clearly outnumbered, his higher elevation gives him an advantage. (Note the dazzling Fire optimism of that observation!) The crisis could prove to be his finest hour, giving him a chance to prove his mettle. At the moment, however, the outcome remains unknown, the only certainty being that Fire won't be contained if the situation gets hot enough.

The figure appears to defend against a physical attack. Less overtly, he may be perceiving an assault on his ideas, convictions, or the soft underbelly of his pride and selfhood. Whatever his concerns, coordinated footwear is obviously not among them—proof of his nonconformist stance. Perhaps it is this oddly shod Wandsman's eccentricity that has brought on the attack. Dare to be different, but be prepared to pay the price.

Then again, the antagonistic Wands could be rising up from within. Who hasn't had to fend off those poking inner voices that throw up "Yeah, but" obstacles every time we aspire to higher reaches? At such times the enemy may be ourselves.

The card combines the Emperor's boundary keeping with the Chariot's intractable sense of purpose. For such a fiery energy, it may seem strange that the figure is clad in soft green, the color associated with the heart chakra and Venus, goddess of love. But having the courage (from the French *coeur*, "heart") to remain true to ourselves despite opposition is a valiant expression of that rarest of virtues, self-love.

A Seven of Wands Story

I climbed out of the smoking, limping wreckage of my Honda
Accord stunned, but without injury. The other driver claimed she
hadn't seen the stoplight. Though I felt fine, I went the next day
to see a chiropractor at a friend's insistence. After a few minutes
of rotating my very supple neck, she announced a treatment plan
so extreme it nearly gave me whiplash—twice weekly visits for the
next three weeks, with more to follow "as needed."

When I got home I inquired about the wisdom of seeing the
chiropractor again. The self-protective Seven of Wands didn't
mince words. I never went back. And my neck is still as flexible as a
flapjack.

Seven of Wands Attributes

Key word:	Forcefulness
Being:	Defiant, aggressive, feisty, defensive, resistant
Doing:	Showing force, protecting yourself, holding your ground, pushing away unwanted demands, resisting advances
Shadow:	A defensive attitude when openness is needed, oversensitivity to criticism, bad tempered; creating self-imposed obstacles
Reversed:	Apathy, timidity, resignation; being defenseless or overpowered, relaxing your defenses
	Possible Advice
Reversed:	"Relax—you have nothing to prove and no need to defend." "Let it in."

Eight of Wands

Swifter than arrow from the Tartar's bow.
—William Shakespeare

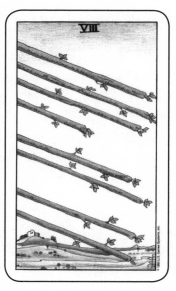

The Eight of Wands shows an instance of high activity, when the air crackles with energy and life jumps into warp speed. A volley of Wands race through the sky at such height, you can almost feel the force of it. Whether you see them moving up or down, the elemental rocketry seems bound to hit its target as it whistles through the bright blue air.

Like signals zapping through phone wires, the Eight of Wands represents the rapid-fire energy of messages sent and received, ideas seized and implemented, projects planned and launched. Whatever the activity, swiftness is assured. We're ready and responsive, and we get results in record time.

For all the excitement, there is order here, as demonstrated by the neatly bombarding Wands. As in the Wheel of Fortune, beginnings and endings are emphasized in the Eight of Wands, albeit with faster turnarounds and less cosmic mystery.

An Eight of Wands Story

My father once developed an infection from knee surgery that extended his hospital stay. Every day that he lay in bed, he became more discouraged. My mother and I brought humorous books and lively stories to cheer him up, but in his weak condition he showed no interest.

Once at home, I asked, "What can I do for Dad?" and pulled two cards. The first was the Eight of Wands, reversed. This told me that the very things I thought might hasten his recovery—buoyant reading materials, *New Yorker* cartoons, and perky assurances that he would soon be up and moving again—were not helpful. His mind and body needed quiet and rest, not the stimulation I offered. The intent of this reversed card was seconded by the slow-moving Six of Swords, a card signifying gradual recovery.

When I visited Dad the next day, I made a point of just being present with him, instead of trying to rush him out of there with my words and thoughts. It immediately felt right. He was released from the hospital the following week, his spirits lifting higher each day.

Eight of Wands Attributes

Key word:	Movement
Being:	Lively, motivated, communicative
Doing:	Acting quickly, sending or receiving messages or proposals, traveling, launching activities or events, multi-tasking, pursuing multiple interests, experiencing a transition
Shadow:	Overstimulation, intense but meaningless activity
Reversed:	Slowness, delay; missing the target, running out of steam, putting on the brakes, taking it easy
	Possible Advice
Reversed:	"Slow down!" "Reprioritize your activities."

Nine of Wands

Great works are performed not by strength but by perseverance.
—Samuel Johnson

A man keeps watch before a row of Wands that stand both as monuments to his battles and markers of his territory. Despite the verdant hills and calm summer sky, he looks about with apprehension. His achievements haven't always come easily (as his bandage attests), and he's resolved not to let his guard down should the need arise to prove himself again. He tightens his jaw and his grip on the Wand as he braces for the next foray into Fire.

Although capable of putting his strength to the test, this fellow lacks the spirit and agility of the warrior Wandsman in the Seven. Gone too is the ambition of the adventure-hungry dreamer in the Two. He is no longer roused by calls to heroism. What's left is a kind of raw, edgy determination to preserve his hard-won stability. He will battle if he must, but perhaps only grudgingly.

At its brightest, the Nine stands for the indomitable spirit of the survivor. "I may be wounded," the figure proclaims, "but, by God, I'm still standing!" As a card of advice, it urges us to stick to our guns and, even in our losses, never to accept defeat.

A Nine of Wands Story

Under the repressive leadership of a new boss, my client Sophia and her coworkers gradually found themselves in a "protect your posterior" climate in which all productive energy was diverted by a more pressing need to avoid blame and keep their jobs. Though she saw her boss as a tremendous obstacle, the Nine of Wands in Sophia's Self-Image position showed her determination to keep the job and the customers she loved. To do so, she had made the decision to take fewer risks on the company's behalf and never let her guard down around her employer.

"I'm staying put," she said, as if providing a caption for the Nine of Wands. Meanwhile the Moon, looming in the Possible Outcome position, promised only fluctuation. Sophia's tough-it-out strategy soon waned. I received an e-mail a month later that she and a coworker had quit their jobs.

Nine of Wands Attributes

Key word:	Perseverance
Being:	Tough, courageous, resolute, stoic, vigilant, stubborn, wary, tense; a survivor
Doing:	Bracing for challenges, showing endurance, refusing to buckle under pressure, "holding up the fort"
Shadow:	Hypervigilance, paranoia
Reversed:	Lacking persistence, giving up, surrendering in trust
	Possible Advice
Reversed:	"Find an easier way." "The war is over—go home."

Ten of Wands

The fire which enlightens is the same fire that consumes.
—Henri Frédéric Amiel

In Hindu cremation rites, the dead are engulfed in flames as an offer to Agni, the fire god. This ritual, *antyeshti*, is known as the "final sacrifice" and has its counterpart, perversely, in the Ten of Wands. We see the consuming aspect of Fire, with the overburdened, burned-out Wands-bearer apparently bent on self-sacrifice. It would come as no surprise if the kindling he is collecting winds up as the pyre for his inadvertent self-immolation.

There must be less strenuous ways to carry such an armload, but given Wands' taste for speed over efficiency, the man has grabbed his cargo in haste, blinding him to less painful alternatives. Psychologically, he may feel a sense of servitude or, conversely, carry the brunt of an overly responsible "Leave it to me" attitude, stubbornly denying his need for assistance. Here too is the workaholic laboring under his overcommitments.

Just as surely as the Wands-schlepper's stooping strains his back, operating too long in overdrive pushes the immune system to its limits and makes us susceptible to injuries and illnesses. The Ten shows the point at which we've gotten too caught up in the action to know when, or how, to stop.

Extreme as it is, the card as advice may speak to the importance of persisting in goals despite great burdens. As many Fire-fueled runners and body-builders can attest, sometimes you've got to go for the burn!

A Ten of Wands Story

Early in my Tarot practice, a woman in her early thirties came for a reading about her troubled long-distance relationship with a man. Not satisfied with the information that came up, she made a second appointment a week later. That appointment was followed by a phone call in which she, presuming a personal interest on my part, proceeded to unload more details about her increasingly complex relationship.

In those days I was quite weak in the boundaries department, so I spent twenty minutes in full Rescuer mode, offering my golden advice for every problem she voiced. When the call ended, I pulled a Tarot card to find out why I suddenly felt so depleted. "You took on somebody else's stuff and made it your problem," said the Ten of Wands as he shuffled by, groaning under his load.

Ten of Wands Attributes

Key word:	Overload
Being:	Weary, determined, overworked
Doing:	Shouldering burdens, taking on too many responsibilities, testing your limits, toughing it out
Shadow:	Servitude; refusing to ask for or accept help, taking on blame, acting like a martyr
Reversed:	Unburdening, lightening the load, delegating, walking away from responsibilities, not taking on others' "baggage"
	Possible Advice
Upright:	"Keep going—you've come too far to let things drop." "It's up to you to carry the load."

Page of Wands

The value of identity, of course, is that so often with it comes purpose.
—Richard Grant

The Court figures in the suit of Wands inhabit the desert, where the heat of the sun is most intense, the vegetation rare and precious. The Page looks with understandable awe at the greenery sprouting from the Wand. He senses its magical potential with an excitement matched only by his frustration at not yet having mastered it (Fire wants it all and wants it now).

Three pyramids form the backdrop for the Wands Court cards. They connote the uplifting of body, mind, and spirit. The upward-glancing Page stands at the threshold of a newly inspired direction. Although he has no idea where the path will take him, something tells him it will be fun, challenging—the adventure of a lifetime. Like a whisper of encouragement, a feather rises from his sixth chakra, the intuitive energy center.

We feel the Page's influence when drawn to something that could accelerate our personal growth and enable us to be and express more of who we are. Some feel the quickening of spirit when nurturing a budding talent or business, others when exploring opportunities that had once seemed out of reach. His tunic is decorated with salamanders, animals believed by the ancients not only to survive fire but to *inhabit* it. Likewise, the Page knows he has his hands on an opportunity to discover his own magical potential. The time has

167

come for him to strengthen his faith in himself and, as the flame motif on his boots suggests, step more lively in the dance.

A Page of Wands Story

It's easy to feel great about a relationship when everything is going well. But the real tests of partnership are the snags. Madeline and her husband, Clark, were caught on the barbed wire of their twelve-year marriage. She asked me point-blank if the relationship would survive. I suggested we "go direct" and ask her Higher Self what energy to bring to the relationship. There, without drama, was the Page of Wands.

"What feeling do you get from the card?" I asked. "It looks hopeful," she responded, somewhat surprised. I offered that the little flame on the Page's hat was a sign of something still worth kindling in the marriage, some spark of growth potential. "And there are buds on the Wand," added Madeline with a hint of appreciation.

Madeline and Clark are still married. I sometimes wonder if Clark ever learned that it was a little Page that inspired his wife's recommitment.

Page of Wands Attributes

Key word:	Eagerness
Being:	Intrigued, hopeful, inspired, trustworthy; a beginner
Doing:	Embarking on self-development, sensing your potential for creative or spiritual expansion, pursuing adventure
Shadow:	Sampling but never committing
Reversed:	Discouragement, inability or unwillingness to make a fresh start

	Possible Advice
Reversed:	"Find other adventures to pursue."
	"Protect your dreams from those who would shatter them."

Knight of Wands

Life is either a daring adventure or nothing.
—Helen Keller

The scarlet flicker that began on the helmet of the Page of Wands blazes into flaming plumes on the Knight; he takes the inspiration and runs with it. While all the Knights are driven by passion for a cause, passion *is* the cause for the Knight of Wands. If it hastens the pulse, spikes the adrenalin, or raises the stakes, this Knight charges after it.

Impatient with details, he is apt to say yes before knowing the full demands of his commitments; whatever the challenges, he'll meet them head-on. The Knight rides in the salesperson revved up to meet the monthly quota, the extreme sportsman egged on by risk and danger, and the tourist eager to visit three countries in two days.

Like Fire itself, the Knight is inclined to attract attention. He is eager to show what he's made of, and if there is applause for his efforts, he'll happily repeat the performance. Recognition is its own tantalizing reward. When he is done dazzling us, he tips his gleaming helmet and dashes away, pumped up for the next adventure.

Just as Fire moves in no predictable manner, the Knight can be erratic, chasing after any shiny object that happens to pop into view. However, if things don't move fast enough, he may find it difficult to stick around and see them to completion. Notice that the horse is as orange as the lion in the Strength card. The hint here is that if the rider is ever to attain Queen and King maturity, he must learn to temper appetites with restraint in the service of his mission. Such discipline is what separates the journeymen from the masters.

A Knight of Wands Story

A young client, Maggie, was making an effort to sound calm on the other end of the phone: "I just heard about a job opening in my local library and want to know if it's worth pursuing." I silently asked for guidance and shuffled the cards, and the Knight of Wands leaped into my hand. "The answer is Yes," I said, "and judging by the card that came up, you'd better fill out the application ASAP."

She did so and was on the job the following week.

Knight of Wands Attributes

Key word:	Vigor
Being:	Energetic, enthusiastic, confident, daring, self-motivated, feisty, restless, sexually adventurous; a thrill seeker
Doing:	Competing, taking risks; rousing the support of others; pursuing creative, physical, or sexual adventure; creating excitement; coming to the rescue; acting on impulse
Shadow:	Arrogance, overeagerness, recklessness; a hothead

Reversed:	caution, self-restraint, doubt, reluctance or inability to move forward
	Possible Advice
Reversed:	"Cool your heels. Don't go charging into this situation." "Slow down. Take a more rational or contemplative approach."

Queen of Wands

Nine-tenths of education is encouragement.
—Anatole France

The Queen of Wands is the soul of Fire. She is that part of us that is deeply moved by the human effort to rise above limitation, innovate, and win. She is the pride and admiration we feel when a friend receives a diploma after years of struggle and self-sacrifice. She is our slack-jawed awe at the commitment of Olympic athletes and the urge to rush backstage and praise a performer for knocking our socks off. The Queen is our profound appreciation for all expressions of creativity, courage, and spirit, wherever and in whomever we find them.

The Queen is right at home amid the lion motif, symbol of fire and sexual power, and the sunflower, emblem of solar radiance. The Queen has chosen her cat for its independence and devotion, traits shared between them. Like Bastet, the feline goddess-protector of children and home, the Queen is fiercely loyal to those fortunate enough to have her in their court. Whomever she trains her Fire upon flourishes like the sunflower.

The Queen is intimately acquainted with her soul's longing to reach beyond restraint, and she intuitively recognizes that spark when it appears in others. These qualities make her a generous encourager of people. The Queen tells you, "I believe in you. I know you can do it. You've got what it takes to do whatever it is you desire. I'm behind you all the way." She is the champion of dreams, healer of despair. The Queen, as a person or as an inner energy, keeps the fire burning.

Her determined jaw and commanding posture suggest intolerance for doubt and pessimism. The Queen does not want to hear negativity, but she does not deny it, either. Her response to the downbeat is to transform it by holding to her vision of the possible.

Nevertheless, she has a chillier side. Her magnanimous loyalty and protectiveness is just as present in the pushy stage mother relentlessly promoting her child, or in the family whose blind loyalty to its own makes them stand by each other's most inexcusable behaviors. But at her most majestic, she uses her Wand to light up the world, showing us our brilliance and stoking our faith.

A Queen of Wands Story

"That's my mother," said Shawn, a forty-five-year-old Tarot student. "No wonder the card's reversed." Shawn explained that, since childhood, her mother's constant disapproval had severely undermined her confidence and esteem. "My mother," she said edgily, "has made it very hard for me to believe in myself."

While the reversed Queen of Wands symbolized Shawn's mother, it also represented—*as within, so without*—Shawn herself. Mother's unsupportive voice had long ago taken up residence in daughter's psyche. Though Shawn's ego felt justified in blaming her mother for her esteem issues, the card showed it was up to Shawn to nurture the positive qualities that her mother had failed to acknowledge. Shawn's task for self-empowerment now was to turn the throne right side up, settle into it, and crown herself Queen.

Queen of Wands Attributes

Key word:	Faith
Being:	Faithful, creative, self-assured, passionate, optimistic; a cheerleader
Doing:	Nurturing the qualities of Fire in yourself or others, championing the human spirit, offering encouragement, helping others find their strength, showing loyalty, exercising willpower
Shadow:	Blind loyalty, a domineering attitude
Reversed:	Self-doubt, squashed enthusiasm, disapproval; giving the cold shoulder, withholding praise or support for self or others
	Possible Advice
Reversed:	"Hold back. Your support or loyalty is misdirected." "Warmth and willpower aren't enough; be more strategic."

King of Wands

Make no little plans; they have no magic to stir men's blood.
—Daniel H. Burnham

What happens when the fiery Knight of Wands develops the discipline to harness multiple talents, channels them into constructive outlets, sticks with them long enough to achieve mastery, and wins the admiration of a kingdom? Answer: He becomes the King of Wands. Given the impulsiveness of the Fire/Wands suit, the crown isn't easy to come by. And with it comes responsibility.

This enterprising King is accountable for making his efforts successful, not just original and exciting. He has a genius for strategy and promotion, whether he's blazing trails in the worlds of business, sports, art, or entertainment. He knows how to draw the spotlight to himself and get the support he needs to win.

His winning style opens doors; others immediately respond to his confidence and glamour. He can often go far on charisma alone. The King has bold ideas, likes to move quickly on them, and generally has no trouble getting the resources to do so. Unlike the Knight of Wands, he no longer chases opportunities—he creates them. As an entrepreneur or business leader, his intuition serves him royally, resulting in gainful (though at times short-lived) ventures.

The King is a natural leader but, maverick that he is, not always a good team player. He may be impatient with people he perceives as

174

dull and risk-averse. He may struggle to listen to others and barely tolerate those holding opinions contrary to his own.

Curiously, the pyramids that appear on the preceding three Court cards are missing here. Perhaps by this omission the deck's creators are showing us the King at the point where the weight of his responsibilities has eroded the idealism that drove him to his success. The salamanders' joined heads and tails complete the circuit on his mantle and cloak, signifying the totality of Fire in the suit of Wands.

A King of Wands Story

Seth announced to the Tarot class that he had been certified by his boss and mentor, Wyatt, to cofacilitate the man's successful self-development seminars in cities nationwide. Eager to see how the cards might comment on the news, he laid out a Celtic Cross spread. I watched as Seth's eyes went immediately to the card in the Outcome position—the King of Wands, reversed. "I don't like seeing *this* here," he said with sudden concern. Seth's reaction told me he was interpreting the reversed card as a pending failure of his abilities, or perhaps his boss reneging on the offer.

I drew Seth's attention to the other cards, which solidly affirmed the rightness of his promotion, especially the Chariot shouting "GO!" as his Higher-Self Advice. Given Seth's drive, my feeling was that the reversed King indicated only that he would experience the frustration of not reaching Wyatt's level of mastery as fast as he wanted. Kings are made, not born. "You're obviously qualified, Seth," I said, "so why not let the card be a reminder that you've got room to grow?" Seth preferred my interpretation, and he has undoubtedly been growing in his mastery of the seminars he leads to this day.

King of Wands Attributes

Key word:	Vision
Being:	Driven, disciplined, successful, charismatic, enterprising, competitive, competent; a risk taker
Doing:	Challenging, motivating, or inspiring others; maintaining a powerful leadership position; trailblazing; promoting or profiting from creative ideas; building upon your accomplishments
Shadow:	Arrogance, bossiness, overresponsibility
Reversed:	Thwarted leadership, denial or distrust of power, delayed achievement; being less driven or competitive
	Possible Advice
Reversed:	"Step aside and give others the chance to shine." "Temper your ambition."

Cups: From the Heart

Water, verily, is greater than food. . . . Meditate on Water.
—Chhandogya Upanishad

Element: Water
Astrological signs: Cancer, Scorpio, Pisces

Water moves in all living things. Mystics say it is the source of life; scientists, the universal solvent into which all ultimately merges, unifies, and dissolves. Whereas Fire rises, Water descends. Even in cloud form, it eventually falls to earth, filling in the hollow places, soaking through the dry ones. Like the roots it nourishes, our deepest parts thirst for the saturation of the Divine, yearning to flow fearlessly, formlessly in perfect bliss. Substance of the soul realm and of the undulating unconscious, Water fills the wells of memory, mystery, and imagination, shimmering moonlit as we guess at its depths.

In virtually every culture, sacred vessels are integral to water rituals of cleansing and spiritual regeneration, from the Catholic chalice and the Jewish *mikveh* (ritual bath) to the purifying water bowls at Shinto shrines. In the secular sense, the Cup is a feminine symbol denoting both the containment and outpouring of pure feeling—the contents of which are highly changeable. We raise our Cup in celebration of relationships, spill our joy and tears from it, and in hardening times, seal it in ice.

Ace of Cups

My cup runneth over.
—The Psalms

The Ace of Cups signifies the highest potentials, opportunities, and gifts offered by the elemental energy of Water. The card's Fountain of Life design is awash with Christian symbolism. The hand of the Almighty holds up a chalice representative of the Holy Grail, which is believed to have received the blood of Jesus at the crucifixion. A white dove, symbol of the Holy Spirit, deposits a sacrament of communion into the chalice. Five streams miraculously rise and descend into the water below, denoting the outpouring of divine love into the sensory world.

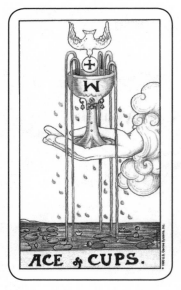

At the center of the vessel hang three tiny bells emblematic of the trinity of body, mind, and spirit through which the waters of divine love flow. The twenty-six cascading droplets correspond, in the Kabbalistic number system, to the tetragrammaton (see page 36), a sequence of letters that stand for the unknowable, unutterable name of the Creator. Thriving in the element are lotus blossoms, the Hindu and Buddhist symbol of spiritual perfection.

Like the Star, the Ace of Cups symbolizes the infinite supply of love available to all who become open receivers. It augurs the call to deepen our capacity for feeling, open the heart to others, and see ourselves—and all beings—with compassion. Like a cool glass of water, the Ace of Cups offers refreshment and renewal.

An Ace of Cups Story

Delia, a former Tarot student, pushed her grocery cart toward mine. "I'm so glad I ran into you," she exclaimed. She recounted the details of a recent Past, Present, Future reading in which the Ace of Cups signified her future. "I knew the Ace of Cups was about things like spiritual gifts and relationship opportunities," she said, "but I really had no clue how those kinds of energies were about to play out in my life. I was just happy it was a positive card."

Delia said that a few days after her reading, she got a phone call she'll never forget. "It was my daughter calling to tell me I was going to be a grandma. I can't imagine a more spiritual gift than that, can you?"

Ace of Cups Attributes

Key word:	Blessing
Being:	Peaceful, grateful, benevolent, joyous, inspired, spiritually enriched
Doing:	Giving or receiving love or blessings, connecting to Source, healing, cleansing, hydrating, making a spiritual commitment
Shadow:	Unrealistic insistence on purity; idealizing a relationship

Reversed: a feeling of spiritual disconnection, soul emptiness, feeling unworthy of spiritual abundance

Possible Advice

Reversed: "This Cup is empty. Seek nourishment elsewhere."
"Your emotional boundaries are spilling over. Ground yourself."

Two of Cups

Let yourself be silently drawn by the stronger pull of what you really love.
—Rumi

Opposites meet. And by the looks of it, they're off to a good start. It is a scene of attraction, courtship, and pledging. The Cups align at the couple's third and fourth chakras (will and love, respectively) and show their commitment to meaningful exchange.

Their respective Mars-red roses and Venus-green myrtle garlands point up their differences; nearly identical profiles show their commonality. Enough alike, yet enough different, it's a strong basis for relationship. The distant house hints at these two energies converging intimately under one roof, presaging the Ten of Cups.

Take away its romantic storyline (what fun is that?), and the card depicts the energy of mutuality and trust. The couple represents agreements, formal and otherwise, and the dependence on the other to fulfill them. The stateliness of their pose underscores these practical, functional benefits of partnership, the kind that keeps businesses running and countries cooperative.

At its deepest level the Two of Cups echoes the Lovers' theme of making peace with our inner opposites. Instead of the Lovers' angel, a lion presides to fire up the feeling between yin and yang below. Coiled between the couple is the Caduceus. This symbol of healing signifies the auspiciousness of the pairing and its potential for mending division.

A Two of Cups Story

My reading for Pam confirmed her frustration with the woman whose struggling small business she financially supported—her life partner, Maureen. The strain of working at her demanding corporate job and keeping Maureen's daycare-for-dogs enterprise afloat was everywhere on Pam's face. I saw the Two of Cups, reversed in the Higher-Self Advice position, as counseling Pam to dissolve this financial arrangement and, quite possibly, the relationship itself. Yet as right as these prescriptions seemed, I felt strongly that Pam, not I, should provide them. I asked her what she wanted.

The words tumbled out. "I want to stop being the bank for her business." She paused. "And that will probably destroy us." I recommended couples counseling. With Pam at the breaking point, counseling offered the only hope for bringing the Two of Cups to its upright position.

Two of Cups Attributes

Key word:	Attraction
Being:	Cooperative, compatible, intimate, in love
Doing:	Coupling, bonding, sharing, establishing a business partnership or contract, finding mutual understanding or agreement, reconciling, exchanging vows
Shadow:	Overdependency on the other, unrealistic expectations for the relationship
Reversed:	Disagreement, incompatibility, absence of attraction, lack of reciprocity, inequality, separation, independence
	Possible Advice
Reversed:	"Demand a refund from the dating service." "Amend or dissolve the contract."

Three of Cups

A cheerful heart has a continual feast.
—Book of Proverbs

The Two of Cups displayed an intensity common in the initial stages of infatuation and courtship. There we saw a passionate awareness of opposites. The Three shows us a more joyous expression of the feeling sparked in the Two. A playful affection nurtures the dynamic that will sustain it long after romantic entrancement fades.

In this card, appreciation ripens for the pleasures of relatedness and for life itself. There is growing emotional generosity, too. The loving vibration that was exclusive in the Two expands here to embrace others.

A scene of communal love and fellowship greets us. Good feelings abound. Three figures reap the rewards of fertile friendships amid harvest-time golds and oranges. They hoist their goblets as if toasting, "Here's to us!" The illustration is derived from an ancient Greek image of the Three Graces, a trio of sister goddesses who attend Aphrodite, goddess of love. Here we see Aglaia, representing radiance; Euphrosyne, joy; and Thalia, fruitfulness.

A Three of Cups Story

As soon as we arrived at our hotel in Vienna, two of my traveling companions insisted we go sightseeing. It was an excellent proposition; the conference we were attending there would leave little time to spend outside the hotel. But feeling the beginnings of a cold along with the exhaustion of spending the last twenty hours awake, I wanted only to soak in the tub and collapse into my king-size bed.

I did a reading about it, fully expecting the Four of Swords to turn up and prescribe the bed rest I craved. But the sociable Three of Cups had other plans for me. I turned off the bathwater, grabbed my camera, and enjoyed the company of my fellow travelers in a whirlwind tour of Vienna.

I highly recommend the pastries.

Three of Cups Attributes

Key word:	Delight
Being:	Convivial, sociable, joyful, playful, affectionate, warm, loyal
Doing:	Joining in, thriving in friendships, experiencing emotional breakthroughs, extending good will, enlarging a family, finding your "tribe"
Shadow:	Overdependency on group acceptance or activities
Reversed:	Thwarted gratification, absence of support, feeling that you don't belong, separating from a group, acting autonomously, canceling the party
	Possible Advice
Reversed:	"Don't push for harmony—let things be." "This is not your circle—bless them and move on."

Four of Cups

There comes a time when one asks even of Shakespeare,
even of Beethoven, is this all?
—Aldous Huxley

The day is clear and calm, the earth soft and green, and three gleaming gold cups lie at his feet. So why does the young man look so discontented? Does he not trust the appearance of the good around him? Has he simply become bored with it all? And what of the chalice offered him by a heavenly hand? Is he overlooking an opportunity or has he, in a fit of false modesty or self-doubt, decided he is unworthy of it?

The conspicuously open space next to the Cups brings an asymmetrical tension to the scene. It simply begs for another Cup. What, though, might a fourth one provide that the three don't already?

The three lined-up Cups suggest that the man has experienced the emotional fullness of the preceding card. However, he may sense that becoming whole requires a greater spectrum of feeling—joy, sorrow, and everything in between. Perhaps the new Cup floating into the picture will fill the gap.

The enigmatic picture of the Four of Cups compels us to project our own motives onto it. In any given reading, the young man may be scolded as a procras-

tinator, praised as a discriminating realist, envied as an unrepentant independent, or dismissed as a thankless lout. However we view him, there is no mistaking his discontent.

A Four of Cups Story

Twenty years after Paolo's divorce, he complained he had not found someone suitable for a long-term commitment. Handsome and charming, he had no trouble attracting many desirable women. But each time he'd inevitably discover some deal-breaking fault in them and terminate the relationship.

It surprised neither of us when the Four of Cups made a prominent appearance in two readings I did for him just twelve months apart. Whereas the same card might, for someone else, represent a temporary discontent, for Paolo it was a Please Pay Attention card, a notice to examine his chronic patterns of romantic dissatisfaction and dissolution. I pointed out that until he confronted his deep-seated resistance to commitment, no woman could meet his expectations, and his unhappy "revolving-door dating" would only continue.

Paolo eventually broke the cycle. I recently learned he is engaged to be married.

Four of Cups Attributes

Key word:	Discontent
Being:	Suspicious, reluctant, obstinate, jaded, disenchanted, apathetic, bored, self-absorbed
Doing:	Refusing an offer, demanding proof, distrusting others' intentions toward you, procrastinating
Shadow:	Being spoiled, pouting, making others guess what you want, never being satisfied, being unable to appreciate the goodness at hand
Reversed:	Accepting an offer, going after your true desires
	Possible Advice
Upright:	"Wait for a better offer." "Notice the gift."

Five of Cups

Thou shalt forget thy misery, and remember it as waters that pass away.
—Book of Job

A lone figure mourns three spilled Cups, emptied of joy and pleasure. Cloaked in grief, he (or she) confronts what can never, in the same form, be replaced. There is a great stillness here, though not a peaceful one. It aches with absence.

The Five of Cups shows us the inevitability of emotional pain in response to loss and disappointment. From the consuming black void within, we struggle to reckon with the death of dreams, loved ones, or parts of ourselves. At these times the rest of the world ceases to exist. In the figure's solitariness we recognize that all our losses, even those we share keenly with others, are ultimately felt as private losses.

What's unclear from the image is how long this person has been standing in sorrow's grip. His attention goes to the irretrievable past. In the extreme, he may be immobilized by an inability to let go, standing like a somber obelisk in monument to what was.

Just as plausibly, it is not mourning that lowers his head, but the agony of self-recrimination, the downward pull of lingering regrets. The inability to forgive ourselves robs us of our spirit and condemns us, like the figure in the card, to a life draped in shame. In a more generalized way, the Five of Cups may describe a psychological attitude in which one routinely expects and experiences only pain and disappointment.

Despite the card's central silhouette of despair, all is not lost. The landscape is bucolic. There is movement in the rolling hills. A river rushes through the bridge's dual portals, mirroring the life-bringing choices of the two remaining Cups. The gray sky is a blank slate, reminding at every moment that we can choose to write our lives from the perspective of what we have or what we have lost.

A Five of Cups Story

"What do you need to grieve?" I asked Andrew, a gentle giant of a man in his mid-fifties. He leaned forward to take in the details of the Five of Cups in the Higher-Self Advice position. As he spoke, his voice grew so faint I had to lean across the little table. I learned that within a ten-year span he had attended the funerals of more than a dozen friends who had succumbed to the AIDS virus. His unconscious response to the enormity of these losses, many in rapid succession, was to *feel less*. Yet, as his awareness of pain diminished, so did his capacity for pleasure and joy.

Andrew said that only a few days before the Tarot reading, his daughter had suggested he see a therapist about his melancholy. I told him this was an excellent idea. "She thinks I need a good, long cry," he said. Andrew's Higher Self, speaking through the Five of Cups, emphatically agreed.

Five of Cups Attributes

Key word:	Loss
Being:	Sad, remorseful, disappointed
Doing:	Mourning a past or anticipated loss, blaming yourself
Shadow:	Getting stuck in the past, wallowing in regrets
Reversed:	Moving on from mourning and regret or, conversely, refusing to deal with such feelings altogether
	Possible Advice
Upright:	"Acknowledge your losses so you can move forward." "Give full expression to your grief."

Six of Cups

Sow good services; sweet remembrances will grow from them.
—Madame de Staël

You are looking at the Hallmark card of the Minor Arcana. A valentine. In a quaint courtyard, a boy gives a flowering Cup to a very young girl. Pure white petals pop up from the Cups around them. Love is in bloom, though not the romantic variety of the Two of Cups, nor the ecstatic sort of the Three.

The feelings flowering in the Six of Cups are innocent, sentimental, and tender. The boy exhibits the affection we may feel toward a child, a cherished friend, or one whose delicacy stirs our devotion and protectiveness. The boy is more mature and capable than the girl, and he gives happily with no thought to receiving in kind. She, quite literally, looks up to him, like a younger sister to an older brother.

The girl raises her hand in readiness to receive. In this simple gesture lies a profound truth—to obtain the gifts of the Universe, we must open to it, allow it. The Divine may be sensed in even the smallest kindnesses, such as in acts like an unexpected present, a compliment, a call from a friend—things done from the heart. When the offering is sincere there is no need for guardedness, as the retreating sentry in the background suggests.

Look beyond the sentiment, and the girl's mittens suggest a coddling in which one is kept a child. This shadow aspect of emotional dependency is similar to the one we will see played out in the Six of Pentacles.

A Six of Cups Story

Synchronicity and enchantment are so often kindred spirits. While I was writing about the endearing Six of Cups, my eleven-year old godson, Roble, walked into my office and presented me with a table-top bonsai tree. Enough said!

Six of Cups Attributes

Key word:	Affection
Being:	Sweet, charming, kind, tender, sentimental, childlike, protective, shielded, pampered
Doing:	Acts of kindness; offering or accepting gifts or compliments, fondly reminiscing, enjoying familial bonds, savoring simple pleasures
Shadow:	(Giver) placating or coddling, trying to buy affection (receiver) childlike dependency
Reversed:	Rejection of (or failure to recognize) a gift or affection, disenchantment, a break from an idealized past, parent-child conflicts
Reversed:	*Possible Advice* "Don't let sentimentality cloud your judgement." "It's time to bring the relationship to a more mature expression."

Seven of Cups

Everything that deceives may be said to enchant.

—Plato

Nowhere is the imaginative nature of Water more apparent than in the Seven of Cups. Transfixed, a man beholds a puff of Cups containing the extraordinary contents of his fantasies and dreams—fairytale castles and dragons, earthly treasures and accolades, mystical reveries. These figments appear so real that he yearns to touch them, though they will disappear into thin air.

The card's showiness might seem appealing if not for the man's shadowy depiction. What accounts for the character's physical vagueness is that, in practical terms, he is not present. He is off in his own world, head in the clouds, overshadowed by the cinematic spectacle of his private matinee. It may be a gratifying place to be for a while, but it's not without its frustration. The skull on the front Cup warns that unless he chooses to make something of his fantasy material, he is doomed to a life of dead-end dreams.

The Seven of Cups is the lure of get-rich-quick schemes, miracle cures, and mind-altering chemicals. The same energy is behind our myriad collective trances, from celebrity fixations to allowing the symbols displayed by our politicians to distract us from substance. When reversed in readings, the card may be asking us to "snap out of it," to examine how we are deceiving ourselves and the costs of that deception.

191

At best, the card depicts the imagination's menu of possibilities, some of which we may choose to make real, others to savor as pleasant fantasies.

A Seven of Cups Story

Instead of enjoying a beautiful autumn drive through downstate Illinois, I once found myself worried that someone might break into my apartment back home. I vividly imagined the doorframe wrenched away, the intruder working quickly through each room, and me reporting the losses to the insurance company. My mind also played a future scene in which I would be shaking my head and telling friends, "If only I hadn't gone away that weekend."

The part of me that feared this might be a premonition was ready to turn the car around. The part that figured it was mind junk kept driving. When I got to my destination I asked the cards, "What action should I take in response to this feeling?" Had I been shown the alarmed Knight of Swords, I might have raced right back to defend my home—and called for a SWAT team stakeout in the interim. Instead, I drew the fanciful Seven of Cups. "Relax," it assured me. "It's your imagination, not your intuition. Stop worrying and enjoy your trip." And I did.

Seven of Cups Attributes

Key word:	Entrancement
Being:	Imaginative, dreamy, whimsical, confused, tempted
Doing:	Fantasizing, daydreaming, musing, entertaining future scenarios, taking mind-altering substances
Shadow:	Habitual escapism; being clouded by illusion, not dealing with reality, hallucinating

Reversed:	Thinking more concretely, coming down to earth, putting dreams into action, resisting flights of fancy, denying yourself the freedom to dream
	Possible Advice
Upright:	"Muse awhile. Let your mind drift."
	"Entertain the possibilities."

Eight of Cups

Solvitur ambulando. It is solved by walking.
—Saint Augustine

As in the Four of Cups, there is a chasm in the arrangement of these Cups that suggests something is missing. Yet unlike the Four, the figure on this card doesn't wait around for things to change. He leaves the Cups behind (or takes one with him) and heads upward in the direction of rocks green with the promise of growth. Perhaps the trail will take him to the open sea, far from the shallow waters of this protected little inlet.

The moon evokes the contemplation of inner depths and shadows. That which once brought pleasure no longer seems as real now, no longer seems enough. Significantly, the Cups are left intact; he hasn't kicked them over in blame and frustration, nor given them an angry whack. He leaves them be and, without looking back, quietly walks away. Does the moon's pensive expression reflect that of the traveler? Or is there vigor in his leave-taking, as his red garb suggests? The answer may be both—and the journey bittersweet.

The Eight of Cups announces emotional turning points in which the old life is abandoned. As is true of all the cards, there is the potential for extremes; in this case, the person who cannot be satisfied or who takes off when relationships hit certain predictable cycles. But when the call to move on is organic, as the image on the Eight of Cups implies, we are better equipped to make our break in peace.

An Eight of Cups Story

Margaret, a Tarot student, was due to have her baby in two weeks. She anxiously asked me what it meant that her husband had drawn the Eight of Cups in a reading about the big event. "This card seems to say he'd rather leave the baby and me," she said, "but I know that's not true. He wants this baby more than anything."

The card certainly didn't rule out the possibility that some part of the man longed to flee the responsibilities of parenthood—what parent hasn't had that impulse? However, I told her the more likely meaning of the card was that her husband instinctively recognized that impending parenthood had brought him to a point of departure; he would need to leave behind the freedoms and social pleasures of their childless years and move into the unfamiliar and demanding role of father. The card showed him on a journey toward maturity, not a retreat from his wife and child. Though Margaret knew this intuitively, she welcomed the confirmation.

Eight of Cups Attributes

Key word:	Departure
Being:	Reflective, dissatisfied, hopeful, eager for change
Doing:	Walking away from the life you know, leaving a relationship, abandoning a dream, seeking meaning or fulfillment by going in a different direction
Shadow:	Emotional withdrawal as a way to avoid responsibilities
Reversed:	Staying with it, delaying a departure, denying the call to leave
Upright:	*Possible Advice* "Bless it and move on." "Take a long walk."

Nine of Cups

While you are upon earth, enjoy the good things that are here.
—John Selden

Here we meet a man who nearly has it all and is not thin on appreciation. He folds his arms contentedly and sits before nine Cups arranged like trophies at an awards dinner. The blue table draping suggests a waterfall, an outpouring of pleasure from the Cups above it. This is the first time in the suit that the Cups appear on a manmade object, a clue that the feelings of fullness may include material, not just emotional, pleasures.

His costume suggests a man of means. His expression shows he enjoys his treasures—whatever they happen to be. What might be the secret of his success? His matching red hat and socks could offer a clue.

These items symbolize the principle *as above, so below*—the interconnection of mind and matter—as do the yellow sky and floor. The fellow held a vision for creating his desire, felt passion for it, never questioned his worthiness, and now savors its manifestation. He is the essence of the artist posing proudly before his exhibition or the parent boasting about much-loved children.

Despite the card's aura of happiness, some people react negatively to the figure, assessing him as smug, greedy, or overindulgent. Some home in on a defensive quality, as if the character were saying, "Look, but don't touch." (If you resent waiters bringing spoons for everyone when they deliver your dessert, meet your patron saint.) But for most Tarot readers the card comes as a welcome affirmation of security, fulfillment, and well-being.

A Nine of Cups Story

The Nine of Cups lay reversed in the Self-Image position for Dominique, a young art-gallery owner. "I'm fine with showing other people's work," she told the Tarot class, "but I guess I'm afraid to show my own." Indeed, the reversal of the card was consistent with Dominique's doubts about her artistic merit and her fears that exhibiting in her own gallery could appear self-congratulatory.

When we finished discussing all her cards, Dominique came back to the Nine of Cups and tapped it impatiently. "I don't like this one upside down," she said. "Then turn it right side up," I said. "You mean

I can do that?" she asked. "Cool!" When she turned the card to its dignified position, the class applauded. She exhibited her work a short time later.

Nine of Cups Attributes

Key word:	Satisfaction
Being:	Happy, content, gratified, emotionally secure
Doing:	Indulging; getting your wish; enjoying sensual, emotional, and/or material pleasures
Shadow:	Complacency, overindulgence, greed, smugness
Reversed:	Incompletion, lack, disappointment, feeling undeserving, denial of satisfaction or pleasure
	Possible Advice
Reversed:	"Don't linger too long at the bar or buffet." "Don't rest on past success—innovate."

Ten of Cups

It was a dream of perfect bliss . . .
—Thomas Haynes Bayly

"There's a pot o' gold at the end of the rainbow." "Home is where the heart is." "Happily ever after." In the Ten of Cups, all the clichés apply. Every conceivable experience of unconditional love and joy— friendship, tenderness, passion, harmony, appreciation—gushes forth in one idyllic picture. Of all the experiences depicted in the Minor Arcana, this is as good as it gets.

A couple stands side by side, cocreators of a reality so beautiful, so expansive, they must step back to take it all in. With their arms outstretched they hail the rainbow of Cups, symbol of the overarching awareness of divine love and blessing at work in their lives. With their palms upraised they not only offer thanks but open themselves as vessels to receive the continued good that effortlessly comes to them.

The children are proof of the couple's love multiplied, continuing into the future. Yet the past, too, figures here. The woman's dark, trailing skirt reminds us that the memory of pain never leaves us; it only deepens our appreciation for present happiness.

A Ten of Cups Story

Perhaps it's due to the basic anxiousness that drives people to Tarot readings, but in ten years of reading the cards, I have rarely seen the Ten of Cups describe a person's present situation. Most times it shows up as something denied or wished for, rather than what is.

At a local theater fund-raiser, a white-haired woman in her late sixties approached my table. I instantly felt warmed by her smile and look of pleasant curiosity as she sat down. "A good soul," I thought. Her hands floating over the backs of the cards, she drew out a few, which I placed into a Life Journey spread (see page 309).

There, elusive as the Asian Slipper Orchid, was the Ten of Cups in the center of the spread—"Where you are now."

"This is a beautiful card to have in this position," I said, slightly awestruck. I then touched on the spiritual implications of the Ten of

Cups, the abundance that comes from seeing ourselves, our loved ones, and all of creation, with deep appreciation. As I spoke, she never stopped smiling. I asked if she wanted to respond. Her blue eyes sparkled as she told me the obvious:

"I love my life."

Perhaps that is the secret to summoning the Ten of Cups.

Ten of Cups Attributes

Key word:	Homecoming
Being:	Serene, blissful, emotionally fulfilled, liberated
Doing:	Loving unconditionally, appreciating abundance, living your dreams, enjoying family or community harmony
Shadow:	Expecting the bliss to last forever
Reversed:	Dashed hopes, absence of loving support; distrusting Utopian-appearing situations, leaving a place of emotional comfort
Reversed:	*Possible Advice* "Adjust your expectations." "Sweet as things are, it's time to move on."

Page of Cups

One learns through the heart, not the eyes or the intellect.
—Mark Twain

I can remember scooping up samples of pond water for third-grade science class and being surprised at the myriad life forms swimming under the microscope. Who could have guessed there would be so much activity in a single jar of water? The Page of Cups makes a related discovery. His childlike curiosity leads him to fish into his unconscious—aquatic home to the imaginative, spiritual, and psychic—to catch a glimpse of its inhabitants. What he finds may surprise or amuse, alienate or intrigue, frighten or calm. However he looks at it, he has begun to make contact with his depths.

The Page is fascinated with these gradually surfacing powers. He arrives in our consciousness when we notice synchronicities, get hunches, muse over a dream, or dip our toes in the waters of psychic development. The Page of Cups may have led you to find this book.

The Page's fresh emotional outlook is reinforced by the lotus motif, the symbol of purity introduced in the Ace. His innocent, trusting nature enables him to merge comfortably in most social situations, and he is apt to see his own goodness reflected in those he meets. His soft, billowy sleeves and hat depict his willingness to go with the flow in matters of the heart, whether in caring friendships or in relationships that could blossom into romance.

The easygoing Page may feel out of his depth, however, when relationships become too complex. His trusting nature makes him slow to perceive hidden motives. If he feels threatened by discord, he will use charm or sentimental appeals to appease the person and restore good feelings, rather than follow the conflict into turbulent waters. But unless he risks the occasional shark tank, the Page may become the perpetual people-pleaser, trying too hard to be liked.

A Page of Cups Story

Dorie never got a good look at the man she passed on the sidewalk that night. Seconds after she had said hello, he knocked her to the ground and ran off with her purse. Though physically unhurt, the attack left Dorie feeling fearful and unsafe wherever she went. She described the incident in the Tarot class a few days later and asked for counsel.

The advice was poignant—the open-hearted Page of Cups, reversed. I felt its message was not that she stop seeing the good in people, or distrust every stranger. Rather, the prescription for the soft-spoken Dorie was to project greater boundaries and less vulnerability on the city streets. She had lost a part of her innocence, and it looked as if the Page, its childlike face turned upside down, had also.

Page of Cups Attributes

Key word:	Sensitivity
Being:	Lighthearted, sensitive, affable, loyal, imaginative, charming, emotionally vulnerable
Doing:	Flirting; flattering; making friends; discovering spiritual or esoteric interests; getting hunches; exploring the unconscious through dreams, creative writing, or therapy
Shadow:	Gullibility; a people-pleaser
Reversed:	Distrust, fear of being hurt, unwillingness to begin a relationship, resistance to explore emotional or psychic material, emotional maturation
Reversed:	*Possible Advice* "Be careful to whom/what you're giving your trust." "Strive for more emotional independence."

Knight of Cups

There is a passion for hunting something deeply planted in the human breast.
—Charles Dickens

The Page of Cups beheld a fish that signaled an initiatory encounter with feelings, inner mysteries, and the imagination. But the Knight is not a newcomer to these realms; the fish on his tunic declares his devotion to mastering the qualities of Water. The slow gait of his horse shows the reverence the Knight holds for his quest, one that will take time and patience. The stream he approaches has not yet opened into the oceanic mastery we will see in the Queen and King.

All the Knights ride in service to their respective missions. The wings on the helmet and boots of the noble Knight of Cups bespeak his call to follow and uphold the loftier, more idealized aspects of Water—humanitarianism, altruism, and romance. Thus, the Knight may take the guise of the choir seeking to uplift the congregation with heavenly hymns, the volunteer raising funds to aid disaster victims, or the worshipful paramour pledging eternity (for now, anyway) to his or her beloved. That which moves the heart and soul inspires the Knight of Cups.

Unlike the other Knights, he is not gloved. In chakra analogs, hands are extensions of the heart center. That his are uncovered shows the deeply human quality of his loving intentions, whether toward a significant other or his fellow human beings. As for his armor, well, who can blame this sensitive soul for wanting to protect his refined sensibilities from the harshness of life?

True to the suit, the Knight has an enduring vision of harmony that makes him a passionate peacekeeper. He personifies the Rescuer archetype, driven to protect or liberate the vulnerable and hurting. Gallantry of this sort may be truly compassionate or, as a shadow trait, merely compulsive. Another shadow tendency of the Knight—one he shares with the Seven of Cups—is seeking and dreaming yet avoiding the finding and doing. Or he may reach the end of his romantic quest only to find himself unable or unwilling to deal with its blunt realities: the vacation home in paradise needs a new roof; the long-courted lover is bored with the poetry. Though the Knight's heart is in the right place, now and then his feet may need to come closer to the ground.

A Knight of Cups Story

When Chicago's Carson Pirie Scott department store asked me to reprise my role as Santa Claus (my fourth season), I decided to consult my Higher-Self Committee about it. There he was—the Knight of Cups—summoning me to saintly service. How could I refuse?

One afternoon, as I sat sweating under beard and padding, a former Tarot student walked by. "Hello, Elizabeth!" I called out in my rounded Santa tones. Her shock was delicious. Before she could utter a word, I began to muse in a kindly way about specific details of her life—her cat, Emily, her work at the stock exchange, her sister Kathy—things that only the real Santa could know. Her eyes misted over as she thanked me for our chat. When I got home that night I sent her an anonymous e-mail, asking if she'd figured out Santa's real identity. I'll always cherish her reply.

"Dear Santa," she wrote, "While who you are is certainly very important, in this season of possibilities what you *represent* is much more important and so needed in our wounded world. Our encounter was sweet and magical, and I have enjoyed telling it many times! So, dear Father Christmas, please remain a mystery to me! You are a beautiful representation of all that is good in each of us. With much love and affection (and lovely memories), Elizabeth."

There was no sweeter music to the Knight of Cups.

Knight of Cups Attributes

Key word:	Romance
Being:	Dreamy, romantic, courtly, gallant, courteous, sensitive, poetic, humane, self-sacrificing, spiritually directed
Doing:	Peacemaking; selflessly serving others; offering gifts, allegiance, or a love partnership; following your heart; offering forgiveness or making amends
Shadow:	Dreaming without the doing, chasing rainbows
Reversed:	Disillusionment, dashed romantic hopes; abandoning a dream, halting a courtship, looking at things more objectively
	Possible Advice
Reversed:	"Don't let your dreams delude you." "Avoid wooing, soothing, or rescuing."

Queen of Cups

I am certain of nothing but the holiness of the heart's affection,
and the truth of the imagination.

—Keats

The Queen of Cups, gown flowing into the sea, most closely resembles the High Priestess. The comparison is not just visual. Both Queen and Trump preside over the element of Water, each at ease with the liquid inner life. The two icons represent the capacity to feel freely, unafraid of psychic depths.

But where the High Priestess kept the veil between prying eyes and her inner world, the Queen of Cups flows her being openly and expressively (except when deliberately holding back to enhance her mystery and allure). She

sees feelings as natural, valid, and inherently worthy of respect. Her understanding of the human heart makes her an empathetic listener, the first to ask us where it hurts and then, tenderly, to massage our wounds.

The Queen's compassion and psychological insights are complemented by her psychic sensitivity. She is quick to pick up on what is *not* being said, attuned as she is to the sublayers of conversation. She may be drawn to the metaphysical in a "just curious" way or be actively glimpsing past lives and communicating with the unseen world. On the card, the Queen studies her chalice's mystical glyphs, which imply her receptivity to the spiritual and symbolic dimensions of life. The Water Queen is intuitively equipped brilliantly to

205

decipher dreams, Tarot cards, and synchronicities, while preserving a passion for the mysterious.

Yet such remarkable sensitivity has its disadvantages. She can be moody, high strung, obsessed with whatever emotion has taken hold of her. Her psychic receptivity may cause her to sponge up the emotions of others and yet be unconscious of the fact. Or she may try to take responsibility for others' feelings, exposing her insecurities through frequent and unnecessary apologies.

The sovereign is well suited to her seaside location, which enables her to dive anytime into dreams and imagination. Throne-climbing mermaids reflect her love of the charming and whimsical. Doubtless a good story could entrance the Queen to the obliviousness of all else.

The Queen is the essence of the artist, able to channel her unconscious material into form (the chalice). She is the painter who paints without need of approval, though she may be thin-skinned to criticism. She is the actor whose facility for feelings easily evokes those of the audience. Regardless of her endeavors, mere cleverness will never do; the Queen's creations are authentic. Fresh. Soul drenched.

A Queen of Cups Story

Samantha, a talented young singer, had spent the better part of a year pursuing her dream of creating a solo cabaret act in New York. In addition to writing and rehearsing her material, there were the business details that never seemed to end—auditioning for clubs, getting publicity photos, securing rights to songs, and then leaving it all for weeks at a time to wear slinky gowns and drape herself over cars at auto shows.

I knew it would hit a nerve when I asked Samantha to tell me why the Queen of Cups, symbol of the very soul of her artistry, lay reversed in her spread. The question triggered heavy tears. "It's been more than a year since I've sung for an audience," she said. "Sometimes I forget why I'm even doing all this." Samantha was surprised by her emotional response to the card. "I didn't realize how desperately I missed singing until I saw this beautiful lady upside down."

Queen of Cups Attributes

Key word:	Heart
Being:	Empathetic, emotional, artistic, imaginative, dreamy, self-sacrificing, devoted to children; an animal lover
Doing:	Nurturing the qualities of Water in yourself or others, expressing emotions freely, intuiting others' needs, offering emotional support, expressing feelings and imagination in art forms
Shadow:	Oversensitivity, moodiness; getting caught up in others' dramas; an emotional sponge
Reversed:	Emotional blockage, distrust, numbness, artist's block, depression; taking a less emotional approach
	Possible Advice
Reversed:	"Pull back from your emotions." "Resist the temptation to play Mother."

King of Cups

Man is a speck of reason in an ocean of emotion.
—William James

Who but the King of Cups could float evenly on rolling waves and not get wet? Not one drop intrudes. Here is a person able to remain centered in times of turbulence, even though a lot may be stirring beneath the surface. The lotus motif that appeared on the High Priestess card reappears on the King's scepter and armrest, a testament to the maturation of his own watery qualities—qualities he must express with kingly discipline. As a result, he shares his Queen's compassion, imagination, and spiritual capacities, but displays little of her spontaneity. The King decides which feelings he will communicate, and to what degree, based on what he thinks is appropriate to the situation. He believes it is not enough to convey one's feelings; one must convey them responsibly.

The cautious King of Cups is the perfect diplomat, acutely aware that the tone of an interaction is more important than the content. In his world, sudden displays of emotion can be costly, endangering carefully built relationships. The King may have a knack for speaking articulately about his feelings without actually showing them—an exasperating characteristic to those who want more fire from him. The distant fish and red ship suggest that the King relegates his feelings to the background, which frees him up to tend to the emotional needs of his subjects.

Such emotional control makes him an anchor of stability for those in need of a calm and skilled listener. The King is the manager responsible for fielding complaints from employees or customers, but who stays professionally committed to keeping his own strong feelings in check. The archetype will be familiar to every parent who, in a family crisis, has felt compelled to present an unflappable front for the children. The King's natural empathy and talent for reading others makes him an effective actor, therapist, counselor, minister, or caregiver—one not easily manipulated.

However, if taken too far, the King's emotional discipline becomes emotional avoidance; consummate discretion degenerates into paralyzing self-monitoring; and like the shadow side of Strength, wise self-control veers into habitual self-denial. Despite his skill in helping others through difficult times, he may be incapable of asking for support in kind, perhaps due to a belief that nobody could ever understand the intensity he so carefully conceals.

A King of Cups Story

Ruth was the legal guardian of Marlon, her fourteen-year-old grand-son. She enrolled the boy at the local suburban high school, where he was now midway through his freshman year. During the reading, she spoke of Marlon's anguish at enduring cruel pranks and name-calling by a group of his peers.

"He cries as he tells me some of these stories, " said Ruth, "and it breaks my heart. But he's adamant that I not talk to his teachers about it. He says the kids will treat him even worse if the school intervenes. Meanwhile, I'm a wreck."

"The cards agree with Marlon on this," I said, eyeing the King of Cups in the Advice position. "The only action you need to take is to listen and give him emotional support, and try not to get over-whelmed yourself. You're more helpful to him calm." The reversed

Knight of Swords seconded the advice; rushing in to police the situation would not be effective, or wise.

Ruth gave me an update a few weeks later. Marlon's abusers had gradually eased up on him—bored, perhaps, with their own sport. Meanwhile, Marlon had found solace and acceptance in a smaller, more civil band of friends.

King of Cups Attributes

Key word:	Composure
Being:	Sensitive, self-possessed, compassionate, cool under pressure, gentle, trustworthy, emotionally stable, responsible, discreet, self-sacrificing
Doing:	Controlling or concealing emotions, mediating, counseling, ministering, intuiting others' needs, keeping confidences, providing emotional support from a position of strength
Shadow:	Excessive emotional restraint, overresponsibility
Reversed:	Emotional spontaneity; feeling emotionally overwhelmed
	Possible Advice
Reversed:	"Let your feelings out."
	"Allow others to support *your* emotional needs."

Swords: To the Point

As our soul, being air, both holds us together and controls us,
so do breath and air encompass the whole cosmos.
—Anaximenes

Element: Air
Astrological signs: Libra, Aquarius, Gemini

*A*ir is the breath of life. It is omnipresent, formless, invisible—qualities likened to God. Though we cannot see Air, we sense its changing weight and temperatures and the character of its conditions. The same can be said of thought. Its "atmosphere" changes with the thinker and, though unseen, produces discernible effects. Our thoughts create our experiences, whether stormy or calm, foggy or clear. And it is the quality of our breathing that creates the climate of our thoughts (so the yogis teach). To consciously control the flow of breath is to quiet the mind and become more objective about the mental processes that determine one's reality and truth.

The suit of Swords features the most conflict-laden images of the Tarot. The etymology of *sword* is to cut, to cause pain, and—most pointedly—to speak. Indeed, our own thoughts can shred us with anxiety; our words can be used as the most damaging weapons. But there is a deeper message within the troubled depictions of the Swords. The strife of the suit warns that reason alone is no proof of truth, that thinking divorced from feeling is the surest obstruction to spiritual development. Yet the same Sword that deludes and wounds can, with awareness, cut through cloudy misperception. The Sword is emblematic of the discerning, ethical, disciplined mind and of oral and written communication that sparkles with clarity.

Ace of Swords

Be master of mind rather than mastered by mind.
—Zen saying

The raised Sword honors the highest potentials, opportunities, and gifts of elemental Air. It pierces a crown—the mastery of mental energies. The olive branch of Peace and the palm branch of Suffering offer a choice: self-torment or self-liberation? Upon which shall we focus our thoughts and therefore create in our experience? The Ace of Swords, like Excalibur, challenges us to free our thoughts from the granite of the lower mind.

The six falling *yods* refer to *Zain*, the Hebrew word for "sword" and sixth letter of that alphabet. Six also relates to Trump 6, the Lovers, to which early Tarotists assigned the theme of choice. The esoteric meaning here is that the function of the Sword is wisely to decide (*decidere*, "to kill") which options to cut away. The Sword's double edges point up the two sides of every truth and the interplay of paradox.

The Ace heralds intellectual awakening—invigorating ideas, inspired studies, and a passion for principles. Raw notions appear that demand honing and polishing. Powers of concentration intensify. New perspectives emerge, and with them new convictions. Under the influence of the Ace, we are emboldened to seek and seize the Truth. Or, more accurately, the truth of the moment.

An Ace of Swords Story

Jason, a twenty-three-year-old computer specialist, had trouble with his boss. He explained that the man gave vague or incomplete instructions, which Jason would follow inevitably to a bad result. In addition, Jason was never sure if his boss's sarcastic comments were intended as playful asides or sly reprimands. Jason felt intimidated and avoided him as much as possible. "I'm not sure how to deal with him," he said.

The Ace of Swords provided the answer. "Ask for clarity at every step with this guy," I said. "Repeat every instruction he gives and ask for confirmation. Better yet, do it in writing. And if you're not sure if he's joking about something, ask him."

"What if that gets me fired?"

"See the crown at the top of this card?" I asked. "You earn that crown when you state your needs and intentions openly and ask for clarity. If he doesn't respect that, you might eventually make a decision to leave on your own. But you'll leave with your self-respect."

Ace of Swords Attributes

Key word:	Intellect
Being:	Alert, scrupulous, disciplined, honest, coherent, articulate, precise, rational, principled, fair, insightful, discerning, decisive, impersonal
Doing:	Getting the point, checking facts, proclaiming your truth, keeping your promise, broadening the intellect, communicating with clarity, putting it in writing
Shadow:	Overintellectualizing, self-righteousness, clutching ideas
Reversed:	Poor judgment, irrationality, muddy thinking, integrity lapse, poor communication
	Possible Advice
Reversed:	"Approach this matter from your heart, not your head." "Question the integrity of this situation."

Two of Swords

I do perceive here a divided duty.
—William Shakespeare

Perhaps the woman wishes for the certainty of the Ace of Swords as she balances two large Swords of opposing ideas. She might favor either one at this point, yet stonily resists premature judgment. In an attempt to make the most well-reasoned choice, she has affixed herself to a seat of granite and turned her back on the emotional influences rippling nearby.

Though the day is bright the moon looms, implying eclipse. With solar and lunar in effect, the polarities of psychic wholeness—light and dark, action and passivity—must be reckoned with, held in balance. What is needed here may not be decision at all but the ability quietly to hold two contradictory ideas and be at peace with each. In the either/or, good/bad way of thinking to which the suit of Swords is vulnerable, such flashes of objectivity are precious indeed. We saw that detachment modeled to perfection in the High Priestess (also numbered 2),  though she did not have the mental demands faced by the character depicted here. For the figure in the Two of Swords, contemplative nonaction may be the wisest action.

As for the blindfold, the woman may turn a blind eye to appearances to find a deeper knowing within. Or has she blindfolded herself to avoid facing the truth altogether and simply found the strain of keeping the Swords aloft less painful than taking action? This possibility could account for the fact that her hands cover her heart, as if closing off the feelings that might otherwise help her embrace a right decision.

A Two of Swords Story

A client for whom I had once done some freelance writing called to offer me an eight-week assignment. I told him I'd check my calendar and get back to him. On the one hand, the job sounded boring and dizzyingly complex and would compromise some of the time I had available to spend on more enjoyable projects; on the other hand, it paid much better than the enjoyable projects. I decided to get some perspective from the cards.

"What is the greatest good of taking this job?" I hoped for a clear-cut answer, but my inner guidance showed me the Two of Swords, which simply mirrored my own ambivalence. "Taking the job is a compromise," the card seemed to say, "but it won't kill you, either." I took the assignment, humbled by the Universe's suggestion that not all my decisions were pivotal moments in my destiny!

Two of Swords Attributes

Key word:	Indecision
Being:	Unresolved, impartial, discerning, cool-headed
Doing:	Striving to be objective, suspending judgment, embracing paradox, mulling things over, avoiding premature decision, compromising, staying mentally balanced amid change
Shadow:	Chronic self-doubt, procrastination
Reversed:	Lack of objectivity, choosing sides, making a decision, taking action
	Possible Advice
Upright:	"Listen to both sides of the story." "Embrace paradox. Don't look for 'right' or 'wrong.'"

Three of Swords

The heart that breaks open can contain the whole universe.
—Joanna Macy

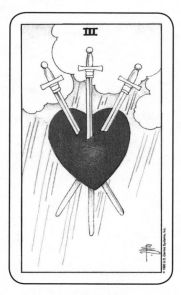

No blood oozes from the punctured heart in the Three of Swords, but that does little to ease the emotional rawness confronting us here. As is true of any great loss or betrayal, suffering is without antidote. It must simply be allowed to run its course. But Air's tendency is to obsess on the suffering, foist shame onto it, or use it to justify a protective shutting-down of feeling. As a result, the pain gets stuck in the mind-body, never decreasing in intensity. Our identity becomes fixated upon our wounds.

Ever so gently, the Three of Swords offers an image of healing within the heartache. Recalling the waters cascading from the Ace of Cups, a cleansing rain falls, dissolving our resistance to pain into a larger pool of consciousness. If we allow ourselves to take in the full hollowing impact of our sorrow, we may begin to sense that ours is not an isolated experience; the same cruel Swords may pierce the illusion of separateness and open our hearts to the suffering of all.

A Three of Swords Story

The cards can serve as powerful affirmations that we are moving and changing in the ways we desire. The Three of Swords appeared reversed in the Current Emotional State position of a spread

217

I customized for my friend Louise, who was just weeks away from the end of an acidic divorce. When I explained the significance of the card, she pumped her fists in the air triumphantly.

"Upside down like that, it's like the swords are sliding out naturally," she observed, "rather than I having to yank them out!"

Three of Swords Attributes

Key word:	Wounding
Being:	Injured, heartbroken, remorseful, self-recriminating, sensitive to criticism, skewered by the truth (as in a Tower experience)
Doing:	Letting in pain, making (or reeling from) hurtful remarks, showing empathy
Shadow:	Taking everything as a personal attack, never forgetting an injury; a victim
Reversed:	Protecting the heart, letting go of pain (or numbing it), forgiveness
	Possible Advice
Upright:	"Let the pain in. It's the first step toward healing." "Tell the hurtful truth with kindness."

Four of Swords

In returning and rest you shall be saved.
—Book of Isaiah

The Four of Swords stabilizes the wounds sustained in the Three. Recovery will require peace and quiet, a state exaggerated in the eternal repose of a knight in effigy. Three Swords hang above the sarcophagus—the mind's painful preoccupations suspended. After times of battle and strife comes a calling-away to repair the psyche, create a sense of order, and recover one's strength.

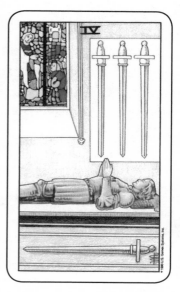

The knight faces the leftward direction of the unconscious to welcome the healing release of sleep and dreams. Below, a single sword (the Ace) points in the same direction, underscoring the purity of purpose beneath his psychic recharging. The world can wait.

The scene is nearly devoid of color, like the bland but calming hues of a hospital room. The only stimulation is a stained-glass window symbolizing the spiritual dimension his intellect may have ignored and through which he now seeks solace. However, the inspiring window is sharply divided—spirit and matter split apart by the ego-mind. Although his hands are joined in the traditional Hindu *mudra* that signifies opposites coming together, it will take many more hushed vigils for the knight to know the peace of inner unity. It is enough that his respite brings a much-needed rest.

Unlike that other withdrawn figure, the Hermit, the reclining knight of the Four of Swords is more in need of relief from the mind than engagement with it; more hungry for quiet than meaning. Meditation is in order. If nothing else, the card calls for us to hang out the "Do Not Disturb" sign, lay low, and slow the neural firings for a while ("Let the brain drool," as my friend Bob says). From restoration comes rejuvenation. But not—as we'll see in the remaining Sword cards—if we continue to identify solely with the fears cranked out by the untamed mind.

A Four of Swords Story

The reversal of the Four of Swords in Glen's Present position signified the unexpected revival of his sex life. The catalyst was twenty-six-year-old Miranda, the first woman the sixty-three-year-old retired businessman had dated since his wife's death six years earlier.

"Miranda's as surprised as I am about this," Glen said. "I thought I was destined to live out the rest of my days on the couch."

The Knight, through the love of a maiden, had risen from the sarcophagus.

Four of Swords Attributes

Key word:	Respite
Being:	Meditative, quiet, tired, inactive, listless, self-protective
Doing:	Canceling your appointments, resting, recuperating, laying low, de-stressing, sheltering yourself
Shadow:	Retreating from life, escaping from feelings or responsibilities
Reversed:	Reengaging in life, refusing to take time out; sleep deprivation
Upright:	*Possible Advice* "Quiet the mental chatter and step away from outer dramas." "Rest and recuperate."

Five of Swords

Who overcomes by force, hath overcome but half his foe.
—John Milton

The Fives of the suits introduce upsets and upheavals to the stability of the Fours. Here a man claims the spoils of victory as two defeated figures retreat into the background. Wind rages through the conqueror's hair, chops the waters, and slashes clouds into razors. There is violence in the motives here, if not the deeds. Something has been seized by force and has left conceit and division in its wake.

If the man had a look of concern, we might suppose he was a peacemaker who had just broken up a quarrel. If he appeared worn or stoic, we could project nobility onto his winning. But his smirk renders him unsympathetic. We intuit that whatever victory he has achieved has been unfair, undeserved, and shaded with meanness. Even the visual perspective shows him larger than the two whom he has put down, effectively diminishing them.

The gloating attitude of the central figure is epitomized in Gore Vidal's quip, "It is not enough to succeed; others must fail." The card pushes us to examine how we use our power, not just in conflict situations, but in our day-to-day interactions. "How do I treat others I perceive as weaker than myself?" "Do I punish, not just counter, those who cross me?" "Whom do I judge and exclude with my righteous attitudes?"

The Five of Swords can reveal a domineering attitude in which a person, fighting feelings of deep inadequacy, is compelled to maintain a one-up position in his relationships. Anyone whose power he perceives as equal or greater than his is especially threatening and must be disarmed—bullying, cutting remarks, and ridicule among the likely weapons.

Equally insidious, the card can represent the "energy vampire" in which the abuser quite unknowingly sucks the life from his victims with nonstop talking, complaining, or the vacuum of his own unconscious anger. The result is as damaging to the recipients as if the intentions had been overt, leaving them feeling drained or resentful. The card asks us to notice with whom and in what situations we are the aggressor, the unwitting vampire, or one of the overpowered people in the background.

A Five of Swords Story

Cherise, a psychotherapist in Atlanta, stopped sending money to her daughter, Jordan, when she suspected the young woman's drug problems. Jordan, who lived in Colorado, admitted her addiction and asked for money to pay for substance-abuse counseling. "I told her I'd pay for the counseling," Cherise said, "but that I would pay the counselor directly rather than send Jordan the money." Jordan angrily refused the terms of the offer. A heartsick Cherise feared being shut out of her daughter's life, but she resisted the temptation to try to win her back with conciliatory gifts.

Cherise nodded solemnly at the advice of the Five of Swords, which sat at the top of her Celtic Cross spread. The figure in the foreground validated Cherise's attempts to disarm her daughter of her weapons of self-destruction. The card's retreating figures confirmed her powerlessness to save her daughter from herself.

222

Five of Swords Attributes

Key word:	Overthrow
Being:	(Sword holder) overbearing, unfair, hostile, self-serving, divisive, jealous, spiteful, abusive, predatory; a killjoy; (background figures) depleted, defeated, degraded, sabotaged
Doing:	(Sword holder) gossiping, ridiculing, criticizing, having the last word, hogging the spotlight, winning at the expense of others; Me First; (background figures) giving in, conceding defeat
Shadow:	Failure to recognize or correct these qualities
Reversed:	Ending a toxic relationship, moving toward a win-win situation
	Possible Advice
Upright:	(Sword holder) "Don't enable the destructive behavior." (background figures) "Surrender. You can't win this one."

Six of Swords

I am not afraid of storms, for I am learning how to sail my ship.
—Louisa May Alcott

The Six of Swords is a card of transition. After the fiasco of the Five, the Six paddles toward more tranquil shores. This is hardly a pleasure cruise—the vessel is laden with Swords—but there is calm and forward movement nonetheless. The two Swords separated at the left of the boat echo the truce held in the Two of the suit; the adjacent Swords point to the peace achieved in the Four.

A ferryman pilots a skiff for a hooded figure and a small child. But the Swords don't oppress here, surrounded as they are by a much larger, benevolent force—the water itself. The water is not deep enough to overwhelm (the pole pushes against the lake bottom), but it is big enough to contain whatever pain these Swords represent.

The cloaked person looks downward as if weighted by troubles, though the child leans forward attentively. This attitude puts the child in alignment with the ferryman. (If you look at the pole as dividing the boat, the child shares the ferryman's portion.) With his pole in the water, the ferryman makes contact with the unconscious guidance that navigates the journey. At the same time, his pole, like a Wand, provides the Fire required to propel them away from heaviness and toward the peace of mind awaiting on the tranquil blue shores. When difficulty is all one can see, the first step to recovery is finding the strength to put an oar in the water and one's eyes on the horizon.

A Six of Swords Story

Elaine wanted to go to Italy on a summer vacation with a friend, but, as an occasionally unemployed person, she was certain that the trip would put her in unmanageable debt. We asked, "Given the trajectory of Elaine's financial situation, what is the wisdom of taking this trip?" Elaine grimaced at the Six of Swords. "Well, that doesn't look like much fun," she said.

I told her what I saw in the card—that even if she decided to go, her legitimate anxieties about the price tag could weigh her down and make her an uptight traveling companion.

"And that is *not* the way I want to see Italy," she said, sounding more decisive than disappointed. "I'll go another time, after I've saved up some money."

Six of Swords Attributes

Key word:	Recovery
Being:	Pensive, melancholy, cautiously hopeful
Doing:	Coping, riding out rough times, getting by despite troubles, slowly recuperating, seeking asylum
Shadow:	Living an unremittingly "blah" life, depression
Reversed:	The end of a troubled journey, a canceled excursion
	Possible Advice
Reversed:	"Travel more lightly—unload some baggage." "This sad trip is not for you."

Seven of Swords

Where secrecy or mystery begins, vice or roguery are not far off.
—Ben Johnson

One can almost hear this fellow chuckling as he tiptoes away with the Swords he's stolen from the camp of open tents. The inhabitants congregate in the far distance, unaware as yet that they've been had. The absconder looks sure of his cleverness, but the card hints that his underhanded deeds will catch up with him—handling swords by the blades is a very shaky undertaking. He'll eventually get cut.

The setting and exotic costume call to mind carnivals, places of hokum, and flim flam. When you look at the card, do you look mostly at where the man is looking . . . or where he is walking? Magicians and con men alike use diversion to operate their skillful deceptions, drawing our attention to one hand while maneuvering covertly with the other. It comes as no surprise that the card is traditionally associated with intentional deceit, even if, as in the example of the professional magician, the deception is purely for entertainment.

The Seven of Swords slips into our lives whenever we conceal our true feelings, wants, and intentions, either by saying or doing the opposite or by pretending that everything is just fine on the surface. The Sword stealer is there when we hide our hearts behind our cleverness, using words and wit to keep others at a distance. At its most complex, the figure is the emotional outsider who compulsively uses charm to distract others from getting too close, only to rob herself.

Yet there are times when being a little sneaky (or "artfully indirect") is the smart thing to do. Myths and fairy tales are overrun with characters whose cleverness and cunning outwit the evil ogre or witch and save the day. Jesus used parables to convey ideas that, if spoken plainly, would have been too radical and threatening to the already hostile status quo. Closer to home, anyone who has ever planned a surprise party, felt compelled to compliment a friend's unflattering outfit, or sweet-talked a growling Rottweiler while inching out of the room knows the wisely practical side of the tiptoeing Seven of Swords!

A Seven of Swords Story

Dan and Art thought they'd be together forever, but after fourteen years, issues surfaced that threatened the future of the relationship. Their home was a minefield of resentments. Attempts to talk through their problems only intensified the tension.

Dan came for a reading in the hope of learning the result of the couples counseling he and Art had recently begun. Instead, we approached the question from a more empowering angle: "What energy should Dan and Art bring to the relationship at this time?" The Seven of Swords confirmed the delicacy of the situation: "Proceed with caution." They would be wise to save open confrontations for the counseling sessions and not attempt them at home. As Dan scrutinized the image, he concluded that the two still-standing Swords looked "solid." It proved to be an intuitive observation—the couple recently celebrated their eighteenth anniversary.

Seven of Swords Attributes

Key word:	Evasion
Being:	Elusive, indirect, secretive, subversive, clever, sneaky, calculating, tactful, superficial
Doing:	Avoiding confrontation, sidestepping issues, hinting, manipulating, diverting attention, disarming tension through humor, getting away with something
Shadow:	Hypocrisy, lies, deceit
Reversed:	Candor, directness, telling it like it is
Upright:	*Possible Advice* "The situation calls for caution, discretion, or diplomacy." "Use your humor to disarm the 'opposition.'"

Eight of Swords

I have never been contained except I make the prison.
—Mary Evans

Why does this woman stay put despite loose restraints and no visible captors? Yet there she stands, blind to escape options. Whereas the blindfolded woman in the Two of Swords carefully weighed her options, this woman may believe she has no options or that they're too frightening to consider.

At times we may find ourselves in restrictive situations: "I can't go—my parents want me to stay in tonight." "I'd love to try a more creative approach, but the client has my hands tied." The Eight of Swords is akin to the Hanged Man or Devil to the degree that one feels bound by circumstances. Certainly, some are more binding than others, and this card represents the gamut. But like the loose chains in the Devil, the Swords do not completely surround the woman; she is not really confined, she only thinks she is, and her thinking makes it so.

The figure's back is against the wall of Swords, which, to her limited vision, makes her imprisonment seem tangible. Thrust deepest into the soil, a single Sword stands apart which, like the Ace of Swords, represents the larger, more objective truth of her situation. She turns in its direction, perhaps intuitively sensing its potential to free her, though her mental filters prevent her from seeing it. No matter what beliefs we live by, we are in essence bound by them, blinded to whatever possibilities lay outside them. As Schopenhauer

228

saw it, "We often take the limits of our own vision for the limits of the world."

The challenge of Swords/Air is to make the mind a garden (like the Magician's) wherein we feel the strength and peace of being richly rooted in the present moment. Cultivating the awareness that our Being has more substance than our thoughts frees us from the prison of continuous doubts, resentments, judgments, obsessions, and projections. As Magicians, our trick is to loosen the grip of what William Blake called the "mind-forged manacles," otherwise known as normal consciousness.

An Eight of Swords Story

In ten years of giving readings, the restrained maiden has elicited mostly shudders of aversion—until I read for Doreen. The card's position described her relationship with her boyfriend. She smiled at it. "Oh, I like her!" she purred. "She looks so protected."

I learned that Doreen equated the Swords with the sense of safety she enjoyed in the company of Bobby, a physically intimidating man and possessive lover. I suggested somewhat gingerly that she consider the costs of her voluntary restriction, particularly as her other cards showed struggles with self-esteem. Doreen merely shrugged at this. I didn't press the issue—the last thing I wanted was for Bobby to come after the Tarot reader who put ideas in her head!

Eight of Swords Attributes

Key word:	Restriction
Being:	Frustrated, confined, stifled, hemmed in, blind to possibilities, held hostage by real or perceived limitations
Doing:	Resisting or accepting limitations or restraints

Shadow: Ignorance of your own confinement, passive-aggressive behavior; acting helpless, holding narrow views

Reversed: Clarity; overcoming restrictions

Possible Advice

Upright: "Accept that, for now, your hands are tied."
           "Restrain yourself from action or comment."

Nine of Swords

Let not our babbling dreams affright our souls.
—William Shakespeare

The Eight showed how we imprison ourselves in thoughts and situations of our own making. As frustrating as that was, the Nine presents an even more injurious picture—the mind nearly at the breaking point—a culmination of every false and fearful facet in the troubled suit of Swords. A figure, hair prematurely gray with worry, buries her face in her hands in the dead of night.

Her gesture is almost a literal depiction of "losing face," the shame of having one's faults exposed. But shame is just one of many possible daggers disturbing her rest. Throw in guilt about the past, anxiety about the present, dread of the future, self-recrimination, self-pity, visions of doom, or an endless mental replaying of unpleasant moments long gone. Within this tortured psyche lies the shadow side of the Hermit— introspection gone berserk.

Swords scale the wall like the oppressive thoughts mounting within her. A carving on the tomblike bed depicts a figure rising in alarm as an attacker lunges forward. Its low placement on the image implies that she may not even be conscious of the basis of her anxieties.

We have all had nights, if not weeks or months, like the person in the Nine of Swords is having. Such disturbances are not always the product of gloomy self-absorption. The nightly news, illness, concerns about loved ones, or the plight of the earth itself can be enough to put nails in the mattress. But just as the stained-glass window provided a calming influence in the Four of Swords, the Nine's bright coverlet, a "comforter," offers a glimmer of hope. Woven into the fabric are roses and astrological symbols, reminders of the perfection of divine order permeating Life—even if, for now, we can only bear to look at it through our fingers.

A Nine of Swords Story

Vanessa was overwhelmed by the financial problems of her church, for which she was the accountant. Most frustrating to her, however, was the response of the church leadership. The minister and board routinely dismissed her thorough (and thoroughly bleak) financial projections as proof of her "negative, lack-based thinking" and instead urged her to "affirm prosperity." Gradually, Vanessa herself began to question the legitimacy of her concerns, even as the capital continued to plummet.

"Am I just short on faith," she asked as I laid out the Celtic Cross, "or am I right in thinking there's reason for alarm here?" The Nine of Swords showed up in an unusual position—Higher-Self Advice. "Your worries are well founded," I said. The card gave Vanessa the nudge she needed to put her impeccable skills in the service of a more responsible employer. She left the job one week later.

Nine of Swords Attributes

Key word:	Anxiety
Being:	Apprehensive, fretful, guilt-ridden, ashamed, despondent
Doing:	Worrying, dreading, obsessing, suffering from insomnia
Shadow:	An unrelieved state of anxiety, shame, or depression; self-pity as a security blanket
Reversed:	Reducing or eliminating anxiety or, conversely, denying its presence altogether
	Possible Advice
Upright:	"Talk about what's keeping you up at night—let it out." "Explore the beliefs underlying your fears."

Ten of Swords

When you can do nothing, what can you do?
—Zen koan

When it comes to cards like the Ten of Swords, one is happy to be reminded that the Tarot is symbolic and not, in most cases, a literal depiction of events! There's no mistaking the message of finality here. This human pincushion is the last word on failure and dead-end choices. Swords/Air symbolize the mind and intellect. The card depicts the certainty of defeat when we make choices from above the neck at the exclusion of feeling and the instinctive wisdom of the body. Dark as the card is, it nevertheless compensates for these omissions.

Notice the location of the Sword that penetrates deepest: the fellow is forced to take his defeat to heart. The sight of the long-neglected water pulls him into soulful reflection. Brought down from his heady world of Swords, the steady earth now grounds him, puts him in touch with the here and now. The dark clouds retreat in the dawn of sunlight's fire, bringing the first rays of hope. And then a most surprising gesture—his fingers curl into a sign of blessing as humiliation gives way to humility.

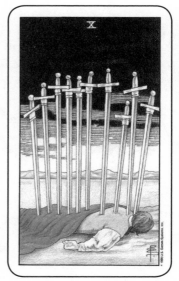

Our fallen figure has learned the hard way, and it hurts. If the lesson has stuck he will not stay there, nor attempt to repeat whatever led him to this result.

As Einstein said, "We will not solve the problems of the world from the same level of thinking we were at when we created them." The figure faces the mountains, the higher levels of thought that—in balance with the influences of Fire, Water, and Earth—inspire wiser choices.

A Ten of Swords Story

Susan, an attractive divorcee, wanted to know which of the men she was dating offered the greatest potential for a satisfying long-term relationship. Her face glowed with expectancy as she pulled two cards, one for each man. No reader likes to give discouraging news, so imagine how uncomfortable it was to see her romantic interests summed up by the Nine and Ten of Swords, respectively.

Fortunately, Susan had a great sense of humor. "Oh, joy!" she exclaimed. "Which relationship shall I choose—pain and suffering, or pain and defeat?" In the same tongue-in-cheek spirit, I suggested to her that the Nine was by far the happier choice, as it had at least one less sword to contend with!

Ten of Swords Attributes

Key word:	Defeat
Being:	Depressed, pinned down, attacked, betrayed, forced to give up
Doing:	Hitting rock bottom, conceding defeat, thinking things to death, facing up to limitations, learning through failure
Shadow:	A defeatist attitude, self-pity; acting like a "doormat," playing the Martyr
Reversed:	Refusing to give in to defeat, avoiding certain failure, slowly getting back on your feet
	Possible Advice
Upright:	"Relax—it's out of your hands." "Try Plan B."

Page of Swords

Make a proper investigation first.
—Buddha

A force of air moves in the Page's direction, blowing his hair. Ideas flow along the current—theories, concepts, truths, untruths. The Page leans back to observe them patiently. The mound gives him a higher, more objective perspective on the notions coming at him.

Not every idea pitched his way will fly with him. Skepticism permeates his inquisitiveness. The Page asks questions. Conducts a little research. Looks for proof. Unless convinced of the substance of an idea, he will let it sail past him.

Compared with the other Pages, who gaze upon the emblems of their suits with newcomers' wonder, the Page of Swords seems to have moved beyond the honeymoon stage. He may already be book smart, articulate, or quick minded. He could be flirting with a philosophy or learning to use his words with greater thought and precision. His bright red boots reveal a readiness to put what he's learning into action.

Even so, his Page status tips us off that he has a way to go before achieving the brilliance of his intellectual elders. And herein lies a concern: In the hands of a novice, a big sharp blade can mean trouble. Somebody could get hurt. The Page may be vulnerable to hastily formed opinions that will come back to wound him later. With the danger of just a little knowledge, he may even imagine that his mental powers are equal to those of his clear-eyed imperial elders. If so, the birds flying overhead may, like circling vultures, be waiting for him to slip up and cut off his own head. Yet it's a mistake the Page in his intellectual exploration must be allowed to make.

A Page of Swords Story

Leila, a successful business owner, was having problems with her five-year-old son, Josh. The boy's frequent tantrums had begun to trigger her own rage, and to her dismay she found herself responding to his explosions in kind. We asked what attitude or energy would help her cope with her son's Emotional Spectaculars.

When the cool Page of Swords appeared, I asked Leila to mimic the figure's stance. "How does that feel"? I asked. "Like I'm above it all," she said. We talked about the value of finding ways to become more emotionally detached when dealing with her son's tirades—and to use her Sword to "cut through the crap" and establish much-needed timeouts for the child.

During a subsequent reading several months later, Leila admitted that she found the Page's psychic distancing a difficult parenting skill. "I'm so easily manipulated by my son," she sighed. "I feel so guilty about being at work so much, and he knows it."

Page of Swords Attributes

Key word:	Investigation
Being:	Emotionally detached, intellectually engaged, intrigued, observant, inquisitive, skeptical
Doing:	Asking questions, grasping concepts, getting the facts, cutting through obstacles, holding your ground, striving for objectivity
Shadow:	Uninformed opinions, spying, aloofness as self-protection
Reversed:	Closed-mindedness, boredom; rejecting an idea, feeling something is "over your head," moving beyond the Page stage
	Possible Advice
Reversed:	"Be more engaged, less detached." "Give your attention to worthier ideas."

Knight of Swords

The mind is not a vessel to be filled but a fire to be ignited.
—Plutarch

Meet the figure so intense that he makes the Emperor, Chariot, and Tower look almost listless in comparison. The blood-red plume and cape streaking from his armor leave no doubt as to his aggressive, if not warlike, intentions. Where the Page faced the wind with curiosity, the headstrong Knight charges into it resolutely, defiantly, taking on all who would challenge his ironclad opinions and ideologies or foolishly attempt to proclaim their own.

In place of the Page's inquisitiveness, the Knight seeks to prove his point. The five birds overhead allude to the Five of Swords, the card of forceful overthrow (note the same jagged clouds). They warn that the headstrong Knight may be rushing toward a similar fate.

Before you decide that you have nothing in common with the Sword-swinging Knight, consider that he also represents the tendency within each of us to "rush to judgment" whether in our words or thoughts. And who has not desperately tried to unsend an email written while temporarily possessed by this medieval avenger? We all unleash the Knight.

Most overtly, the Knight of Swords is the bullying trial lawyer, the religious fanatic hellbent for heaven, and the friend who turns conversations into lectures. The aggressive excesses so plainly in view on the card make this Knight an easy target for our distrust.

237

But the Sword he brandishes is double edged. Like all the Court figures, he has another side. His motives are not always self-righteous, his ways not always arrogant. Effectively channeled, the force of the Knight can be a tremendous inspiration. The Knight rides forth as the victim of abuse who boldly confronts the perpetrator; as the whistle-blower who exposes corruption; as social activists who jab at the complacency of a sleeping citizenry. At his most subdued, the Knight is the impulse to clear the throat, raise a finger, and politely correct inaccuracies.

A Knight of Swords Story

The instant the young man sat at my table, I could sense the storm brewing inside him. I invited him to shuffle the cards, which he did with brooding intensity. Further darkening the clouds was his unmistakable air of resentment, which made me wonder if someone at the party in the next room had pressured him to get a reading.

He had no particular question, so we did a three-card "Life Journey" spread (see page 309). I've long since forgotten the other cards that appeared, but in the Where I Am Now position was the headstrong Knight of Swords. "What battle are you fighting?" I asked. In a stern, guarded way he replied that he had been having arguments with his wife. And then he clammed up as if to say, "End of story." My guidance led me to speak about his issue indirectly— through the card itself. "The Knight of Swords is invested in being right," I began, "and he may *be* right. But look at him—there's a point when the Knight gets exhausted from charging on the warpath and trying to prove his point. What the Knight really wants more than anything is peace, and there's only one way he can begin to get it— by putting down his sword and *listening*, really listening with all his heart, to the opposition." The man sat looking at the card in silence for several moments, his features softening slightly. "This was good," he said with a hint of sadness.

Knight of Swords Attributes

Key word:	Assertion
Being:	Idealistic, courageous, competitive, opinionated, quick-minded, argumentative, aggressive, enlivened by controversy
Doing:	Defending a person, a position, or an ideal; confronting ignorance, incompetence, or injustice; trying to win an argument; fighting for a cause, driving fast
Shadow:	Vengefulness, self-righteousness, fanaticism, running off at the mouth, imposing your beliefs on others
Reversed:	Stifling anger, staying silent, refraining from attack, putting on the brakes, lacking commitment to an idea or cause, taking a less aggressive approach (such as listening)
	Possible Advice
Reversed:	"Down, boy! You're coming on too strong." "Before you charge in, *listen*."

Queen of Swords

For me the greatest beauty always lies in the greatest clarity.
—Gotthold Ephraim Lessing

Before you write off the Queen of Swords for looking too rigid or unfeeling, take a moment to consider what you may have in common. Do you thrill at displays of intellectual brilliance? Exalt at the well-chosen word? Are there firm principles by which you live your life? Do you find beauty in truth? If you answered yes to any of these questions, hail your Queen of Swords, the soul of Air.

For the Queen, clarity is as nourishing and vital as breath. Chief in her priorities is nurturing her own clearheadedness while sometimes inspiring, sometimes insisting on, the same in others. The Sword, incompletely pictured in the Page and Knight, is whole and comprehensive in the hands of the Queen. Like the Ace, it points straight up, rising above the clouds of illusion and confusion. The cherub at her side is emblematic of the purity of ideals that the Queen so uncompromisingly preserves.

Just as the Sword of Justice signified Supreme Intelligence cutting away self-deception, the Queen uses hers with the same intention, albeit with human limitations. In the truest sense, the Queen aspires to be, as John F. Kennedy said of his own aspirations, "an idealist without illusions." Her crown is shaped of the butterflies that eluded the Knight of the suit—thought matured, evolved. The soaring solo bird guides her aims to live by the sterling clarity of the singular Ace.

She upholds her gleaming ideal to measure the quality of her thoughts and conduct, which may explain her stern expression. The Queen can represent people whose constant striving to live up to their high principles—or to get others to adopt them—gives their lives integrity but little joy, moral certitude but little peace. Perhaps it was for this reason that Waite wrote in particular of the Queen's "familiarity with sorrow." Penetrating clarity often follows great pain; the Queen of Swords knows firsthand the ability of the mind to restrict and distort as well as, by a conscious endeavor, to illuminate and heal.

People who closely identify with the Queen may find in themselves her reverence for discipline, her straight-from-the-hip communication style, her passion for precision. They may also come equipped with her shadow aspects. They may pride themselves on their brutal honesty with others without applying the same searing scrutiny to themselves. Conversely, they may be forgiving of others' faults but turn their Swords against themselves with samurai intensity. This hard-wiring for perfection and disapproval is often the voice of an internalized parent who continues to be enthroned in the cloudy corners of the psyche. Yet it is this very haziness that the Queen, in her rightful authority, is committed to clear away by virtue of her psychological insights and disciplined powers of mind.

A Queen of Swords Story

Once, during a period of personal and interpersonal strife, I went to the cards and asked, "What will open my heart?" Had the Queen of Swords appeared in her upright position, I would have been surprised, as matters of the heart are not typically her domain. But the card's reversal was my Higher Self's way of saying, "Ease up on your Queen of Swords attitude—in particular, her shadow qualities."

It asked me to look at the hardness of some of my views and the rigid do-or-die expectations I'd set for myself and for those closest to me. In her reversal, the Queen urged me to lighten up, to be kinder—inside and out—and slower to form opinions. What better practice for opening the heart? To this day, when I feel the tension that comes from my own severest attitudes, I try to breathe, pull back, and reconnect to the feeling of that advice.

Queen of Swords Attributes

Key word:	Discernment
Being:	Direct, insightful, high-minded, discriminating, precise, uncompromising, witty, articulate, stoic, disciplined
Doing:	Nurturing the qualities of Air in yourself or others, seeing with clarity, upholding high standards, acting with honor, rising above distressing thoughts, teaching, mentoring, speaking harsh truths, reprimanding
Shadow:	Cynicism, prudishness, perfectionism, sarcasm; being excessively critical of yourself or scornful of others
Reversed:	Ambivalence, emotions clouding the truth or fear of claiming it; succumbing to worry, making allowances in your principles, softening
	Possible Advice
Reversed:	"Embrace imperfection." "Don't take things so seriously. Have some fun!"

King of Swords

The voice of the intellect is a soft one, but it does not rest until it has gained a hearing.
—Sigmund Freud

The King of Swords is the king of compromise. Whereas the Queen's Sword is upright to signify the pristine clarity of her convictions, the King's Sword leans in sympathy with the fact that, within the societal sphere of his influence, there is no pure ruling on what is true, right, and good for everyone all the time. Ideas about morality, truth, and justice are mired in complexities. It takes the force and intellect of the King of Swords to wrestle with the abstract, pin it down, and pull from it something that can be reasonably useful for the tribe.

KING ♂ SWORDS.

Like the King of Cups who sets aside his feelings, and the King of Wands his unbridled ambitions—each for the benefit of the kingdom—the King of Swords demonstrates a disciplined fairness by considering views other than his own. The two birds on the card signify the dualities the King must actively contend with, issues that had immobilized the figure in the Two of Swords. Though he privately recognizes the wisdom of paradox—that things can be at once true and false, beneficial and harmful—he is responsible for moving his Sword in a particular direction. If his ruling proves ill advised, he will use his evaluative powers to find out what went wrong and amend it accordingly.

The King's decisions have influence whether by virtue of a strong personality, an authoritative job, or social position. Awareness of this power makes him fair and scrupulous in its exercise. Here is the researcher taking pains to keep personal bias out of her work, the jury scrutinizing the legalities of a case, the grandparent making a point to spend equal time with the wicked grandchildren as well as the endearing ones. The King is committed to the rational and equitable running of things.

A winged cherub activates the clear seeing of his sixth chakra. Yet the idealism of the preceding Swords Court personalities is tempered in the King. While the Queen and King are equally possessed of strong convictions, his role responsibilities may dictate a shift from "What is right?" to "What is best under the circumstances?" Unlike the Queen's immovable stone dais, the King's throne rests on a patchy mound of earth—the practical considerations in which his judgments must be rooted. Once he (or the powers that be) issues a suitable decision, he becomes, like the Emperor, a stickler for compliance and consistency. The butterflies that crown his Queen and give her intellectual freedom are concretized in the stiff motif that backs the King.

The King of Swords is perhaps the most complex Court figure in the Tarot, and without a doubt the most ambiguous. He can be read as a moral person doing his best to make fair and balanced decisions or an unfeeling despot supporting blatantly unjust laws to preserve the status quo. On the relationship front, he may attempt to use logic and abstractions to distance himself from his feelings or to defend against becoming emotionally vulnerable.

A King of Swords Story

My friend Nancy's artistic talents blossomed during her years in Spain. Her paintings featured provocative images rendered in lush Mediterranean colors. At the time of her Tarot reading she was living in Chicago, hoping to find representation for her work. Like many artists, she confessed to being sensitive to criticism of her work. She dreaded taking her portfolio to galleries where her deeply personal pieces would be judged on their commercial value.

The King of Swords waiting in Nancy's Near Future reminded me of the "Gotcha!" squares on board games that players try to avoid. If she wanted gallery representation, no roll of the dice would enable her to skip around the potential stings of gallery owners' assessments. "He looks so cold," she said.

I proposed that she draw a card that would show her a way to approach the art-business contingent effectively. She closed her eyes and drew a card. The Page of Swords appeared, calmly suggesting that Nancy resolve to take criticism less personally; the implication was that she consider any rejection from the art world's Kings of Swords as just part of the game.

King of Swords Attributes

Key word:	Judiciousness
Being:	Knowledgeable, intellectual, analytical, philosophical, logical, fair, responsible, judicious, orthodox, professorial
Doing:	Showing intellectual leadership, thinking abstractly, writing or speaking with mastery, upholding standards, developing strategies, establishing or enforcing laws and rules, handling legal matters, striving for impartiality
Shadow:	Intellectualizing or dismissing feelings, being domineering; legalistic
Reversed:	Making biased decisions, being wishy-washy, not playing by the rules, suspending judgment
	Possible Advice
Reversed:	*"Feel* more—judge and analyze less." "Break some rules. "

Pentacles: Down to Earth

The earth, that is sufficient.
—Walt Whitman

Element: Earth
Astrological signs: Capricorn, Taurus, Virgo

*E*arth is the element of physical reality. It is the dimension of greatest density, of clay and root, muscle and bone, cause and effect, the work and its result, the time-bound plane in which time and gravity anchor all. And yet, for all its seeming solidity, it is the space of greatest illusion, masking the spirit in nature to all but awakened eyes. The body, too, is divine, as is the sunlight that warms it, the air that fills it, and the water drenching every cell. Mother to body and soil, Earth is our subsistence and the instinct to sustain what is basic, stable, and grounding. Earth rewards our labors with food and shelter and sensual pleasures; and in its most fertile seasons, it showers material abundance.

The Pentacle is a five-pointed star representing the five senses, as well as the five end-points of the human body, famously articulated in Leonardo da Vinci's drawing, *Vitruvian Man*. The circle, symbol of the feminine, ensouls the star, merging spirit and Earth in a sphere of wholeness. In some Tarot decks, particularly earlier ones, the suit is represented by coins to symbolize money and commerce. Although money itself is symbolic (of rewards, exchange, and value), it manifests tangible things and is therefore associated with Earth.

Ace of Pentacles

Mankind are earthen jugs with spirits in them.
—Nathaniel Hawthorne

The hand emerging from the cloud holds within it the tangible potentials, opportunities, and gifts offered by Earth. The Ace of Pentacles is linked with the first chakra, the energy center related to physical comfort and well-being. As such, it inspires us to ground ourselves through proper nutrition, exercise, rest, and leisure activities. It encourages us to create safe, stable home and work environments in which body, mind, and soul may flourish. And it instills awareness of the importance of making common sense our common practice.

The feminine is resplendent in the garden that graces the Ace. An oval archway resembles the Cosmic Egg of the World card. Eggs signify boundaries, safety, and potential. The greatest gift of the Ace of Pentacles may be the sense of coming home, of feeling comfortably rooted, both in our bodies and on the planet. The flowered archway gives us access to the mountains of higher wisdom, but from the grounded perspective of the garden, so that we may put that wisdom to use.

An Ace of Pentacles Story

Shortly after her certification in Reiki (a form of energy healing), Robin opened for business. But her financial investment wasn't paying off. She had few clients. Many sessions were bartered or offered for pay-what-you-can. In just four months of business, she had already received two bad checks.

Robin, cringing, asked about the future for her business. "Not good," I answered, "but we don't need the cards to tell us that." I fought the urge to launch into a lecture from Universal Laws 101 and allowed the cards to have first say on the matter. We asked, "What's the obstacle to Robin's success?" The Ace of Pentacles, reversed, took the words right out of my mouth.

"There's a part of you that doesn't truly believe you have a right to charge for your services," I said. "So, unlike the open hand on the card, you're not open to abundance." My words struck a chord in Robin, who admitted she always felt ambivalent about charging fees for healing work—a belief in disastrous opposition to her desire to operate a practice. It was not just her clients, but also her perception of the value of her work, that needed healing. I suggested she post an image of the Ace of Pentacles near her appointment book and use it to affirm her right to receive in kind fully for her services.

Ace of Pentacles Attributes

Key word:	Prosperity
Being:	Practical, productive, prosperous, grounded, healthy, fit
Doing:	Breaking new ground, seeking wealth and security, offering or receiving money, establishing roots, creating value, tending to physical needs and domestic duties, protecting the environment
Shadow:	Overemphasis on money, security, and the physical
Reversed:	Health issues, lack of financial opportunity, a premature start, refusing to play it safe
	Possible Advice
Reversed:	"Invest elsewhere." "Shift your priorities—it's not about the money."

Two of Pentacles

To dispose a soul to action we must upset its equilibrium.
—Eric Hoffer

The Ace of Pentacles was a lot like the Garden of Eden—forever secure, endlessly bountiful. Now, choices must be made. Do we share, sell, trade, conserve, hoard, or increase our earthly time, money, and resources? The rocking ships on the Two of Pentacles dramatize the unrest we may feel in the sea of such practical possibilities.

If the discriminating lady on the Two of Swords faced weighty either/or decisions, the young man here successfully juggles the dynamic and detail-oriented (but no less consequential) matters of *how, when, where, how much,* and *with whom.* Such prioritizing and alternating of energies is vital to the management of everyday affairs and to overall psychic balance, as the infinity symbol suggests. For example, one's health may require countering a heavy work schedule with an active social life or compensating for extroverted periods with contemplative ones. It is easy to imagine that the green infinity symbol containing the Pentacles is a giant rubber band, as it sometimes takes quite a stretch to keep the demands of one's life moving in a state of flow.

The lad's short, stout legs emphasize his closeness to the pavement, which makes him particularly well grounded in the maintenance of day-to-day affairs. His red tights signify the vitality of his first chakra, which relates to physical sturdiness and survival. Having developed these attributes, he is not upended when life throws him a curve, as his one-foot balance demonstrates. The value of these strengths cannot be underestimated; we all know people (or are them) who fall apart when even small changes or pressures are introduced into their normal routines. Perhaps the juggler wears his clownish hat as a reminder to keep a sense of humor as he strives to keep the balls in the air. With all in constant flux, whose life at certain times hasn't resembled a circus?

A Two of Pentacles Story

Trudy, a fifty-three-year-old office administrator, came to the reading for insight into her relationship with her elderly parents. Of the ten cards in the spread, Trudy seemed most unsettled by the Two of Pentacles, which lay in the Self-Image position. "That's very accurate," said Trudy. "I'm always trying to juggle my time so I can visit Mom and Dad." Then, pointing a perfectly manicured nail at the figure on the card, she added, "But there's something about his goofy hat that really annoys me!"

Trudy saw it as symbol of her tendency always to keep conversation "light and entertaining" with her parents, whom she described as having no capacity for honest emotional exchange. Further, she saw herself as having to "jump through hoops" to please the couple, whose demands were high and thanks infrequent. The court-jester aspect she perceived in the card mirrored a role she was anxious to change. We spent the rest of the reading exploring more empowering "hats" she might try on.

Two of Pentacles Attributes

Key word:	Juggling
Being:	Resourceful, flexible, adaptable, accommodating, willing to please
Doing:	Managing priorities; displaying multiple talents; multitasking; keeping up with change; juggling the demands of family, work, money, and relationships
Shadow:	Having too many balls in the air, trying too hard to keep everyone happy
Reversed:	Being overwhelmed, being unable or unwilling to keep things going, dropping the ball, being ineffective at time/project management, succumbing to extremes, lightening the load
	Possible Advice
Reversed:	"Ask for help or delegate."
	"You're trying to juggle too much—let something drop."

Three of Pentacles

Synergy—the bonus that is achieved when things work together harmoniously.
—Mark Twain

The tensions observed in the Two harmonize in the Three. Now priorities are established, resources procured, and plans put into action. An artisan, an architect, and a monk collaborate on the building of a church. The architect with his blueprint symbolizes the original creative vision, carefully refined. The artisan gives form to that vision through craftsmanship. The monk stands for integrity and ethics in the endeavor, as well as the spirit of service that is, ideally, the function of the church they construct.

Their unity combines vision, skill, and spiritual values in the fulfillment of shared goals. Anyone who has ever been fortunate enough to experience such group synthesis knows that even mundane projects can become sources of immense satisfaction capable of forging deep interconnections and lasting pride. Carved into the archway are three Pentacles. They signify the builders' high standards and the greater good to which their labors are dedicated.

Take away its traditional associations with community and teamwork, and the Three of Pentacles represents an individual's spiritual renovation. The three figures personify body, mind, and spirit in collaboration. The arches form a doorway to a place of yet-unformed potential, which, like stone to a mason, holds the raw materials for unlimited creative expression.

A Three of Pentacles Story

I once worked as a freelance writer with a small marketing company. We were a tightly knit group of people who created entertaining trade-show presentations for many high-profile clients. The Three of Pentacles aptly depicts the synergy we enjoyed as a collaboration of producers, writers, actors, multimedia artists, and administrative staff.

In my eighth year with the organization, the nation's economy tanked, and many of our most lucrative accounts disappeared, practically overnight. I did a Celtic Cross reading about it. In the Outcome position sat the Three of Pentacles, reversed. This was one outcome I knew I had no power to change.

The company went under within the month.

Three of Pentacles Attributes

Key word:	Synergy
Being:	Cooperative, team-oriented, inspired by a collective effort
Doing:	Apprenticing; building a foundation; working constructively; working in community; showing technical proficiency; striving for high standards of service, quality, or workmanship; seeking opinions or consensus
Reversed:	Inefficiency, mediocrity; working at cross-purposes, being in a state of inner or outer discord, operating independently
	Possible Advice
Reversed:	"Reconsider the team you're working with or the project itself."
	"Make this one a solo effort."

Four of Pentacles

All you are unable to give possesses you.
—André Gide

The material order and stability that Fours represent is rendered in this picture of a royal figure lording it over four Pentacles. Behind him stands a thriving center of commerce from which he has derived his holdings. We last saw the theme of possessions in the Nine of Cups. But where that character took great pleasure in his prosperity, this one exudes only a determined protectiveness. For him there is no joy in the having—having is its own reward.

The drive to acquire is suggested in his fiery red shoes and robe, while his dark cape insinuates greed lurking in his motives (the card is traditionally called "The Miser.") As though fearful of theft, he secures two Pentacles to the pavement with his feet. The Pentacle rising above his crown implies that money remains at the top of his priorities, while the gray skies and pavement underscore not only materialistic stability, but the static quality of such an exclusive orientation.

The blocking of the Pentacle at the heart and throat centers hints that his relative security comes at the cost of his feelings and self-expression. It's a familiar dynamic—people prove their prosperity by buying things, mistakenly believing that possessions will somehow provide the experience of soul and wholeness from which they feel disconnected. Like the man clutching his Pentacles, they remain alone, though the crush of material distractions temporarily inures them to the pain of their isolation.

We wouldn't be giving the Four of Pentacles its due without rightly acknowledging its empowering component. Now and then, holding back energy (money, time, resources) may be exactly the means to restore balance. When we have been leaking energy— overgiving, overdoing, overspending—it serves us to put more value on a miserly attitude than giving in to the fear of appearing selfish.

A Four of Pentacles Story

Morgan waved me over to her table in the Tarot classroom. "I asked how my friend Todd affects me," she said, "and I got the Four of Pentacles, reversed. I don't get what it's saying, especially reversed."

"Upside down, the figure may be losing resources," I said. "Do you spend too much money when you're with Todd?" Morgan laughed at this, assuring me both of them were notorious tightwads.

"Then how might your dynamic with Todd leave you feeling ungrounded and not in 'possession' of yourself?" Morgan laughed again, this time in rueful recognition. She disclosed that Todd's entertaining yet oversized personality made her feel like a houseplant in a hurricane. Though she adored him, she often felt exhausted in his company. The reversed Four of Pentacles card showed her the problem and, when considered in its upright position, a solution—claiming her boundaries, putting limits on the amount of time spent with Todd, or finding some way to stay rooted in the hurricane.

Four of Pentacles Attributes

Key word:	Conservation
Being:	Financially stable, frugal, acquisitive, self-protective, stubborn
Doing:	Holding onto money, conserving energy or resources, claiming ownership, protecting investments, looking out for yourself, clinging to security
Shadow:	Hoarding, holding grudges; miserliness, self-absorption
Reversed:	Letting go, sharing, divesting, releasing what had been clutched or hoarded, losing ground; financial instability, a weakening of psychic boundaries
	Possible Advice
Upright:	"Hold onto what you've got." "Get hold of yourself—conserve your energies."

Five of Pentacles

How camest thou in this pickle?
—William Shakespeare

Once again, the stability of the Fours breaks down as the Fives usher in crisis. This time, it's finances. Health. Home. Issues of survival. A weary, rags-clad couple trudges forward on frostbitten feet, the man with the aid of crutches, and crude ones at that. Bandages encircle his head, though his expression reveals that they do little to ease the pain. As if circumstances weren't deplorable enough, he wears a bell, the kind forced upon lepers to warn the public of approaching contagion. (Many people instinctively recoil from the card when they first encounter it, as if it had the power to transmit the conditions it depicts!)

The artist has incorporated the Pentacles into a stained-glass church window, perhaps to convey the idea that spiritual wealth, not material success, offers true refuge. The couple's failure or refusal to see this light in the darkness suggests a deeper impoverishment.

As a psychological simile, the card personifies the perpetual loser, in which one's wounds and setbacks are allowed to define one's existence. According to the Law of Attraction, such a mindset creates and reinforces every subsequent run of bad luck. "Poverty hides in thought," said Kahlil Gibran, "before it surrenders to purses."

The woman on the Five of Pentacles represents unconsciously held beliefs about self-worth—highly disabling ones, in this case. Unconscious attitudes are far more influential, so she is shown leading the man (the crippled ego), who dutifully follows. If the unconscious programming is not addressed, the self-punishing, wayward trek will continue.

A Five of Pentacles Story

Based on the preceding cards in Evangeline's Celtic Cross spread, I knew the Five of Pentacles was about her money worries. Though a self-described "child of the Great Depression," Evangeline said her parents were never destitute and that she and her husband had lived comfortably, if modestly, for their seventy years. But a lifelong fear of poverty preoccupied her. Her startling comment, "There are people with money, and then there are the rest of us

258

poor slobs," made it painfully clear where she put herself (and me!) on the spectrum.

When a Tarot reading reveals a lifelong toxic attitude, especially one so perversely cherished, all a reader can do is point it out and hope for the best. A poverty of spirit, not finances, was Evangeline's real problem. I suggested to her that if she continued to view her life through the lens of lack, well-being would always be out of reach. The Five of Pentacles reminds us that the only true security is that which is anchored within.

Five of Pentacles Attributes

Key word:	Hardship
Being:	Cast out, alienated, impoverished, crippled by circumstances, steeped in drudgery, ill
Doing:	Going through hard times, struggling to get by, expecting the worst, complaining, commiserating, neglecting basic needs
Shadow:	Believing deep down that you deserve your hardships, suffering yet refusing assistance
Reversed:	Coming in from the cold, beginning to recover from setbacks, accepting help, overturning a disabling situation (or a disabling consciousness)
Upright:	*Possible Advice* "Though temporary, this struggle must be endured." "Focus on the spiritual opportunity in the situation."

Six of Pentacles

*A gift consists not in what is done or given, but in
the intention of the giver or doer.*

—Seneca

An impressive recovery from the plight of the Five. Resources return and are shared, fostering harmony. The giving of the Six releases the hoarding of the Four, and movement returns. A man of means tosses coins to two in need. He bears a resemblance to the similarly costumed (and prosperous) figure in the Nine of Cups.

The resources circulate. Merchant scales suggest the percentages of generosity are given from practical, socially expected considerations rather than loving-kindness. No matter—the needs are mutually met, even if a decided power imbalance colors the relationships.

It is power that makes the Six of Pentacles so intriguing. The merchant clearly holds a one-up position in relation to the beggars. He has what they need and is in a position to choose if, when, and how much to give. The dependents kneel in deference. If that smells of tyranny and subjugation, we have only to remember that no bank loan has ever been applied for and granted, no car keys requested and relinquished, without this dynamic asserted. Power imbalance does not imply its abuse.

Only in intimate relationships does the Six of Pentacles proffer shadows. Here we find the specter of codependency, the unspoken agreements made between people that keep them chained to mutually toxic behaviors. The merchant may be the spouse who calls the shots when it comes to how much money, approval, or attention is extended to the partner, who, though feeling undeserving, begs for it. In another scenario, the beggar may be the person who plays Helpless in order to be taken care of by a person playing emotional or financial Rescuer. Add to these examples the countless ways in which people degrade themselves to get their needs met and then resent the obligation they feel toward the people providing them.

Power dynamics are played out in as many ways as there are people; they shift from relationship to relationship and, within those relationships, from moment to moment.

As with all the cards that feature more than one figure, the question is, with which character in the Six of Pentacles do you most relate? Are you the dispenser or the receiver? Or the one apparently still waiting?

A Six of Pentacles Story

Dee fell in love with Tom's paintings, and then with Tom. He moved in with her. She was happy to pay for his art supplies and didn't mind that he was frequently unable to split their living expenses. When Tom was grumpy and down on himself—a trait she attributed to his artistic sensitivity—Dee gave him pep talks or little gifts to cheer him. Whenever Tom's mood or money was low, Dee was there to fill him up.

But after two years with her dependent partner, Dee had second thoughts. "I'm definitely this one," she said of the benefactor in the Six of Pentacles, "but I also feel like the beggar, waiting for Tom to pitch in a little." A few minutes later Dee's cell phone rang. She rolled her eyes. It was Tom. She apologized for the interruption and took the call into the other room. I could hear her assuring him, repeatedly, that she would come home within the hour.

Six of Pentacles Attributes

Key word:	Dispensation
Being:	(Merchant) successful, charitable, supportive, benevolent; (beggar) submissive, needful, appreciative
Doing:	(Merchant) rewarding others, paying attention where it's due, making donations, sponsoring or mentoring others; (beggar) petitioning, receiving financial assistance or grants
Shadow:	(Merchant) being patronizing, keeping others dependent, "buying" love; (beggar) feeling degraded, begging for attention, having to "earn" love, settling for too little
Reversed:	Payment withheld, loans denied; fearing to ask, refusing charity or assistance, restoring the power balance
	Possible Advice
Reversed:	(merchant) "Examine your motives in giving." (beggar) "Don't put yourself in this position." (both) "Strive for more equality or reciprocity."

Seven of Pentacles

And when is there time to remember, to sift, to weigh, to estimate, to total?
—Tillie Olsen

A gardener leans on a hoe and takes a pause from the exertions of working the land. Amid rolling mountains, tall vines teem with plump

Pentacles. The gardener appraises them. His tunic is orange, a color signifying the fertility and harvest hoped for in his efforts. So what accounts for his pensive expression? Perhaps the yield has not yet reached his expectations.

The gardener's hoe handle resembles a modified Wand, which alludes to the drive that tills the soil of any purposeful endeavor, as well as the inevitable restlessness that takes hold when the fruits of our labors seem to dawdle indifferently in the face of our deadlines. However strongly we expect progress while tending our careers, projects, relationships, and self-development, there are periods that test our commitment.

Tests are central themes in all the Sevens. Will the Wands warrior win the battle? Will the dreamer choose a Cup or continue to fantasize? Will the Sword thief get away with it? For the Seven of Pentacles, the test is whether he will stick with what he has been growing. The answer, like the image, is inconclusive. Just now, he evaluates.

Despite our most controlling efforts, the things we cultivate ripen by their own timetables. Still others fail to take root. The Seven of Pentacles illustrates that all we can do is plant the seeds, nurture them to the best of our abilities, and patiently allow Nature to do what it will.

A Seven of Pentacles Story

Jerzy's violent temper got worse after the divorce, in which his American wife, Stacie, received full custody of their young son,

Peter. Fearing for their safety, mother and son fled Poland to live in Baltimore near her family. As Peter got older, he longed to know his father, yet felt intimidated when the man used guilt to pressure him to visit. After many discussions among Stacie, Peter, and his child psychologist, it was agreed that the boy was ready to stay with his father for one week, with Stacie on call in a nearby hotel.

Two weeks before the departure, Stacie came for a reading. "I don't want Peter to pick up on all my doubts and anxiety about this trip," she said, "but part of me wonders if it's still too soon to leave him alone with his father." We invited Stacie's deepest wisdom to weigh in on the matter. A gardener herself, she visibly relaxed a little when she saw the Seven of Pentacles in its advisory position. It was time to step aside and let Peter, who had thrived under her care, grow on his own. Stacie wrote me a few weeks later to report that despite a few rough moments, Peter's visit had gone better than expected, though much healing still lay ahead for father and son.

Seven of Pentacles Attributes

Key word:	Assessment
Being:	Evaluative, concerned, disappointed, impatient for results
Doing:	Taking stock of how things are progressing, assessing value or performance, learning from feedback, leaving things be
Shadow:	Always second-guessing your efforts; overevaluation
Reversed:	Abandoning what failed to meet expectations, changing plans or priorities, acting upon evaluation; lack of assessment
	Possible Advice
Reversed:	"Plant seeds in more fertile fields." "Enough evaluating—act."

Eight of Pentacles

He did each single thing as if he did nothing else.
—Charles Dickens

The Seven of Pentacles' doubts about the purpose or progress of projects have been chiseled away in the Eight. A craftsman's apprentice works diligently at producing what appears to be, quite literally, racks of hanging Pentacles (the suit is not the most imaginative!). But it is plain to see that what he lacks in innovation he makes up for in skill and discipline.

Carving his designs by hand onto stone disks is undoubtedly a demanding operation, one requiring the right tools, concentration, patience, and lots of practice—attributes useful beyond the carving of Pentacles. The man's red tights underscore the passion with which he applies himself to his earthy assignment, while his blue blouse testifies to the earnestness of his approach. The Pentacles are lined up progressively on the mounting board. More wait to be added. There is satisfaction in the work here. Things are evolving nicely.

A small town lies in the distance. Even though the miser in the Four sat before a thriving mecca, there was no road to relieve him of his self-centered isolation. Here, a pathway is highlighted, symbolizing the interdependence of the apprentice and the community of which he is part. His ever-improving skills have value for others, who reward him in turn.

The Eight of Pentacles is a symbol for the striving for self-perfection. Work helps us achieve this by presenting opportunities to

265

build character, discipline, and maturity alongside our craft. Jean de la Fontaine observed, "By the work one knows the workman." Ultimately, what we do may not be as important as the spirit in which we do it.

An Eight of Pentacles Story

Imagine my shock when, on my first day as a Tarot student, the instructors informed us we'd be giving readings to the public in just three days. My Virgo ascendant immediately kicked into Perfection mode. I was determined to memorize as many card meanings as I could, and I meticulously cataloged information from three different texts.

On the evening of the public readings, I went to the classroom to collect my emergency reference books and notes, only to find the door locked and the facility manager gone. Reality set in: I would have to do the readings without a safety net.

"What energy should I bring to my card readings tonight?" I asked, somewhat breathlessly, and drew the Eight of Pentacles, reversed. The upside-down card was no mystery. "You've hammered away at your studies," it said to me, "now don't *work* so hard. Go with the flow." I did as instructed, and that evening of trial-by-fire readings remains one of the most exhilarating experiences of my life.

Eight of Pentacles Attributes

Key word:	Meticulousness
Being:	Steadfast, industrious, disciplined, skillful, methodical, proud of your work, precise, detail-oriented
Doing:	Perfecting a skill, taking classes, doing homework, attending to detail and craftsmanship, doing something repetitively, improving yourself, repairing

Shadow:	Monotony, boredom
Reversed:	Disruption of routine, lack of effort or discipline, inattention to detail, unsatisfying work, low output; messing with the formula
	Possible Advice
Reversed:	"Vary the routine. Take a more flexible approach." "Do something more satisfying or constructive."

Nine of Pentacles

Life begets life. Energy creates energy. It is by spending oneself that one becomes rich.

—Sarah Bernhardt

The lady in the Nine of Pentacles is arranged so elegantly in her luxurious setting, and with such a confident air, it is as if she were posing for the cover of a magazine featuring the scoop on her great success. Since Nines signify completion, she is the pinnacle of self-won achievement. She has truly come into her own, developing material abundance and the grace to appreciate it.

For the first time since the Two of Pentacles, color returns to the sky—a bright yellow—for there is a luminous clarity in the way the lady views herself and her attainments. In the most simple and profound sense, she understands that her life is exactly what she has made it. And the lady has it made. Her success is well managed. The grouping of six Pentacles below her hand implies that she exercises the generosity learned in the Six of the suit. The three Pentacles at the right suggest her mastery of synthesizing (recall the Three of Pentacles) the vision, skill, and ethical standards necessary for meaningful gain.

A falcon perches on her gloved hand. Its hood demonstrates the role that discipline has played in her success. The dreams to which she gave flight have landed, fully realized, thanks to her grounded, ordered efforts. The snail attests to the patience her achievements have demanded. That patience doesn't always extend to others, however. The lady may be fussy about who she lets in her garden, disdainful of anyone tracking mud across her perfect lawn or trampling her prize vineyard. Everything must be "just so."

Her flowing gown bears the emblem of Venus shown on the Empress. She shares in common with that archetype a love of plenty and savors the perfection of the pleasures afforded. An aura of fertility completes the linkage. The lush clusters of ripe grapes surrounding her have ancient associations with Mother goddesses, while the card's number assumes additional significance as the time between conception and birth.

A Nine of Pentacles Story

Nick, a young real-estate agent, was ambivalent about the prospect of moving in with his girlfriend, Ellie. "I love her," he said. "I'm just not sure if I can live with her." Chief among Nick's reservations was that Ellie lived with her twelve-year-old daughter, whom he characterized as "very sweet and very troubled." Further, a growing frequency of turbulent mother-daughter exchanges was turning his already cold feet to subfreezing.

"What is the greatest good of Nick continuing to live alone?" we asked. The Nine of Pentacles presented itself, the perfect symbol of the home and lifestyle Nick described as comfortable, orderly, and "totally under my control."

"What is the greatest good of living with Ellie and her daughter?" drew Trump 18—the unpredictable, psychically volatile Moon. "So is that card saying 'yes' or 'no'?" he asked anxiously. "That's up to you," I said, "But be assured that it offers the kind of intense emotional atmosphere you've already gotten a taste of."

Nick shuddered. I could see that leaving his tidy Nine of Pentacles garden was not likely to happen!

Nine of Pentacles Attributes

Key word:	Fruition
Being:	Successful, prosperous, efficient, independent, self-reliant, privileged, refined, disciplined
Doing:	Thriving, appreciating your accomplishments, living an ordered life, enjoying Nature, beautifying or upgrading a property or business
Shadow:	Perfectionism, intolerance for physical imperfection or emotional messiness
Reversed:	Property issues, lack of discipline, frustration from unmet goals, financial dependence
	Possible Advice
Reversed:	"Focus more on teamwork and partnership and less on purely personal gains." "Get comfortable with imperfection."

Ten of Pentacles

A state that is prosperous always honors the gods.
—Aeschylus

The affluence cultivated in the Nine has become *de rigueur* to the lifestyle displayed in the Ten. The clothes are exquisite, the estate sprawling, the barn enormous, and the dogs as well bred as their owners. Nature adds to the overbrimming power, prestige, and privilege with its blessing of a crisp blue sky.

To understand the family in the Ten of Pentacles, it is helpful to contrast them with the other family of the Minors, the Ten of Cups. The Cups family radiated love beneath an arc of Cups; they needed only one another to be happy. The Pentacles clan stands below an archway of stone engraved with a crest, symbol of social identity, heritage, status, and the expectations attending these. The Cups couple united in joy; the lord and lady of Pentacles Manor stand together to uphold the responsibilities of their wealth and social standing. Thus the two cards show Family as love and Family as institution, respectively.

This should not imply that the Pentacles family is unfeeling. The child, pets, and smiling woman suggest otherwise. Rather, the card shows us a group held together primarily by material priorities—name, possessions, traditions—as opposed to emotional ones. An analogy: working for a company. In the best circumstances the employees feel a sense of belonging and security. They may behave altruistically, subverting personal needs for the good of the organization. They may show loyalty and expect it in return. The company may even describe itself as a family. But nobody expects the workplace to fulfill complex emotional needs. So it is with the Ten of Pentacles.

The affiliation shown is that of tribal belonging with its requisite roles and rules of membership. You'll recall that such organized belief systems were overseen by the Hierophant, whose distinctive checkerboard motif appears to the left of the archway. Roles and rules have particular solidity and finality in the suit of Pentacles, as does the number 10, which calls to mind the mighty Ten Commandments as well as the uncontestable authority of any list with ten items in it ("Ten Tips for Financial Success"). The dogs sum up the hierarchical pack loyalty that further distinguishes the card from the free-flowing Ten of Cups.

Ten also refers to the end of old cycles and the beginning of new ones. The white-bearded elder looks to his grandchild as the promise of the next generation; the child sees in the elder a link to her past and future. As for the man's extraordinary cloak, perhaps it signifies that with age comes the freedom to show our true colors. Forming the Kabbalistic Tree of Life the ten Pentacles emphasize the card's message of completion and abundance.

A Ten of Pentacles Story

Three months after the death of her life partner, Karen, my friend Kathy drove out of Los Angeles to embark on what she later called a "Trail of Tears across the United States." During her stop in Chicago, I gave her a Celtic Cross reading. A lantern beamed from the spread's Outer position. Who but the Hermit could have depicted so eloquently both her trailing of the past and her questioning about what lay ahead?

The other particularly affecting card was the Ten of Pentacles in Hopes and Fears. The card represented her desire to find a place for herself in Karen's family as a way of feeling closer to the woman she had loved. But in reality, the family did not recognize the relationship between the two women. "I felt invisible at the funeral," Kathy says. "In their orbit, I didn't exist."

In the Ten of Pentacles' white-bearded figure, I saw Kathy the outsider hovering unacknowledged. The image underscored what Kathy's inner sage already understood: Karen's family considered themselves to be "Members Only."

Ten of Pentacles Attributes

Key word:	Inheritance
Being:	Secure, traditional, conservative, wealthy, ensconced in a stable system or environment, status-minded; a club member
Doing:	Profiting handsomely; drawing from trust funds; receiving a pension or inheritance; participating in socially sanctioned activities; fulfilling a traditional role; ensuring the longevity of a property, position, or institution
Shadow:	Elitism, ethnocentrism; fitting in at any cost
Reversed:	Feeling disenfranchised, being disinherited, having a shaky financial foundation, being outside the system, being unconventional; scandals in family, church, business, or government
	Possible Advice
Reversed:	"This affiliation doesn't suit you." "Norms be damned—be unconventional."

Page of Pentacles

*Your work is to discover your work and then with all
your heart give yourself to it.*

—Buddha

The Page of Pentacles shows us a young person discovering and appreciating the physical realm. How delicately he holds the Pentacle, as if it were a bird alighting there or something praiseworthy plucked from the greenery underfoot. The Page is enthralled with the world around him. He wants to know the nature of things, how life works.

"What shall I make of this?" the Page seems to ask, observing the Pentacle. While all the Pages are eager to learn, this one does best when he knows he will be able to apply knowledge in tangible ways. Once convinced of an endeavor's practical, material, or aesthetic value, the Page invests in it. The Page of Pentacles follows courses of study through which he can hone a bankable skill, a healthier body, or a beautiful craft.

On the other side of the coin, the Page does not always pursue the obvious payoff. He may pour himself into the study of zebras or the history of the steam engine, simply because these things interest him. To the Page of Pentacles, all knowledge is valuable if it helps broaden his understanding of the world.

A Page of Pentacles Story

"Where am I in my life right now?" asked Casey, randomly pulling the Page of Pentacles from her deck. Though the twenty-six-year-old Tarot student admitted she had previously found the card boring, it took on new relevance in light of her question. Most evident was the correlation between the Page's role as a learner and her own anticipation of entering law school—a generous gift from her parents. In the Pentacle itself she saw the golden opportunity that had been placed in her hands, the realization of a long-held dream. Even the height at which the Page holds the Pentacle triggered Casey's association with the lofty expectations she held for her education.

Casey continued to gaze at the card for a few silent moments. "Okay," she concluded, "I guess the card's not so boring!"

Page of Pentacles Attributes

Key word:	Interest
Being:	Studious, patient, curious, eager to learn something useful
Doing:	Apprenticing, learning by doing, setting practical goals, exploring opportunities that pay off, discovering latent skills, starting a health-improvement program
Shadow:	Pursuing purely practical avenues to the exclusion of emotional or spiritual needs
Reversed:	Inability or unwillingness to pursue study or opportunity, doubt about the value of something; moving beyond the Page stage
	Possible Advice
Reversed:	"Follow a more productive or lucrative course." "Reconsider the value of this endeavor."

Knight of Pentacles

Duty is carrying on promptly and faithfully the affairs now before you.
—Goethe

Have you ever said with conviction, "If I want the job done right, I'd better do it myself"? Turned down a party invitation because you had a school assignment to complete or a bathroom to clean? Worked more than one job at a time to meet financial goals? If so, you've met your Knight of Pentacles.

There are Knights who are more exciting and romantic, but none as solidly dependable. Here is the good soldier, Mr. Fix-it, the worker bee. He is the farmer working tirelessly under the sun, measuring the success of each day by the quality of his output. Where it took enthusiasm, romance, and righteousness to incite the other Knights to action, the Knight of Pentacles requires only necessity and reasonable rewards. Task-oriented and highly disciplined, he puts nose to grindstone because it's got to be done. Period.

No-nonsense though he is, the Knight works best with a little inspiration. Rich, furrowed fields roll below him; a burst of greenery crowns his helmet. His commitment is greatest when he knows that his efforts yield growth and that others are counting on him. He looks above, not at, the Pentacle, for his focus is not on ideals but on the real nuts-and-bolts work the suit calls him to do.

The sober Knight's impressively grounded approach explains the stillness of both horse and rider. One gets the sense that he makes

275

no move without methodically evaluating its usefulness, efficiency, and safety. When it comes to money, he is the sensible shopper in search of the best values, or the person hunting for secure and steady work.

Taken to extremes, the Knight becomes so busy carrying out his duties that he loses sight of deeper needs. He becomes his own task-master, a victim of overresponsibility. When life gets reduced to a time clock or productivity chart, the Knight needs to get off his horse kick off his boots, and feel the soil between his toes—advice that would be heartily endorsed by the Queen of his suit.

A Knight of Pentacles Story

My sister, Jan, and I sat in her backyard admiring our cleanup efforts from her fiftieth-birthday bash the night before. Given the very full week of pre-party shopping and preparations, it was the first time we had been able to just sit and relax. She asked for a Tarot reading, which featured the Knight of Pentacles as her "energy to focus on."

In his solid, steady way, the Knight advised Jan to recover from the week's excitement and get back on track—return the rental equipment, pay the party bills, and diligently resume her work schedule, and normal diet. Jan sighed at my description of the Knight's grounding mission. "This week has been great," she said, "but the card is right on—I'm eager to get back to my routine." For the next few days I made a point to consume as much of the rich party leftovers as I could, so that Jan could at least return to her healthy eating patterns. That's just the kind of brother I am.

Knight of Pentacles Attributes

Key word:	Duty
Being:	Unhurried, practical, purposeful, productive, predictable, reliable, duty bound, self-sacrificing, stubborn, cautious
Doing:	Fulfilling obligations, offering assistance in practical matters, seeing projects to completion, acquiring or offering money and security; job or house hunting
Shadow:	Inflexibility, overresponsibility, work addiction, resigned to drudgery
Reversed:	Avoiding responsibility or, conversely, taking a less pragmatic, more inspired approach to work
	Possible Advice
Reversed:	"Pursue this with more joy and less obligation." "The workhorse needs time off."

Queen of Pentacles

To be rooted is perhaps the most important and least recognized need of the human soul.

—Simone Weil

The Queen of Pentacles feels a profound appreciation for Earth: its ordinary wonders, the endless pleasures it brings to the senses. Her influence is felt in those moments when the beauty of the natural world calms the mind and revitalizes the spirit. The Queen holds all of life—and the Pentacle symbolizing life's physical blessings—with a maternal reverence, ever mindful that what is cherished must be cared for. She is the soul of Earth in all its enchantment and in all its dusty realism.

The Queen of Pentacles enjoys the most picturesque of the views depicted on the Court cards. But the surrounding water, sky, trees, animals, and mountains exist not merely as backdrops; she feels herself to be warmly in relationship with them. A deep-green cowl cascades from her crown to the ground. She feels at home in Nature and takes inspiration from it. The pear motif on the throne relates to the sensuousness of the feminine energy she embodies. As did the lady in the Nine of Pentacles, the Queen emanates the sexual and financial fertility of the

Empress—a point underscored by the appearance of the rabbit.

The Queen's red gown and shoes represent her active participation in the grounding energies of Earth. She is that part of us that revels in the rhythms of gardening, cooking, craft-making, massaging, being massaged, and virtually every physical sensation that leaves us feeling contented and whole. She is our love of comfort and our taste for luxury, even if the latter is pursued with the Queen's eye on frugality. The goat head on her throne alludes to Capricorn, an Earth sign associated with faithfulness and pragmatism.

True to her suit, the Queen puts a high value on stability. Her cautious, conservative bent leads her to thrive among the familiar. The Queen reigns within the couple that prefers a quiet night at home to going out on the town, the business traveler who never packs a bag without his comfy slippers, and the club member who works hardest at preserving the group's traditions.

A creature of habit, the Queen finds fulfillment in the small daily rituals that provide a sense of continuity, safety, and well-being. She is the inexpressible satisfaction that comes in the quiet hours when the house is locked for the evening, the dishes washed, and the children safely to bed. On the other side of the coin, her dependency upon routine can make her fearful of change.

Above all, the Queen has a nurturing way. Her purse and home open to friends in need.

She is a rock to many, offering wise, homespun advice that puts emotionally uprooted folks back on their feet. In her comforting embrace, the world seems a safer place.

A Queen of Pentacles Story

Tarot student Jeremy wondered about pursuing a relationship with Dirk, a man who had failed to provide a good excuse for missing the lavish home-cooked meal Jeremy had prepared for their second date. He called on his Inner Match Maker and asked, "What is the greatest good of offering Dirk a rain check?" (read: "Should I dump this guy?"). He grimaced as he pulled the Queen of Pentacles, reversed. Dirk, as the rescinded hospitality of the upside-down Queen made clear, was not worthy to sit at Jeremy's table. The other students and I quickly assured him that we, unlike ungrateful Dirk, would never snub such an invitation. Two weeks later, we raised our glasses before a wonderful meal at Jeremy's place, toasting our wishes for the fulfillment of his love life.

Queen of Pentacles Attributes

Key word:	Domesticity
Being:	Warm, peaceful, homespun, hospitable, earthy, nurturing, sensual, faithful, worldly-wise, security-minded, efficient

Doing:	Nurturing the qualities of Earth in yourself or others, communing with Nature, nesting, preserving traditions or the environment, fostering a sense of calm, enjoying conveniences, enjoying crafts and hobbies, cooking, savoring beauty, taking care of health and home
Shadow:	Resistance to risk or change, inability to engage the world beyond home or family
Reversed:	Feeling uprooted and off-center, withholding hospitality; disruptions in routine, health issues

Possible Advice

Reversed:	"Get out of the house more."
	"Ask for help in running the household."

King of Pentacles

A prince wants only the pleasures of private life to complete his happiness.
—Jean de la Bruyère

The King of Pentacles contemplates his material success from a throne of solid black. He has learned a thing or two about turning a profit. Hard work, patience, good instincts—and occasional stubbornness—have paid off handsomely. Even his gown boasts his prodigious fruitfulness. Adept at creating abundance, he is rightful King of his suit. His crown sprouts roses and lilies, the same flowers observed in the garden of the original master of manifestation, the Magician.

The King holds the scepter of the Empress. But where the Empress held it above her head to signify the divinity of Nature, the King holds it lower, designating the things of Earth under his disciplined control. Though he is expert at gainfully harnessing

280

natural and human resources, his armored foot straddling the stone boar suggests the possibility of a dominating attitude toward these things. Whereas the soulful Queen of Pentacles felt in partnership with Nature, the King may see it as something to control, buy, and sell.

The bull heads connect him to Taurus, the security-loving astrological sign. His armored boot, heavy cloak, and stone fortress make him the most protected of the Kings. The risks he takes, though few, are carefully measured. His caution slows up his decision making, but when he acts, the delay often proves to have been wise. However vigilantly he protects his assets, the King has a taste for the finer things in life. He wants the best that he can comfortably afford, and he willingly pays top dollar as long as he is convinced of a thing's value.

The character of the King is personified in successful investors or business persons, accountants, bankers, and those whose personal or professional situations require a disciplined eye on the bottom line. The King may also be the contented retiree with money in the bank, an active golf-club membership, and a reputation as a big tipper at all the best restaurants. He enjoys the rewards and symbols of status and gives generously to those charities able to prove their fiscal responsibility.

Lastly, the essence of the King extends beyond his financial abundance. He can be a person of modest means, but with great worldly experience who shares what he has learned for the functional benefit of others. He might be a master of a skill or trade or a teacher in a technical school. At his least formal, the King is that always-sensible friend who gives us golden advice about money, though he wouldn't take a penny for it.

A King of Pentacles Story

Katie swore that the King of Pentacles never once appeared in a reading she did for herself—and she'd been reading the cards for seven years. "He probably figured he had nothing to say to a forty-two-year-old bookstore clerk who makes under twenty-five thousand dollars a year!" said Katie, laughing. "I mean, what's the point?"

So when the King had recently shown up in a reading, Katie took note. The card was the Higher-Self Advice about her finances. To Katie, it made perfect sense.

"I'm tired of living hand-to-mouth," she said. "With my Buddhist leanings, I'd always had this idea that security and material possessions were just illusions, so I downplayed their importance. But I'm not twenty-two anymore. I want to be able to buy beautiful clothes and go out to dinner and see shows and not have to budget every single dime. I really want to change my relationship with money and find a better source of income, and the King was my soul's way of saying 'Yes, Katie, it's time.'"

King of Pentacles Attributes

Key word:	Security
Being:	Successful, traditional, financially secure, conservative, emotionally stable, patient, generous, stubborn; a benefactor; a master tradesperson, CEO, or physician
Doing:	Attracting wealth, bargaining from strength positions, managing money effectively, maintaining a well-run business or property, enjoying retirement, giving charitably, indulging a taste for the finer things in life

Shadow: Resistance to change, lethargy, overattachment to
              possessions, fear of losing wealth or status

Reversed: Problems related to home or real estate, poor money
              management, bad investments, lost revenue

              Possible Advice
Reversed: "Don't get too set in your ways—welcome change and
              innovation."
              "Reconsider this investment."

Part Four

Reading the Cards

God speaks to us as softly as he can and as loudly as he has to.
—Rafi Zabor

Intimate Conversations:
Reading for Yourself

There is only one journey. Going inside yourself.
—Rainer Maria Rilke

*D*oing readings for yourself is like having a heart-to-heart dialogue with up to seventy-eight parts of yourself. In fact, the same cards will sometimes come back to converse again and again. My friend Ben went through a period where the mournful Five of Cups showed up in nearly every reading he did for himself. When the persistent card even popped up in answer to his question, "What energy should I bring to my social life?" he was ready to yank it permanently from the deck!

Whether repetitively appearing cards vex or comfort us, like recurring dreams they are trying to get our attention. The beauty of the Tarot is that we can use it as a tool for consciously grasping the messages sent from the unconscious—the Magician acting in concert with the High Priestess. The better we know and trust ourselves, the greater the clarity of our solo readings.

Nevertheless, reading for yourself can be challenging. Fixed attitudes about the issue in question may blind you to the cards' true message. Fear of misreading a card may constipate your intuition. If you are highly self-critical, you are apt to exaggerate the negative aspects of the spread. While it is ultimately for our benefit to *work through* these obstacles—becoming clearer channels to soul and Source—sometimes the best thing we can do is take a walk outdoors and come back to it later. Or walk away from it altogether.

The biggest obstacle to getting a clear reading is anxiety about the question. Once, while heading downstairs on my way to the airport, I missed a step and watched my ankle bend at a nasty angle. The pain paled in comparison to worries that my injury might prevent me from enjoying my eagerly awaited conference in Minneapolis. Even worse, if I *did* make the trip, I might need to find a doctor, get X-rays, or God forbid, a cast—any of which would present a major logistical hassle so far from home.

To my relief, I was able to make my way back upstairs with only an occasional wince. I grabbed an ice pack and, with only minutes to decide whether I should risk making the trip, pulled out my cards. Self-pity, the nearing flight departure, and mounting frustration at the almost certain self-sabotage of my mishap made it difficult to concentrate. With life-or-death intensity I asked, "What does my spirit say about going to Minneapolis with my foot in this condition?" The triumphant Six of Wands turned up—reversed. I snapped the cards back into their container.

"I'm not going," I announced stoically to my partner, Rich. "You'll be fine, Paul," he said. "You're able to walk on it, right? Just keep ice on it again when you get to the hotel. You'll be sitting during the majority of the conference anyway." Fortunately, my intuition told me to follow his advice, not my fear. I wound up having a wonderful time with full mobility and only intermittent aches.

The moral to the story is, if you're all worked up about the question, don't read the cards. If you went to a reader who was as agitated about your question as you were, you'd head for the exit doors. Anxiety is a psychic block. At sharp enough levels it can create a negative attraction in the reading, causing cards to appear that completely distort the truth of the situation and have you believing the worst. Therefore, it is best to create a measure of High Priestess-like detachment from the issue before you attempt the reading, even for questions that don't raise your pulse. Allow yourself to become curious without getting overly serious.

When *Not* to Read for Yourself

To love oneself is the beginning of a life-long romance.
—Oscar Wilde

Tarot readings demand mindful presence. If you feel tired or scattered, you probably lack the energy and concentration to be a clear channel for your reading, let alone apprehend its meaning. Don't do a reading for yourself if you're feeling spacey or if:

You're down on yourself. Anger, worry, or periods of low self-esteem compound the tendency to find the worst in your reading (and therefore in yourself). Act as if you were reading for someone you love. If emotions make this difficult, wait until you're feeling more generous toward yourself before you pick up the cards.

You're obsessed. If you don't agree with the cards you get, doing multiple readings in hope of "better" answers will only intensify your turmoil. If you have a strong attachment to seeing the reading turn out in a certain way, have someone else read for you.

289

To Be or Not to Be: Tarot and Prediction

What lies before us and what lies behind us are small matters
compared to what lies within us.
—Ralph Waldo Emerson

Fifteen hundred years ago St. Augustine wrote: "God will not permit man to have knowledge of things to come; for if man had a foresight of his prosperity, he would become arrogant and careless; and if he had an understanding of his adversity, he would become listless and despairing."

I disagree—in part. God does permit such foreknowledge, a fact apparent to anyone who has ever had a prophetic dream, spot-on clairvoyant reading, or uncanny Tarot prediction. However, I agree with St. Augustine's point about the disruptive affects of seeing what's in store for us tomorrow. As soon as we believe something is inevitable, we relinquish our sacred power to create our own destiny. If the prediction is negative, we invite doubt, worry, and anxiety. And with our thoughts focused on a fearful future, we, by virtue of the Universal Law of Attraction, greatly increase the likelihood of its coming about. Even if we dismiss the prediction as being improbable, the power of the suggestion may affect us adversely on an unconscious level.

A positive prediction can also have a disempowering effect. Rosy readings about the future have the potential to press our psychic snooze button. Believing the job we'll be applying for is already "in the bag"—because the cards told us so—may rob us of the edge needed to ace the interview. Banking on the accuracy of a Tarot reading that shows a financial windfall "just around the corner" may encourage an overconfidence that makes us careless with the money we have today—and leave us in despair if the reading proves a dud.

Still, intuitively peeking at the future is not "wrong." Mindfully approached, it can assist us in our growth path. If a card shows you a desired outcome, you can choose to see it as a validation of your current efforts and consciously use the image to further magnetize that outcome to you. If a card shows a disastrous finish, you can examine how—by your expectations or actions—you might be setting yourself up for it and take steps to avoid it. If you feel the undesirable outcome is not within your power to control (such as your employer's company going out of business), you can prepare yourself to enter that reality with full awareness and acceptance. We cannot always change what is or what will be, but we can choose how we will respond to it.

A disappointing Outcome card may be the soul's way of saying, "Yes, but not now," or, "No, and for reasons you'll appreciate later." At such times, these factors may be well beyond our capacity to comprehend and can drive us crazy if we try. Considering that the archetype associated with the future is the capricious Wheel of Fortune, we are wise to stay light and loose in our response to predictions.

Another argument for viewing the future with detachment is that oracles are so often ambiguous. In ancient Greece, the psychic priestess known as the Oracle of Delphi informed King Croesus of Lydia that if he stuck to his plan and attacked Persia he would "destroy a great empire." The emboldened Croesus carried out the attack, never considering that the doomed empire would prove to be his own.

The Croesus factor was evident in my reading with my friend Meribeth, an accomplished choreographer who eagerly awaited news of a possible graduate school scholarship. The Outcome card in her Celtic Cross spread was the beneficent Six of Pentacles. As it turned out, the card was accurate—money was generously dispensed—but it was Meribeth who forked it over. Not only did she not receive the scholarship, she wound up having to postpone her schooling and use her finances to assist her mother, who had suddenly taken ill.

In a world of wonder, there are few guarantees. Things can change, and do. Unless a future-oriented Tarot card evokes in us an intuitively unshakable recognition or a jolt of genuine precognition, the best response to spreads with predictive messages is a respectful "Thank you for sharing." We can then use the information gleaned to examine mindfully the choices we are making that may have prompted the unconscious to show us that particular scenario.

If we like what the spread shows us, we can more consciously affirm it in our thoughts and actions. If we do not like what we see, we can do what we can to change it, prepare ourselves to accept it, or decide to live fully in the present and not get hung up about it.

Ultimately, it may be for our greater good that the futures indicated in readings are ambiguous and unreliable. Even without predictive readings, many of us already live too much in the future. Unable to accept the present moment, we wonder and worry what tomorrow, next week, or next year will bring, what-if-ing our way through life.

Yet, the power that the Tarot—and all the great mystical philosophies—implores us to claim is the irreplaceable, always available, spiritually potent *now*. As we learn to live more in harmony with our Inner Being, the need to know the future becomes less compelling. We find peace, and our greatest potential, in each moment.

Preparing for Readings

What in me is dark illumine, what is low raise and support.
—John Milton

The Oracle of Delphi performed an elaborate series of invocations, meditations, prayers, and burnt offerings to become a worthy and open channel to the messages of the gods. Given the naturalness and ease with which people today are learning to tap into intuitive guidance, such ceremonial formalities seem extreme. At the other extreme, consulting the cards gets cheapened when approached with the same casualness as, say, reading one's e-mail.

Cultivating an attitude of reverence moves the reading from the mundane into the numinous. Like the Delphic Oracle, mindfully preparing for guidance preserves divine mystery, quiets the mind, and sharpens attunement. Below are some suggestions to help make your readings more than yet another download.

Card Care

The cards are your soul tools—ones you may wind up using for many years. Store them in a bag or box that feels special. Some surfaces you'll work on may be slippery or dirty; protect your cards by laying them on a silk or cotton cloth.

Environment

Find a peaceful space. Many people do readings in front of homemade altars or on the floor of a favorite room of the house. Other readers take their cards to the kitchen table, where nourishing vibes may already thrive. Whatever the place you choose, de-clutter it. Clear space invites clear mind and enhances your receptivity. Turn off the TV, radio, cell phone, or other potential distractions.

If you are drawn to ritual, consider using candles, crystals, scents, religious figurines, or music to enhance the feeling of the sacred. Such items visually support your intention to create a welcoming space for guidance. Consistency with your ritual will help you access the receptive state more readily each time.

Clear Intention

Write down your question, no matter how simple it may be. Unless you do, you risk forgetting how you phrased it. There is a dramatic difference, for example, between asking, "What energy will support me in today's meeting?" (prescriptive) and "What *is* the energy of today's meeting?" (descriptive). If you forget to write down your question and then discover, while looking at the cards laid out before you, that you are hazy about what you specifically asked, clarify the question, write it down, and reshuffle. If you proceed without doing so, you risk walking away with a false understanding of the divinatory message intended.

Breath

Breathe deeply through your nose before you begin. As you inhale, imagine your body and the area immediately surrounding you filling with white light. Exhale with an audible "Aaahhhh," picturing any anxiety or tension leaving your body and dissolving in the white light. Do this at least three times, gently increasing the depth of each breath.

Invocations

Before or during your shuffle, set a sincere, receptive tone for the reading. Offer a prayer, state an affirmation, or invoke guidance from a higher plane of consciousness. I have provided some examples:

I calmly set aside any fears, worries, and desires for a specific outcome in this matter and open to the wisdom of my highest and deepest Source.

Holy Spirit, rearrange my perceptions. Let me see this situation through divine eyes.

As I do this reading, I become a clear channel to my expanded being, receiving only information that is for my greatest good and therefore for the greatest good of all.

I invite my Highest Self (guides, angels, healers, etc.) and all loving energies who have at heart my greatest good to be part of this reading, to offer insight and guidance.

Okay, Angel Committee, talk to me! I need some insight and direction.

Shuffling the Cards

As with any Tarot ritual, how you choose to shuffle the cards is a matter of personal choice. One method involves scrambling the deck face down, fanning it out, and allowing your intuition to direct you to pull the cards. Many people who prefer this approach use their nondominant hand, symbolic of the unconscious, to pull the cards to which they feel drawn. If you prefer a messier approach, consider the "Chaos" shuffle described next.

1. Spread the deck face down on a clean surface or cloth. Using both hands, scramble the cards around in wide swirls as if you were finger painting. This ensures a nice, random combination of cards in upright and reversed positions.

Keep your focus positive as you shuffle. Affirm and expect clear guidance. Sometimes the mindfulness you experience while shuffling will trigger the intuitive "Aha" you're looking for before you even lay out the cards. There will be times, too, when a card literally pops out of the deck as you shuffle. Make note of the card before putting it back in the deck. Don't be surprised if you find that the card figures significantly in your question or reappears in your spread.

2. Once the shuffling feels done, begin to bring the cards together by gathering no more than one to three cards at a time until you're holding a single, solid deck. Always keep the deck in the same position as it was when you stacked it; if you or the person you're reading for inadvertently reverses the position of the shuffled deck, it may throw off the accuracy of the reading.

3. Pull as many cards from the top as are required for the particular spread and lay them into the designated positions. Flip the cards over from right to left like the page of a book. However, if you prefer to flip them over from top to bottom or from bottom to top, be sure you do so consistently in each reading. .

Whichever shuffling method you choose, take your time with it. We spend so much of our days hurrying, the act of shuffling the cards is often our first opportunity to slow down and center ourselves.

Less Is More:
Keeping It Simple

Out of clutter, find simplicity.
—Albert Einstein

ccasionally, I see books featuring spreads crammed with questions that demand—in a single layout—"What do I want? What do I *really* want? How will I feel if I get what I want? How will I feel if I *don't* get what I want? What should I do if I don't get it?" and so on. Obsessive spreads like these leave me gasping for breath. They cater to the most controlling and fearful impulses of the ego.

Using the Tarot to micromanage every facet of a situation undermines the fundamental trust in guidance that divination invites. As a firm believer in the keep-it-simple approach, I find that a good, well-worded question can be answered with breathtaking clarity with one or two cards. For example, a friend once asked, "How can I meet the right guy for me?" She pulled two cards. The first was the Four of Swords, reversed. This inverted card told my introverted friend she needed to get out more. The second card, the Queen of Wands, advised her to claim and express her natural warmth, confidence, and sexual magnetism—qualities she had unconsciously put into storage following a previous, unsuccessful relationship.

There are no rules governing the number of questions for readings. I find, however, that the busier spreads are not necessarily more illuminating. Just as clutter in a sacred space is distracting, so is an excess of cards in a spread when a few will do. Ultimately, what gives a reading impact is the power of the question, not the number of cards. To honor tradition, though, here I will move from "more" to "less" and begin with the classic ten-card spread.

Mastering a Standard: The Celtic Cross

We are the hero of our own story.
—Mary McCarthy

The Celtic Cross has been popular ever since it appeared in Arthur Edward Waite's *The Pictorial Key to the Tarot* in 1910. Although there are many variations on the spread, all of them provide a template for looking at a single issue or question from ten perspectives. It presents the Big Picture of a situation.

The spread works particularly well for readings in which the person for whom you're giving a reading does not want to reveal the issue in question but is eager to see if the cards pick up on it. In this case, all you need to do is shuffle the cards, lay them out into the Celtic Cross, and see what comes up.

The Celtic Cross is also the spread of choice when you or your querent have no specific question, but would just like to check in and see what's up at the moment. At such times you may simply want to ask:

What area of my life wants my attention at this time?

The preceding is an example of an "open" question. By asking open questions you invite your inner guidance to determine the topic. If you do have a particular area of your life that you're curious about, consider narrowing the question to:

What are the energies surrounding, or factors affecting,

my _____?

    relationship

    work

    studies

    family

    health

    spiritual development

    business venture

    dreams or goals

    special occasion or event

With a little creativity, you can also use the Celtic Cross for readings that go beyond the personal. The spread can accommodate questions that address collective expressions of consciousness—organizations, industries, communities, nations, and the world itself. Some sample questions:

How is the company handling the reorganization?

What is going on in the health-care industry today?

What is the picture of the United States at the moment?

Although any broad topic is suitable for the Celtic Cross, avoid closed-ended questions such as yes/no, or overly specific questions such as, "What skills do I need for employment in the aerospace industry?" If the resulting spread raises additional questions, you can always follow up with a spread configured for more targeted questions (see Create Your Own Spread, page 310).

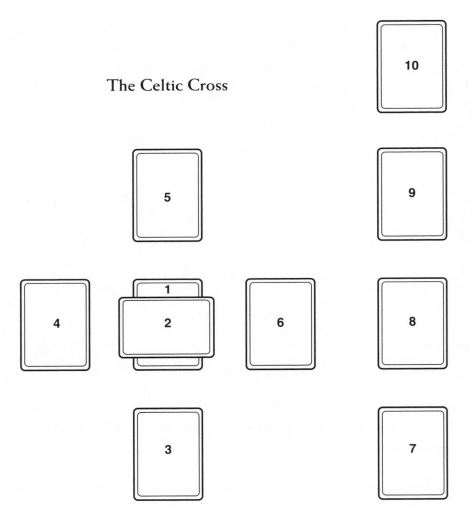

The Celtic Cross

1. *Inner.* This is a picture of your internal experience of the situation in question. *How does the issue affect you? What are your feelings about it? Do you contain or express these feelings?*

2. *Outer.* This is your outward experience of the situation. It shows the people, conditions, or energies that are in conflict or in concert with your inner experience. *What central theme do the Inner and Outer cards suggest? Do they complement or contradict one another?*

3. *Past*. This position shows the roots of the present situation or a particular person or event that figured importantly in its origin. It may also show the expectations you initially brought into the situation. *How might your experience in the past be affecting the situation today? What foundation has the present been built upon? How has it evolved?*

4. *Recent Influences*. This depicts a very recent (last few hours, days, or weeks) attitude, experience, or action relevant to your situation. Sometimes it indicates the recent influence or actions of another person. *How are recent events affecting your current feelings and choices?*

5. *Higher-Self Advice*. The only card of advice in the Celtic Cross, it shows the path toward which your Inner Wisdom is guiding you in the matter. *What is your inner guidance directing you to know, do, or become in this situation? How does the advice confirm what you already know or feel? How receptive are you to acting on this advice?*

6. *Near Future*. This indicates a probable next stage of the issue— an upcoming challenge, opportunity, or partial completion. *Does your Near Future card surprise you . . . or does it confirm your expectations about where things are heading?*

7. *Self-Image*. This is how you see yourself in relation to the issue. Cards in this position usually support or complement the card shown in the Inner position. *What role do you see yourself playing in this situation? Does your self-image support or hinder you in this matter?*

8. *Environment*. This card shows the environmental influences of the issue—the home, workplace, institution, social structure, or person that plays a key role in the situation. *What larger factors have an impact on the situation? Who are the key people or environmental influences that thwart or support your efforts?*

9. *Hopes and Fears*. The card in this position may show you a hope, such as health, or a fear, such as financial ruin. Yet the position is called Hopes *and* Fears because they sometimes intertwine. Our hopes and fears merge when we wish to marry, yet fear the loss of the single life, or when we seek a job promotion and worry over the

added responsibilities. The card may also show us our unconscious expectations, which, to our benefit or detriment, can strongly determine the result of the outcome. *How might your hopes and fears about this issue affect the possible outcome? How are your hopes or fears determined by the past of the situation? By your self-image?*

10. *Possible Outcome.* This gives an idea of how the situation is likely to result given factors both in and out of your conscious control. The Possible Outcome card may indicate quantifiable events such as weddings, births, and graduations. More often, it shows not a definitive conclusion but a state of being that may or may not reflect a change from the present.

If you are not pleased with the possible outcome, how might you attempt to alter it? What other cards in the layout show how you may be moving toward this result? How does the Higher-Self Advice card offer support?

Interpreting the Celtic Cross

Here are some guidelines to help you understand the message mapped out before you:

1. As soon as the cards are laid into the spread, tune into your feelings. What overall mood or story does the spread convey? Do the cards give you a feeling of heaviness or lightness? Movement or inertia? Notice how this initial glance affects you.

2. Which suits are represented? Generally, Wands signify the energies of excitement and enterprise; Cups, relationships and feelings; Swords, conflict and struggle; Pentacles, work and stability. Does one suit dominate the spread? Which, if any, is missing entirely?

3. What is the ratio of Major to Minor Arcana? A prevalence of Major Arcana may call attention to universal themes, soul-level

issues, and karmic lessons. Spreads with mostly Minor Arcana may reflect more ordinary situations.

4. Are the majority of cards upright or reversed? Reversed cards are not "bad," but a preponderance of them can indicate greater personal struggle than when they are in the upright position.

5. What numbers repeat? In their upright positions the Nine of Wands, Cups, and Pentacles, for example, could emphasize accomplishment.

6. What general theme is apparent in the spread? Victory? Love? Loss? Doubt? What story seems to be unfolding? What pattern is suggested in the relationships among the cards?

There may be times when the results of an open reading (such as, "What's going on with me right now?") seem to cover more than one area of your life. You may be unable to decide if the cards are talking about your recent dabbling in oil painting or your visit with the Dalai Lama. Consider that the reading may be showing you both. Parallel themes emerge when there are similar patterns of energy expressing in different areas of your life.

If you're stumped by one or more cards that don't seem related to the overall theme in the layout, avoid force-fitting their meaning. For example, if seven cards in the spread are clearly about a friend's betrayal, the other three will not arbitrarily represent an auto purchase, a Peruvian vacation, and an upcoming dental appointment—unless these all relate directly to the betrayal.

In most cases, the Celtic Cross layout organizes our awareness by directing it to one specific area of our lives. A spread about a health concern may show, for instance, how one's work, family, studies, or relationships influence, and are influenced, by the health issue. The continuity is intact. No matter which cards pop up in your spread, they will each address a facet of the same central issue, rather than send you chasing random tangents.

Celtic Cross Example: Annette

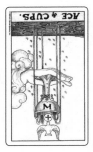

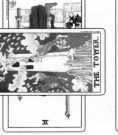

Note: Before you place a card in the crossed Outer position (as in the Tower card shown above), notice whether it is upright or reversed.

Annette is a married woman in her mid-fifties. Her Inner state was represented by the Two of Wands, reversed, which showed her actively pursuing something longed for. "I met a former lover at my high school reunion," she said. "We've started things up again."

"What are you trying to keep from falling apart?" I asked her, pointing to the Tower, reversed, in the Outer position. "Everything," she answered. In addition to masterminding colossal efforts at home not to blow her cover, she was being pressured by her lover to get a divorce.

The Six of Swords in her Past position captured the just-floating-on-the-surface quality of her thirty-eight-year marriage. In contrast, the affair had given her a profound sense of renewal, as the presence of Judgment in her Recent Influences indicated. Yet by showing her the Ace of Cups, reversed, her Higher Self advised against offering or accepting the chance for renewing the relationship.

The Moon reversed in her Near Future position showed what would become her continued efforts to resist the intense emotional tides that threatened to pull her under. In an attempt to cope, she found herself emotionally pulling away even further from her husband, an attitude personified by the reversed Queen of Cups in the Self-Image position. The reversed Ace of Swords attested to the absence of truthful communication in her Environment.

The reversed Sun in Hopes and Fears told of her lack of optimism for a satisfying outcome with either man. And with the reversed Knight of Swords as her Possible Outcome, it was plain that she would neither confront her husband with the truth nor her lover with her resentment of his demands that she leave the marriage.

The stress of keeping up the deception and appeasing her lover threatened to bring Annette, and both of her relationships, to the breaking point. I expressed my concern that the Tower and Moon—two powerful, unconscious forces—were, in their reversed positions, evidence of nearly superhuman suppression on her part. As hard as she tried to prevent it, a collapse of some sort was inevitable.

Chakra Check-in Spread

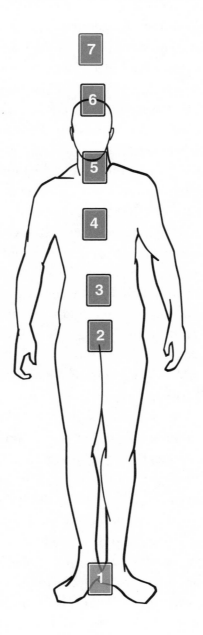

The chakras are seven areas of psychospiritual energy that vibrate in response to the patterns of our thinking, emotions, and behaviors. As such, they are dynamic, not fixed; they contract and expand in sync with the contraction and expansion of consciousness. The degree to which the chakras are open or closed, balanced or imbalanced, is a barometer of how your energy is flowing.

Draw the outline of your body on a piece of paper, or lie on a large sheet of art paper and have a friend trace your life-sized body outline onto it. Draw the card positions onto your body outline as they appear in the diagram. Shuffle the cards. Lay out each card from bottom (feet/root) to top (head/crown).

Rather than ask specific questions for this spread, simply collect your impressions about what the cards may be telling you about how you're managing your energy, chakra by chakra. Use the table in appendix D to become familiar with the characteristics of each chakra. For an in-depth look at the subject, I recommend Anodea Judith's *Eastern Body, Western Mind: Psychology and the Chakra System*.

Solution Spread

When in doubt, do the right thing.
—Anonymous

In this simple spread for finding a possible solution, consider your relationship to the image appearing in the Problem card.

Background   **Problem**   **Solution**

Spread for Yes/No Questions

Nothing is more difficult, and therefore more precious, than to be able to decide.
—Napoléon Bonaparte

The Tarot can be an effective aid in making quick decisions. For "yes/no" questions, pull one card from the deck. Ignore the card itself and consider only its position. An upright card signifies "Yes"; reversed, "No." The hastiness of this method lends itself to the kind of questions you could decide with a coin toss, such as, "Is Saturday best for Bingo?" For issues of greater consequence, consider a more substantive spread.

Exploring Options

It's when we're given a choice that we sit with the gods and design ourselves.
—Dorothy Gilman

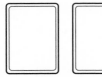
Benefits of Option A

Benefits of Option B

Benefits of Option C

Essential for All Options

When the stakes are high, you may wish to gain some insight by exploring the various, specific options under consideration. Ask,

"What are the benefits of each option?" and you will have more to base a decision on than a mere yes or no. If you seek further input on the matter, follow up with more targeted questions.

Spreads for Soul Questions

Our subconscious mind remains the path to divine archives that are in touch with all that ever is.

—Jan Harris

Soul questions are the take-a-deep-breath questions that probe the nature of your purpose and spiritual progress. A period of quiet contemplation or meditation is suggested before doing a reading on these questions, though somberness is neither required nor useful. When I facilitate these readings in my classes, there are often peals of laughter at the surprising cards that come up. I recommend you not attempt all four readings within one sitting; one reading will give you plenty to reflect upon. If you feel led to draw more than one card for a particular question, do so.

Life Journey Spread

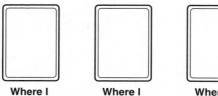

| Where I
Have Been | Where I
Am Now | Where I
Am Going |

Let Go/Grow Spread

What I Am Called to Let Go **What I Am Called to Grow**

Gift Spread

What I Have to Give the World **What I Am Open to Receive**

Past-Life Spread

What Past-Life Issues May Be Current Today?

Create Your Own Spread

It is better to know some of the questions, than all of the answers.
—Mark Twain

Write down your questions and, before you shuffle, intuitively decide how many cards you'll draw for the responses. For example, you may feel that one card will be sufficient to answer the question, "What is the energy to bring to the relationship?" but that three are needed for, "What are my motives in pursuing this relationship?" Your unconscious guidance will cooperate with whatever layout you create—but it needs a layout to know which cards to place where. As you pull each card, place it into the space you've assigned for it.

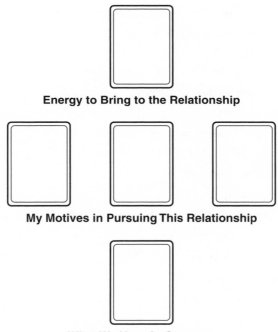

Energy to Bring to the Relationship

My Motives in Pursuing This Relationship

What We Have in Common

When it comes to creating your own spreads, you may find that many of your questions can be drawn (with a little customizing) from the ones listed below. Where the word *it* appears, substitute *situation* or *relationship* as your question requires. Each of these questions can be used alone or in combination with others. Decide how many cards you'll draw in response to each question.

What is the nature of it?

What was it before?

What created it?

What beliefs feed it?

Where is it heading?

What is its potential for (happiness, creativity, financial success, intimacy, etc.)?

What is its purpose?

How do I feel about it?

What energy do/should I bring to it?

What value do I/others bring to it?

What do I want/need from it?

What does it want/need from me?

What supports/hinders me in it?

What energy do I/others bring to it?

What energy/value do I get from it?

What makes me do/want it?

What role do I/others play in it?

What are the opportunities/challenges in it?

What action(s) should I consider taking in it?

What is the spiritual lesson in it?

How can I heal/resolve it?

What should I let go of?

Where am I stuck?

What should I explore further?

What will move me in the right direction?

What am I avoiding or resisting?

Who can help me?

What is hidden?

Clarity First:
Asking the Right Question

A problem well-defined is half solved.
—John Dewey

To get the right guidance, ask the right question. The question is as important, if not more so, than the answer itself. Our questions reveal how we feel about ourselves and our lives and how honestly we're willing to look at the substance therein.

Many people's questions reveal the passivity with which they live their lives. They see themselves primarily as reacting to events rather than being cocreators of them. Negatively phrased questions such as, "Why can't/won't/doesn't something work?" "Why is my partner such a jerk?" or the oft-heard, "Why can't I find love?" presuppose a powerlessness to achieve desired ends.

If you find that your question smacks of self-pity, self-recrimination, blame, or hopelessness, rephrase it. Instead of asking "Why can't I find love?" ask "How can I bring love into my life?" or "What do I need to let go of to have the relationship I desire?" It seems a small thing, but the shift can be transformative. By reframing the question in a positive way, you become instantly aware of the assumption of limitation in the original question. A sense of possibility returns. The breakthrough begins before a card is drawn.

Here are examples of how a disempowering question can be rephrased to reconnect you or your querent to an awareness of choice in the matter:

Disempowering	Empowering
Why is my son so mean to me?	How do I contribute to the problem? How can I best respond when he treats me unkindly? What will help us reconnect?
Does the UPS man love me?	How do I perceive the relationship? What do I want from him? What does the relationship need at this time?
Am I talented enough to pursue a professional acting career?	How do I perceive my acting potential? What drives me toward this career? What will help me achieve success (as I define it)?

Notice that the questions in the left column have an external focus. In each example, the person is looking to find peace, happiness, or resolution through knowing the minds and opinions of others. The belief underlying these questions is, "They hold the key to my happiness and success. I do not." In the second column, an attitude of personal responsibility (not to be confused with self-blame) replaces powerlessness. The questions reflect the accountability that comes when we look within for solutions, rather than making our well-being contingent upon the behavior of others.

314

Whether reading for yourself or others, choose the question carefully. Does the question reinforce feelings of powerlessness, blame, and fear . . . or self-respect and creative possibility? If the question itself brings your energy down, rephrase it in a positive way.

Asking about the Future

You are lost the instant you know what the result will be.
—Juan Gris

Asking questions about the future is like checking the weather report. A forecast helps us be prepared—to make or change plans, to set or adjust expectations. Similarly, we may do a Tarot reading to help foresee the outcome of a situation that, like the weather, is beyond our ability to control. When we ask, "What effect will the merger have on my recent employment?" or "Will Roger call and apologize?" or "What will be the result of my friend's trip to Africa?" we are acknowledging our genuine powerlessness to influence these events.

Yet people have a tendency to approach every question about the future with the same sense of watch-and-wait. We ask, "What will happen?" forgetting that attitude and effort play a huge part in determining events. A client of mine once inquired listlessly, "Am I going to vacation in Switzerland this year?" The distinct lack of energy behind her question telegraphed wishful thinking rather than strong intention. Not surprisingly, the answer—the Seven of Cups—was "Not likely." She had the dream but not the steam to make it happen.

"The best way to predict the future," noted Alan Kay, "is to invent it." At each moment, we are planting the seeds of the future through our thoughts and behaviors. You'll recall that the message of the

Magician is to do so consciously, tending those thoughts that grow and develop us.

What are we really asking when we ask about the future? The answers to our questions about tomorrow lie most often in the principles of the Law of Attraction—that which we focus on with passion, and support with action, magnetizes to us. Take the example of a person who wants to know if the seminar she is preparing to give will be well received by the participants. If she asks the Tarot, "Will people like my seminar?" she is really asking:

Given the degree to which I *believe* in the value of my seminar, and the amount of *passion* I feel for giving it, and the strength of the *benefits* that the people will get from it, and the *persistence* with which I am keeping my *expectations* positive . . . what is the probability of people enjoying my seminar?

This elaborately deconstructed question shows—in the spirit of the Magician—just who is really calling the shots in the matter. Suddenly, the passive "Will people like my seminar?" sounds like so much hand-wringing. The answer depends far more on inside forces than outside ones.

If the card that responds to the person's question is an affirmative one, such as the World, the successful probability of her intention is validated. If the answer appears in the negative, such as the Three of Cups reversed, she might choose to follow up with a question such as, "What internal or external obstacles stand in the way?" Rather than interpreting our "no's" as flat denials, we can use the Tarot to explore insights and alternatives concerning the projected outcome.

Listen for assumptions both in your questions about the future and in your interpretations of the cards that come up. Be open to challenging them. Do they reflect a belief in a fixed or fated outcome to which you can only submit? As the examples in the first paragraph showed, some things *are* out of our immediate control (see the Ten of Swords). The choice then becomes how best to respond to them.

Consider your questions about the future with care. Perhaps the best way to approach the subject is by cultivating, in the words of the prayer, "the serenity to accept the things I cannot change, the courage to change the things I can, and the wisdom to know the difference." Yet, if we must err on either side, let it be that we have the courage to change.

In the following examples, questions implying a watch-and-wait attitude are altered to promote an awareness of choice:

Disempowering	Empowering
Will I like the roommate I've been assigned?	What energy should I bring to the relationship?
	What do we have in common?
Will I get the job I'm interviewing for?	What qualities will serve me best in the interview?
	How does this job benefit me?
	How can I best contribute in this job?
Will I enjoy the vacation?	How do I feel about going?
	What is the greatest benefit of this trip?
	What attitudes or energies are most useful for me to bring along?

It must be said that not everyone has the patience for being asked empowering questions. Many would rather be told what is "in the cards" rather than take responsibility, in whole or in part, for their role in creating the outcome. But readings that give information without insight deprive us of the true value of the Tarot. With every draw of the cards, we have the potential to access the knowing places within that are always present, creative, and empowered.

If You Get Stuck

Do you have the patience to wait till the mud settles and the water is clear?
—Tao Te Ching

Sometimes the meaning of a card or two within a spread—or the entire spread itself—will elude you. Mentally straining to make sense of it will disrupt the intuitive process. Below are some suggestions for dealing with divinatory confusion.

Revisit your question. Make sure it is simple, clear, and unambiguous. Rephrase it if necessary and shuffle again. If you're still coming up blank, consider that you may be asking the wrong question.

Do another reading on the same question. Affirm an intention for clarity. If you're still in the dark, randomly pull a "clarifier" card for each point of confusion. The purpose of a clarifier is to provide another take on the card in question, like a synonym.

Meditate on the card(s) in question. Imagine you are having a dialogue with the figures on the cards. Ask them the meaning of their message for you. Or imagine that you *are* the figure on the card. Pursue the feelings or insights that arise.

Record the reading in your journal. And then walk away from the question altogether. Insights often come later, when we're not trying so hard. Don't get hung up on the cards that stump you, especially if you understand the overall intent of the spread. Focus on what you do understand.

Become the Fool. Trust that if the message of the spread is important, you'll get it another way in the right time. Meanwhile, celebrate your own honest, innocent bewilderment—get out of your head, get up on your feet, and dance!

Reading for Others

Reminding one another of the dream that each of us aspires
to may be enough for us to set each other free.
— Antoine de Saint-Exupéry

side from reading for yourself, there is no better learning resource than friends or family. Reading for those
you know provides an opportunity to practice your skills,
experiment with different spreads, and have a patient and forgiving
audience for your inevitable misreads. Expect to be teased about the
"fortune-teller" stuff or warned against the "evils" of the cards—rites
of passage for every reader. But those who know you best will recognize your sincerity and become willing, if not grateful, participants.

Be aware that there are downsides when reading for those most
familiar to you. The fact of your closeness can cloud objectivity,
especially if the issues addressed in the reading involve you in some
way. You may feel inclined to edit out potentially embarrassing
messages or soft-pedal harsher ones and therefore deprive the
querent of the full value of the reading. You may even be tempted to

use your reader role as a platform to offer personal critiques about how they're living their life ("Mom, the cards are telling you to stop calling me every day to tell me what you had for lunch"). Some Tarot readers do not read for close friends or family members for these reasons.

Before You Start: Know Your Biases

To understand everything is to forgive everything.
—Buddha

If a person who asks for a reading thinks the Tarot is a crock and is merely humoring you, don't read for them. But if they're sincerely curious about the messages from the cards, your energy will not be wasted, and your reading will have impact. For this reason, it is essential that you recognize your biases. What beliefs do you bring to the table that will influence your "spin" on the cards? How do you feel about people who have extramarital affairs? What are your attitudes about wealth and poverty? About people of different races, religions, or sexual orientations? What judgments or fears might you hold about illness or depression? Do you tend to categorize people and behavior as either "spiritual" or "unspiritual"?

We all have biases, many of which remain hidden from our awareness. Recognizing them takes work. But the more we understand the "shoulds" quietly underlying our attitudes, the more easily we can prevent ourselves from dumping them on the people for whom we're reading, the very people who are seeking a more objective perspective. It's not always possible to send a bias packing. But when one shows up we can say, "Listen, Bias, I'm doing a reading right now and need to be as clear a channel as possible. So if you'll just go for a stroll until the reading is over, I'd much appreciate it."

Setting the Stage for Readings

Whether invoked or not, God will be present.
—Carl Jung

There is an intimacy inherent in two people sitting together for several private, intense minutes. Your physical and psychological comfort is important. Decide on a position at the table in which you feel most at ease. I like to sit at a 90-degree angle from the querent so that both of us are able to see the cards from the same perspective. Some readers prefer to sit across from the querent. They find the distance enhances a sense of emotional detachment that aids their objectivity. The disadvantage to this setup is that the querent sees the cards from the opposite vantage point to that of the reader, which inhibits the querent's interaction with the cards.

Begin the session by asking the person if they have a question or situation they would like the reading to address. Clarify and refine vague questions; rephrase negative questions as empowering ones. Consider following this with an invocation (silently or aloud) of the higher energies as a way to affirm and create a sacred space for the reading. Next, invite the querent to shuffle the deck using the same methodology described earlier in Preparing for Readings (page 293). If he appears hurried, encourage him to take a few deep breaths and slow down so that he is more centered and present.

When the querent has finished shuffling, pull as many cards from the top of the deck as are required for the reading and place them onto the spread. If the person has no specific question, consider doing the Celtic Cross or a Life Journey spread (see Soul Questions, page 309) to see what's up. In most cases, the themes that surface in these initial readings will determine the focus of the entire session and inform which spreads, if any, are done in follow-up.

Reading from the Gut

When the bird and the book disagree, always believe the bird.
—James Audubon

Some Tarot readers have highly developed psychic gifts. Without a word of input from the querent, they are able to look at the Knight of Pentacles and announce with accuracy, "Your cousin Ernie in New Jersey wants to go into business with you—something to do with scuba equipment." Obviously, information like this cannot be gleaned from the card's image, nor from any published interpretations. In these cases the cards act as the catalyst for the reader's clairvoyant or clairaudient hits.

Although such skills are useful, they are not required to give readings with clarity and depth. Reading the Tarot is an interpretive art. It combines your rational left-brain knowledge of the cards with right-brain feeling about their intended meaning. Spontaneous images of present or future details are just icing on the cake.

If you do readings often enough, you will eventually deepen your rapport with the cards. You may begin to feel that the cards talk to you, evoke bodily sensations, or usher in mental images. You will be able to read a card accurately without having to ponder which of its many possible interpretations may apply. You may look at a spread and feel a Magician-like quickening of energy or, like the High Priestess, a soul-brushed calm and knowing. Guided by this clarity, you tell the querent the meaning of the spread without need of their input or confirmation. Whether or not the querent recognizes the truth of the reading, you do not waver from the message you received.

At other times the spread will stare back at you, mute. If you try to guess your way through, the mental strain short-circuits your receptivity. To mine the meaning of the spread, you may need to ask questions of an intuitive collaborator—the querent herself. I was introduced to the collaborative approach in a 1999 workshop led by Mary Greer, whose subsequent book 21 *Ways to Read a Tarot Card* presents an inspired variety of interactive techniques, some of which are included here. As you will see in the next section, getting the querent's input can provide just as much insight as the reader-as-channeler format. Some of the best readings you'll give may involve a blend of both.

Collaborative Readings

There are two ways of spreading light: to be the candle
or the mirror that reflects it.
—Edith Wharton

In some readings you will need to rely to an extent on information supplied by the querent to decipher the message. This should not be mistaken for deception; as a reader, you are a facilitator in service to the person's higher good. Your job is to understand why the Tarot has singled out these particular cards for her attention—period. Unless you have presented yourself as one who "Sees All, Knows All," there is nothing underhanded in seeking input from her.

Collaborative readings offer more than opportunities for getting help in deciphering the meanings of a puzzling card or two. The questions you ask the querent can take her to the deeper places of her own self-discovery. By taking an active role in unraveling the mysteries of her spread, the querent begins to understand that the answers she seeks are not within you or the cards but within *herself*—an invaluable experience of self-recognition and empowerment.

Collect Your Impressions

If you come up dry on some of the cards in your querent's spread, get down to the basics. Observe whether the energies of these cards appear to move or idle, expand or contract, control or surrender, give or take, express or contain, empower or stifle. Are they fast or slow, bright or dark? Share these impressions with your querent. You do not need to have a clear idea of each card's ultimate message, or of the spread as a whole, to do this quickly and effectively.

Check-in

Once you have conveyed the energetic bare bones of the "mystery" cards, ask your querent if any of your impressions connected with her. Based on your breeze-through, she may be able to tell you with authority what the card or spread is saying, or be able to narrow down a couple of strong possibilities. Continue going through the spread, offering your insights and eliciting her input when necessary to fill in the gaps.

Invite

By asking, "What do you see in the card?" or "What is going on in this picture?" you give your querent permission to free-associate, to use her imagination spontaneously to provide intuitive answers. While great in a pinch, this approach can have tremendous value for the querent even if you are quite certain of the card's meaning.

In a reading for Dean, a newly sober alcoholic, I merely pointed to the cards I felt he would most connect with and let him do the talking. "That was me," he said gesturing to the Ten of Swords. "Rock bottom. Passed out on the floor. I'd still be there if my friends hadn't helped me get back on my feet." His remarkable free associations virtually turned cards he had never seen into pictures from a personal photo album. In any reading, invite the person to say what he or she sees, and then listen. The results may surprise both of you.

Determine Who's Who

Not every card in a spread may refer to the querent directly. Depending on a card's position within the spread, it could indicate another person in the situation. Questions prevent presumptions. Asking, "Where are you in the picture?" helps reveal the dynamics of the relationship.

A young mother took one look at the Five of Swords and explained that the foreground figure was her unruly son gloating over his winning power plays that left her and her husband as the dwarfed, defeated background figures. In the Six of Swords, a client saw himself as the boatman working to keep his marriage afloat and on course amid his wife's depression. And I'll never forget the woman who identified with the horse on the Sun card, explaining that she felt "saddled" by pressures to uphold the happy, aggressively positive image she felt her church expected of her. For these clients, my question "Where are you in the picture?" evoked strong recognition. By asking, not telling, them about the images, they were free to come to their own conclusions intuitively, giving them a sense of ownership in the reading.

Stay Open

Conducting collaborative meanings may require you to set aside your personal interpretations until the querent explores her own, even if you disagree. I once had a client who projected all sorts of undesirable qualities onto the King of Cups. While I found her reaction useful to the reading (to the extent that it was psychologically revealing), I felt that she was missing out on the true value of the card as it pertained to her question. The King wanted to be her ally.

I began gently, sounding a little like a royal public-relations spokesman: "I know you think the King of Cups looks cold and harsh, so let me tell you about some of his wonderful qualities and how I think they might be useful for you." She gradually softened toward the figure, concurring that the King's ability to remain centered in emotional storms was something she desired for herself.

Give Examples

Never underestimate the power of a good "for instance." Discussing a particular card may remind you of other readings you have done in which that card memorably appeared. It often happens that the example you share will correspond perfectly to the querent's situation. There have been times when I nearly held back from giving an example, doubting its relevance to the querent, yet when I blurted it out, I discovered that it unleashed a spontaneous breakthrough in the querent's understanding. Trust what comes up.

At certain times a card may inspire you or your querent to draw parallels to a book, movie, myth, fairy tale, song, or current event that shares the same archetypal characters and themes. Here are just a few analogies that that have come up spontaneously in readings:

Judgment: Hedwig, Harry Potter's message-bearing owl
Six of Pentacles: Oliver Twist's plaintive, "Please sir, I want some more."
Knight of Cups: Romeo comes a-courting
The Hanged Man: Odysseus's wife, Penelope, awaits his return
Eight of Wands: an Internet chat room

Remember, the point of a Tarot reading is to facilitate the conversation between the person and their deeper being, not to wow them with esoteric sophistication. Examples and illustrations are powerful tools for getting to the heart of an issue quickly and resonantly. They often remain in the querent's memory long after the details of a reading have been forgotten.

Effective readings combine many different elements—your intuition, feelings, psychological insights, understanding of the symbols, analysis of the relationships among the cards, your Tarot (and life) experiences, and your rapport with the querent. Ultimately, however, the approach to reading the cards is not nearly as important as the love you bring to the table. The gift of your attention is often healing in itself.

Handling Difficult Disclosures

Give neither counsel nor salt til you are asked for it.
—Italian proverb

Many years ago some clients hired me to give a private reading for their friend at her fortieth birthday party. Both the party and the reading were planned as surprises. And surprised she was. They ushered her into the den where I sat waiting with my cards. Still dazed from the shock of her arrival, she floated onto the chair. We laid out her cards.

My heart sank.

Here was a veritable pincushion of quivering Swords, all sadness, fear, and heartache. (Happy Birthday!) Worse yet, the poor woman had not even asked for the reading. Yet here it was being foisted upon her along with the canapes and champagne.

Affecting a too-casual inflection, I became the Artful Dodger of the Seven of Swords, hedging, minimizing, and dancing around each thorn poking out of the spread. The woman was all too eager to be an accomplice to my crimes of omission. "That card doesn't bother me at all!" she said pluckily at one point, gesturing with her champagne glass to the thrice-skewered heart in the Inner Self position. Even the Eight of Swords' bound-and-blinded maiden, allocated for her Near Future, managed to acquire through my nonchalant narrative a benign grace.

For the record, I should add that I do not use the same avoidance tactics in readings for clients, who get their readings by appointment, not by surprise!

When they ask for a reading, people signify their willingness to look at whatever comes up in the shuffle. Sugarcoating the sour parts will not fool the querent. They will pick up on the hiding, even if unconsciously. When potentially embarrassing or shattering information appears, pause a moment to ask your inner guidance for the right way to communicate it. Your intuition may lead you to deliver the message as a question, an affirmation, a personal anecdote, or even a playful jab. If for any reason you find yourself holding judgments against the person, silently ask that these be dissolved (touching the area of your heart with your fingertips intensifies the release). After the reading, send prayers for peaceful resolution to the person, holding their highest good in your mind and heart.

Moreover, we have all heard stories about reckless readers who have dropped bombs such as, "Watch for a death this year," practically killing their clients with worry over which loved one's shelf life may be ready to expire. To leave a person feeling fearful and powerless is akin to dispensing slow-acting poison. One well-known psychic's tactic was even more toxic: he told a fifty-year-old friend of mine she'd be dead at eighty-three! Such readers seem to relish the drama of these pronouncements with a disturbing disregard of their impact. Equally troubling is that, even if the querent claims to take the information with a grain of salt, their subconscious mind may take it as truth. As readers and guides, we must never underestimate the influence our words can have on another person.

Using our influence to instill anxiety and fear is not only bad form, it's bad karma. As readers we are invited to become soul guides, curtain lifters, healers. With every throw of the cards, we have the opportunity to help people become more objective observers of their own dramas, to show them the machinery cranking behind the scenes, and to remind them of their birthright as free beings to create lives more aligned with their true power and purpose.

When *Not* to Read for Others

The unconscious wants truth. It ceases to speak to those who want something else more than truth.

—Adrienne Rich

As the archetype of intuitive knowing, the High Priestess has a special place in the hearts of Tarot readers. But basic self-care requires us to also honor our professional boundaries (Emperor) and ethical codes (Heirophant). Without all of these key energies in place, we open the door to manipulation, integrity compromises, and burnout. Don't read for others if:

You have the wrong motives. Don't read the cards if you suspect your real reason is to impress a person with your Special Tarot Powers, snoop around in his or her private life, or use information gleaned from the reading to your advantage.

The querent wants you to "prove it works." Skepticism and ridicule are not always the same, but anything less than sincere curiosity creates resistance. If the vibe isn't right, don't waste your time.

The querent doesn't want a reading. If you discover he was pressured by others to get a reading ("My friend insisted"), decline to do it. Unless he's ready and willing, expect mutually unsatisfying results.

The querent is frantic. Avoid giving emergency readings. A querent in panic can pull you off center, diminish your intuitive clarity, and make for a highly unpleasant interaction. Explain that it is in both your interests to reschedule for a time when she is calmer.

The querent's issues overwhelm you. Know your boundaries. If the person asks for a reading on issues outside your comfort zone ("Why did God take my job, home, health, and family from me?"), don't proceed. Recommend seeking the help of qualified professionals.

The querent becomes dependent on you. You may sense in some people a pattern of always looking outside for guidance and validation. For this reason, many professional readers will not read for their clients more than a few times a year. Let your feelings inform your decision to read on a case-by-case basis, or do a yes/no reading about it.

Epilogue

The Journey Begins

To thee no star be dark.
Both heaven and earth
Friend thee for ever.
—William Shakespeare

You've read the book, maybe even done a few readings. At this point you might be excited about the universal and timeless ideas in the cards or the personal revelations they may have prompted. In fact, you may be feeling slightly lightheaded about the prospect that the Tarot could continue to yield insights indefinitely—or, as this book title generously suggests, for life.

That's part of the practical beauty of the Tarot. It's a tool you can use forever, whenever you feel the need to understand yourself or situations in more objective, symbolic ways.

But the "Life" in the title is not just about duration. It's about the joy of using the cards to discover the spiritual opportunities in the everyday and grow in compassion for the seventy-eight courageous, wise, wounded Tarot characters in yourself and in everyone. In seeing ourselves with more kindness and with a greater sense of creative potential, we cannot help but view the world with the same generosity.

In closing, let me share something I've learned about the Tarot that will spare you a lot of pain. The cards, like the High Priestess, make no judgments. Although you may occasionally feel stung by them, their message is, simply, "Notice." Even the cards traditionally seen as negative have a clarifying, not punitive, purpose. If you use the cards to look for truth, then—to borrow the carnival parlance— every card is a winner.

Blessings.

Appendix A

Major Arcana

Major Arcana	Soul Task	Shadow/Excess	Deficiency/Blockage (Reversed)
Fool	Trusting life	Irresponsibility, gullibility, fear of commitment	Overseriousness, fear of risk, denial of Inner Child
Magician	Consciously creating your life experience	Opportunism, grandiosity, pushing for change too soon	Lack of inspiration, weakness of will, randomness
High Priestess	Honoring your Inner Being	Chronic passivity, excessive holding back, secretiveness	Superficiality, denial of the soul, inability to perceive subtlety
Empress	Opening to pleasure, beauty, and abundance	Overindulgence, overmothering, materialism	Lack, money issues, denial of pleasure, stinginess
Emperor	Exercising power wisely	Rigidity, overcontrol, overresponsibility, bossiness	Indecision, disorder, weak boundaries, power issues
Hierophant	Living by a higher code of conduct	Self-righteousness, blind conformity, dogma	Self-expression issues, poor listening, unethical behavior
Lovers	Learning and growing through relationships	Relationship addiction, overidealizing the relationship	Intimacy issues, sexual issues, disharmony, infidelity

Major Arcana	Soul Task	Shadow/Excess	Deficiency/Blockage (Reversed)
Chariot	Putting your commitments to the test	Bravado, overambition, compulsive drive	Purposelessness, low drive, self-doubt
Strength	Becoming strong in spirit	Fear of losing emotional control, overdiscipline	Low impulse control, depression, timidity
Hermit	Seeking meaning	Self-absorption, excessive isolation, overanalysis	Meaninglessness, poor concentration, fear of aloneness or self-examination
Wheel of Fortune	Understanding cause and effect	Attributing all events to fate or chance	Stagnancy, failure to perceive patterns of behavior
Justice	Striving for truth and balance	Harshly judging self or others	Imbalance, self-deception, blaming, denial of truth
Hanged Man	Surrendering to what is	Martyrdom, persecution complex, chronic passivity	Impatience, struggle, resisting new perspectives
Death	Accepting impermanence	Defeatism, pessimism, commitment issues	Overattachment, inability to let go, resisting change
Temperance	Honoring and blending opposite energies	Fear of extremes, conflict avoidance	Excesses or deficits, disharmony
Devil	facing your demons	Denying the existence of the shadow	Liberation from bondage, fear, and illusion

Major Arcana	Soul Task	Shadow/Excess	Deficiency/Blockage (Reversed)
Tower	Finding the spiritual opportunity within the drama	Defeatism, self-punishment, catastrophizing	Preserving a facade, denying inevitability of collapse
Star	Nourishing the inner and outer life	Intolerance for anything but the ideal	Dimmed hopes, creativity blockage, emptiness
Moon	Exploring the inner unknown	Oversensitivity, instability, moodiness, psychosis	Fear or suppression of unconscious material
Sun	Letting your light shine	Self-centeredness, fear or intolerance of negativity	Pessimism, self-doubt, denial of joy
Judgment	Awakening to a more expanded way of being	Insisting that others awaken in the same way and time	Denying the call, complacency, asleep to potential
World	Unifying with the whole of creation	Inability to create useful distinctions or boundaries	Self-absorption, isolation, alienation, disconnection

Appendix B

Number Meanings

One (Ace):	Unity, initiation, beginning
Two:	Duality, choice, relationship
Three:	Synthesis, expansion, birth
Four:	Stability, order, possession
Five:	Mediation, challenge, struggle
Six:	Harmony, equilibrium, progress
Seven:	Tests, victory, commencement
Eight:	Ebb and flow, prioritizing, change
Nine:	Attainment, completion, reflection
Ten:	The infinite, perfection, beginnings and endings

Appendix C

Astrological and Planetary Correspondences

These correspondences are attributed in part to the system devised by the Hermetic Order of the Golden Dawn.

Fool—Uranus	Justice—Libra
Magician—Mercury	Hanged Man—Neptune
High Priestess—Moon	Death—Scorpio
Empress—Venus	Temperance—Sagittarius
Emperor—Aries	The Devil—Capricorn
Hierophant—Taurus	The Tower—Mars
Lovers—Gemini	The Star—Aquarius
Chariot—Cancer	The Moon—Pisces
Strength—Leo	The Sun—Sun
Hermit—Virgo	Judgment—Pluto
Wheel of Fortune—Jupiter	The World—Saturn

Appendix D

Chakras

Chakra is a Sanskrit word meaning "wheel of light." Chakras are the energy centers of the etheric body. In certain cards, the figures' physical details and costume colors suggest chakra correspondences consistent with the interpretation of the card, even though the chakras are not part of the Western Mystery traditions on which the esoteric Tarot is based.

Chakra	Body area	Color	Issues
1st Chakra	Tailbone, legs, and feet	Red	Survival, vitality, security, tribal belonging
2nd Chakra	Abdomen and hips	Orange	Emotions, sexuality, pleasure, nurturance
3rd Chakra	Solar plexus	Yellow	Power, will, discipline, esteem, integrity
4th Chakra	Heart	Green	Compassion, relationship, giving and receiving love
5th Chakra	Throat	Blue	Self-expression, listening, creativity, channeling
6th Chakra	Brow	Indigo	Intellect, perception, insight, clarity, clairvoyance
7th Chakra	Top of head	Violet	Cosmic energies, unity, spirit, transcendence

Bibliography

Case, Paul Foster. *The Tarot: A Key to the Wisdom of the Ages*. Richmond, Va.: McCoy Publishing, 1947.

Choquette, Sonia. *Trust Your Vibes: Secret Tools for Sixth Sensory Living*. Carlsbad, Calif.: Hay House, 2004.

Decker, Ronald, Thierry Depaulis, and Michael Dummett. *A Wicked Pack of Cards: The Origins of the Occult Tarot*. New York: St. Martin's Press, 1996.

Duquette, Lon Milo. *The Chicken Qabalah of Rabbi Lamed Ben Clifford*. York Beach, Me.: Weiser Books, 2001.

Greer, Mary K. *Twenty-One Ways to Read a Tarot Card*. Woodbury, Minn.: Llewellyn Worldwide, 2006.

Harvey, Andrew. *Son of Man: The Mystical Path to Christ*. New York: Jeremy P. Tarcher/ Putnam, 1998.

Judith, Anodea. *Eastern Body, Western Mind: Psychology and the Chakra System*. Berkeley, Calif.: Celestial Arts, 1996.

Jung, Carl G. *Man and His Symbols*. Garden City, N.Y.: Doubleday, 1964.

Payne-Towler, Christine. *The Underground Stream: Esoteric Tarot Revealed*. Eugene, Ore.: Noreah Press, 1999.

Place, Robert M. *The Tarot: History, Symbolism, and Divination*. New York: Penguin, 2005.

Pollack, Rachel. *Seventy-Eight Degrees of Wisdom*. London: Thorsons, 1997.

Skafte, Dianne. *When Oracles Speak: Understanding the Signs and Symbols All Around Us*. Wheaton, Ill.: Quest, 2000.

Waite, Arthur Edward. *The Pictorial Key to the Tarot*. Stamford, Conn.: U.S. Games Systems, 1910.

About the Author

Paul Quinn is a teacher, speaker, and intuitive consultant who uses the Tarot to help others gain insights leading to positive changes and greater well-being. He was listed as a "top talent" in Tarot by *Chicago Magazine* and has been featured on radio programs internationally. For more information, visit either of his Web sites:

www.TarotforLife.net

www.TheSpiritedLife.com

Quest Books

encourages open-minded inquiry into
world religions, philosophy, science, and the arts
in order to understand the wisdom of the ages,
respect the unity of all life, and help people explore
individual spiritual self-transformation.

Its publications are generously supported by
The Kern Foundation,
a trust committed to Theosophical education.

Quest Books is the imprint of
the Theosophical Publishing House,
a division of the Theosophical Society in America.
For information about programs, literature,
on-line study, membership benefits, and international centers,
see www.theosophical.org
or call 800-669-1571 or (outside the U.S.) 630-668-1571.

Related Quest Titles

The Chakras, by C. W. Leadbeater
The Chakras and the Human Energy Fields,
by Shafica Karagulla, with Dora van Gelder Kunz
The Fool's Pilgrimage, by Stephan A. Hoeller
Numerology and the Cycles of Life (CD), by Philip Clark
The Secret of the Runes (CD set), by John Algeo
Tarot and the Tree of Life, by Isabel Radow Kliegman
The Waking Dream, by Ray Grasse

To order books or a complete Quest catalog,
call 800-669-9425 or (outside the U.S.) 630-665-0130.

MORE PRAISE FOR PAUL QUINN'S

Tarot for Life

"A must-read."
—**American Tarot Association**

"Paul Quinn has seamlessly integrated the best of Tarot tradition with a new vision for the twenty-first century. While maintaining respect for the Tarot as a divinatory tool, he also demonstrates its estimable value for personal development and increasing consciousness of one's life path."

—**Kenneth James, Ph.D.,**
Jungian Analyst

"Paul Quinn's valuable book explores the universal spiritual power that lies not only in the ancient symbols of the Tarot, but in our own willingness to find the meaning and message of those symbols deep within ourselves. It is a useful and entertaining guide for every spiritual journey."

—**Rev. Edward Townley, author of**
The Secret According to Jesus

"Thought-provoking and beautifully descriptive. I love Paul's witty and urbane voice, and his sense of humor is a wonderful teaching tool. He is an extremely efficient and visual writer—warm and nurturing—and a fantastic guide."

—**Gayle Seminara-Mandel, Co-owner,**
Transitions Bookstore, Chicago